AL RASHID MOSQUE

Gutteridge
BOOKS

An Imprint of The University of Alberta Press

EARLE H. WAUGH

AL RASHID MOSQUE

Building Canadian Muslim Communities

Published by

The University of Alberta Press
Ring House 2
Edmonton, Alberta, Canada   T6G 2E1
www.uap.ualberta.ca

Library and Archives Canada Cataloguing in Publication

Waugh, Earle H., 1936–, author
Al Rashid Mosque : building Canadian Muslim communities / Earle H. Waugh.

Includes bibliographical references and index.
Issued in print and electronic formats.
ISBN 978-1-77212-339-5 (hardcover).—
ISBN 978-1-77212-333-3 (softcover).—
ISBN 978-1-77212-340-1 (PDF)

1. Al Rashid Mosque (Edmonton, Alta.). 2. Al Rashid Mosque (Edmonton,
Alta.)—History. 3. Mosques—Alberta—Edmonton—History. 4. Muslims—Alberta—
Edmonton—Social life and customs. I. Title.

BP187.65.C2E3629 2018   297.3'59712334   C2018-901687-6
                                                       C2018-901688-4

First edition, first printing, 2018.
First printed and bound in Canada by Friesens, Altona, Manitoba.
Copyediting and proofreading by Joanne Muzak.
Map by Wendy Johnson.
Indexing by Adrian Mather.

The University of Alberta Press gratefully acknowledges the support received for
its publishing program from the Government of Canada, the Canada Council for the Arts,
and the Government of Alberta through the Alberta Media Fund.

 Government of Canada / Gouvernement du Canada

 Canada Council for the Arts / Conseil des Arts du Canada

Alberta Government

To Soraya Zaki Hafez, indomitable spirit, colleague, collaborator, and friend
and
To the many generations of Muslim friends I have known

CONTENTS

FOREWORD

AL RASHID MOSQUE, Canada's first and one of the earliest in
North America, was erected in Edmonton in the depth of the
Depression of the 1930s. The Great Depression notwithstanding,
such a daring project, undertaken by about twenty Arab Lebanese
families, was in tune with the spirit of the developing Canadian
west. The project was envisioned to reinforce the identities and
heritage of Muslim immigrants and their descendants. Over time,
the story of this first mosque, which served as a magnet for more
Lebanese Muslim immigrants to Edmonton, was woven into the
folklore of the local community.

Earle Waugh's *Al Rashid Mosque: Building Canadian Muslim
Communities* recasts and expands the slender folkloric account in a
scholarly style that is accessible to wider audiences in Canada and
beyond. Uniquely, this book provides the first systematic attempt
to narrate an important chapter in the life of Edmonton's Muslim
community. It sheds light on the socio-cultural, economic, and
political heritage of the early Muslim immigrants to Edmonton

and it highlights important areas to consider for future community development. The book also documents the challenges facing the members of Al Rashid Mosque in the aftermath of the terrorist attacks that occurred in the United States on September 11, 2001 (9/11), which had strong reverberations in Canada. Equally important, the book discusses Muslims' entry into the Canadian mainstream, as it identifies emerging issues that the mosque's growing congregation and their descendants may need to address.

Facing a changing landscape, particularly since 9/11, the Al Rashid Muslim community has been challenged to develop appropriate strategies for dealing with racism and Islamophobia. This issue, along with Muslim population growth and other demographic changes, continues to be central to the community.

The most notable thing about the building of Al Rashid Mosque eighty years ago is that the initiators of the project began the important process of institution building. During the early period of Muslim settlement in Canada, some fifty or so years prior to the building of the mosque, the spiritual needs of the pioneers were met in individual or family isolation or through informal gatherings such as praying at each other's homes.

Little did these Arab Lebanese pioneers know that building a mosque was only a precursor to further institutionalization of the Muslim faith in Canada. Thus, the early mosque served as a catalyst for subsequent developments such as engaging dedicated and professionally trained imams. Other developments included the establishment of children's language and religious programs and, much later, Muslim schools such as the acclaimed Edmonton Islamic Academy, built almost fifty years after the first mosque. Today, the process of institutionalizing the faith has spread across the country. For example, as the number of mosques has increased across the country, Canada has also increasingly witnessed the development of Muslim benevolent societies, service associations, professional associations, and university student associations as well as the creation of the Canadian Council of Muslim Women and the Canadian Council of Imams, among other organizations.

Remarkably, in the early years of the Al Rashid project, Canadian Muslim women were actively involved in outreach and fundraising to advance the building of this mosque. With the institutionalization of the faith, Muslim women in Edmonton and across the country continued to play major, multifaceted leadership roles at the local, national, and international levels. Areas of leadership included historical cultural preservation, interfaith dialogue, gender and family concerns, peace-seeking efforts, and community and educational development.

Canadian Muslim identity has been changing over time. Personal identity is a complex configuration made up of many elements including ethnic identity, national identity, regional identity, racial identity, religious identity, linguistic identity, and Canadian identity. These different aspects intersect and interact and yield a large number of combinations that facilitate self-description on the one hand, and navigation in the larger society on the other.

This book offers a wide range of suggestions for maintaining community balance and integration, as well as for addressing new challenges. It is a valuable and timely addition to the growing literature on Canadian Muslims' adaptive experiences in Canada.

Baha Abu-Laban, CM, PhD
Professor Emeritus of Sociology
University of Alberta
April 2017

PREFACE

To travel is to vanquish
—*Old Arab Proverb*

THE AL RASHID MOSQUE, Canada's celebrated mosque, marks its
eightieth anniversary in 2018. So much has changed since it began
its *rihla* (purposive journey) in 1938 that the board of directors
decided that a special effort had to be made to tell its distinctive
story. Their motivations are not hard to discern.

The world's attitudes to Islam have undergone a dramatic
transformation, with violent forces unleashed in the name of the
religion every night on television. Local believers do not recognize
the religion portrayed in the mainstream media; youngsters search
in vain for the meaning of who they are and how to relate to a
portrayal so distant from the peaceful tradition taught by parents
and grandparents. Voices within and without point to the long and
sorrowful impact of colonialism on cherished homelands and the
continued struggle by fellow Muslims for a just and lasting peace

in their countries. In the meantime, generation upon generation of successful Muslims in Canada are seen everywhere—skilled, educated, and sophisticated people in just about every walk of life. They count themselves as members of the Prophet's tradition without all the baggage of the jihadists. How can we make sense of these disparities?

Despite the common perception that the religion of Islam is a tradition "foreign" to the Western world, the fact is that it arose within and adopted much from its birthplace within a Judeo-Christian environment. Born in the trade-route commercial city of Mecca of Arabia in the seventh century (in which both Jewish and Christian communities were known and respected), the religion affirmed many common conceptions with their monotheistic neighbours. The concept of one God, the role of prophets, the importance of law, and the primacy of prayer and devotion are only a small sample of the many influences. Yet the need for a distinctive Muslim identity motivated much of early contact history, and the fledgling formation of state Islam led to political and cultural struggles with other religions and their adherents. As a result, Islam carved out firm theological and legal traditions that have stood the test of time and continue to shape religious consciousness. At the same time, it assimilated and Islamized cultural influences from all over the world as state Islam spread from Spain to China.

The ensuing Islamic civilization was a counterpoint to the powerful Christian civilization centred in Europe, and the two world religions and their state apparatuses vied for superiority in the world. Because Islamic civilization held that the last and final message had been brought by Muhammad (b. 570 CE), challenges and conflicts with the West became part of the civilizational debates. With the Industrial Revolution in Europe, colonial expansion led to incursions, battles, and eventually the overthrow of Muslim political entities, which resulted in internal debates in Islamic countries about how the last and assumed superior tradition could be defeated by an earlier form of religion. Issues about God's purposes for the world and religion inevitably followed. Shifts of colossal proportion became the order of the day, and reformist movements and redefinitions have shaped the Islam we have today, and have powered the rise of jihadists striving to throw off the colonialist past.

It is beyond the purvey of this book to lay out the complexity of Islam's doctrinal development, but a few words might help the interested reader to comprehend the background of our story. Two publications can assist with that task: John Renard's 2015 book, *The Handy Islam Answer Book*, is a basic primer that can steer one in the right belief direction, and the Marshall Cavendish Corporation provides a glimpse of the immense diversity within the house of Islam in its *Islamic Beliefs, Practices, and Cultures* (2010).

For purposes of this history, however, it is important for readers to know that Islam now has more than 1.2 billion followers worldwide, with more than a million in North America. Hence, Islam is firmly rooted in both Canada and the United States, and has been for some time. Our story briefly explores the success of only one of the many possible stories that could be told. Its piety centres on the Qur'an's presentation of key doctrines, such as belief in one God, and the role of the Qur'an as the very word of God delivered to His obedient servant Muhammad, who understood himself to be a prophet sent directly by God to bring His final message to humanity. What formed was a practicing community called an *ummah*, which embraced all those who were obedient to God and His last and final prophet Muhammad. It was a message challenging humans to act justly on Earth since all would face judgement in the world to come. The vehicle for carrying out devotion to God was described as "pillars," of which five were absolutely required: (1) *Shahada*: the public declaration of belief in one God and the message brought by Muhammad; (2) *Salat*: the commitment to pray five times every day (dawn, noon, afternoon, sunset, and evening); (3) *Zakat*: to tithe faithfully by giving charity to those requiring assistance; (4) *Sawn*: to practice an annual fast during the month of Ramadan, during which one gives up food, water, and bodily pleasures during the daylight hours; and

(5) *Hajj*: to undertake, at least once, a pilgrimage to the Islamic holy city of Mecca.

As Islam developed, theological and legal sophistication became its hallmark, and a variety of viewpoints surfaced in Islam's self-understanding. It is not surprising that early on two major directions came to shape the *ummah*: one known as Sunnism, the other Shi'ism. Overriding these differences, however, was a commitment to living according to God's precepts. Thus, while it is true that Islam interacted with the intellectual and philosophical discourses of ancient cultures, it more and more placed its emphasis upon the scholarly articulation of law, known as sharia. Living life justly and fervently in tune with God's precepts took on a regimented form that regulated and structured Islam in ways that ordinary people found as an acceptable way to live before God. Reminiscent of Jewish notions of Halakhah/Torah, sharia became the vehicle for ordinary folk to relate to the Almighty. In addition, cultural differences were bridged because sharia was adaptable to lived environments wherever Muslims happened to be. Furthermore, it eschewed the notion of priesthood and focused on individual spiritual responsibility before God. The result was the perception that Islam could be practiced anywhere, even if no mosque or house of prayer were available. In addition, Islamic flexibility allowed people from many cultures to adapt to it, and it became the worldwide religion it is today. That tradition was transplanted to Canada, forming a vibrant group within Alberta's diversity.

Indeed, the Al Rashid Mosque has been an important focal point of Islamic life in Alberta and in Canada for eighty years.[1] It has gone from being a lonely outpost in the Canadian west—in 1893 the town of Edmonton was still part of the Northwest Territories— to a critical feature of Canada's multicultural landscape. The story of the mosque is one of incredible achievement, of highs and lows,

---

1 Technically, *Al Rashid* should be transliterated with a hyphen and a long "I"; however, all legal documents pertaining to the mosque cite *Al Rashid*, so we have maintained the convention throughout.

of weathering storms, and of becoming a beacon for a religion of great depth and significance. A key element of this story is the shifts the mosque community has undergone, from its desire to partner with community members and others to establish itself in Canada, to negotiating the challenges imposed by forces abroad with discernment, towards a balance between secularist ideologies and genuine piety, and in contemporary Canada, to accommodate to a new status of a distinctive Canadian voice for Islam. What seems so difficult to grasp now, in the face of years of negative perceptions of Islam, is the fact that this community quite positively embraced Canada and its peoples—so much so that they fundamentally sought to enrich the whole country with their culture and viewpoint. The mosque was, and continues to be, a tangible expression of that collaborative attitude for good. It is the vicissitudes of the story, its challenges and its achievements, that I will try to tell here.

Tellingly, the broader Edmonton community has long valued Al Rashid. In fact, the original mosque is now preserved amid the historical artifacts gathered in Edmonton's famed Fort Edmonton Park where it sits as a representative of Islam's long presence in North America, and the only original mosque building from this period still extant in Canada and the United States.

Very often, observers emphasize a particular perspective—doctrinal, racial, social, geographic, financial, or political—in summarizing the Islamic community in Edmonton. Yet such singular explanations indicate that something is missing. The community on the ground is so diverse, and proudly so, that to view it through a single lens lessens it. One has to accept it for what it is: an iconic mosque community, embodying a cultural attitude with a unique and diverse history. And perhaps at its heart, the story of Al Rashid is a distinctively Canadian story.

There are those who contend that Muslim adaptation to North America in the last century really derives from a much longer and more sophisticated relationship reaching back to ancient Muslim seafarers (Pimienta-Bey 2002); scholars have not given much credence to these studies. More recently, however, Nadia Ahmad

(2014) uses a legal lens to argue that Islamic norms have had a subtle influence on law in the western hemisphere post-Columbus. Whatever the outcome of this line of reasoning, it tells us that far from the destructive and disruptive attitude towards America attributed to believers of this religion, the truth is quite the opposite. Muslims found a compatible home in North America and have contributed significantly to their new places of residence.

Unlike some homegrown groups in North America, such as the black Muslim movement in the United States, Al Rashid came about because its founding community was voluntary settlers from abroad. This is an important fact, because it means that the cultural heritage from abroad played a role both in the meaning of the mosque and in the way it was received in Canada. Nor was Al Rashid founded, like many alternative religious groups in North America, as a persecuted collective that sought refuge in Canada's hinterland to practice their religion without public ridicule. Indeed, in some ways Al Rashid came about without great religious purpose. While it is customary now to refer to that founding as an expression of an "Arab group," or as a "Lebanese community," neither identity drove it here. Indeed, to regard Al Rashid as such is a diminution of its history.

Furthermore, beyond conventional treatment of the mosque's founding, this book argues that one cannot discount the Canadian context. That is, the cultural environment of both homeland and Canada were critical for its success, because both those cultures were dominated by adaptation. Newcomers to Canada had to fit accepted norms of practice to succeed. Trends long assimilated in the homeland continued to infuse ideas and interests. As we will see, the Al Rashid of history and the Al Rashid of today have been continuously nourished by both the homeland and the new land. While obviously historical occurrences in Canada irrevocably shaped the mosque's history, links to a distant home played a key role and helped bring the community about. We need to tell the story about how all these elements came together, since they all are necessary for understanding the iconic mosque of today.

Even a cursory look at the history of this mosque community indicates that it has undergone significant, sometimes massive, cultural shifts. From a handful of diverse Arab families knitted together in common social cause, to a sophisticated business and political community migrating towards a Muslim Canadian identity, to a community in the throes of isolation and "otherness" in a suddenly hostile culture after 9/11, to a confident and resilient collective committed to excellence within the Canadian environment, to an engaged element in constructing a multidimensional Canada today, Al Rashid has stood as a bulwark through it all. Al Rashid is a study in a successful process of continuity and change. To provide the reader with a roadmap of this community is our concern here.

This book, then, is an attempt to provide a short history of the Al Rashid community, to portray one way of seeing a most extraordinary institution's trajectory. It tries to sketch that story not as an isolated entity but one intimately connected to both its roots abroad and to its context in Edmonton and Canada. Both have played decisive roles in what Al Rashid is today. Of course, the view presented is selective—no group as diverse and established can be reduced to a short book such as this. I have tried to give a realistic picture of the mosque's history so that today's youth will know and understand how they came to be part of the successful community to which they currently belong. Al Rashid Mosque is a distinctive Islamic creation in Canada, in Edmonton. The community is justifiably proud of its achievement, and Canadians of all stripes can celebrate with it.

The book is divided into five chapters, each of which reflects a decisive trajectory in the community's partnerships for development, and each indicates a refined reaction to either local, Canadian, or international events. Readers should be aware of disparities in the transliteration and spelling of names, many of them derived from diverse sources. We have tried to limit the confusion by choosing a single spelling, but any remaining variations reflect source texts. As historians will attest, telling such a story requires a wide variety of sources and methods. So far as we know, no systematic attempt has been made to outline Al Rashid's history. Working with the community, I have used a number of strategies to gather information. First, there are the insights provided by those who have either written about or been involved in discussing Al Rashid's background—some of whom I have known for almost forty years, including Soraya Zaki Hafez, Richard Awid, and Dr. Abu-Laban. Dr. Ibrahim Abu-Rabi, the holder of Canada's first Edmonton Council of Muslim Communities Chair in Islamic Studies at the University of Alberta, provided much insight while he was with us (see Waugh and Goa 2013).

Second, many who have passed on (may God grant them peace), whom I counted as friends, including Larry Shaban, Saleem Ganam, Muhammad Deeb, and Mahmoud Tarrabain, were influential sources; I have no doubt that my views have been influenced by conversations with them. Then, there are those whom I have interviewed at various times, either recently or for earlier projects, whose insights are also reflected in this story. A complete list of informants is now probably impossible, since some I talked to years ago when I was just beginning to learn about the community. The Provincial Archives of Alberta houses information about early settlers, which has also been helpful, as have a few excerpts from the National Archives of Canada in Ottawa. I have also drawn from earlier studies and lectures, such as those of Drs. Baha Abu-Laban and Sharon McIrvin Abu-Laban, Drs. Regula Burckhardt Qureshi and Salem Qureshi, as well as my own involvement in teaching many of Al Rashid's students over the years. Written and published sources can be found in the bibliography. Local newspapers and news sources, such as the *Edmonton Journal*, *Arab News*, and *Aramco Magazine* have also been useful. I have also consulted various publications and brochures from Al Rashid, some of which appear in the bibliography as well. The fame of Al Rashid has reached many parts of the world, and several films have been made about the mosque, a couple of which are also listed in the bibliography. While I cannot calibrate how much of each of these sets of various resources have shaped my perceptions, I acknowledge that they have all been part of the production of this book.

Clearly, a book like this has a long pedigree. As I have suggested, many authors have sketched important elements in other works, but a few require special mention. Soraya Zaki Hafez, long associated with the community, and with whom I have worked on many projects, consistently urged me to take on the task. Her perceptive understanding of women's roles and her emphasis on women's centrality to the mosque's achievements have made this a more nuanced work. Dr. Baha Abu-Laban, a colleague at the University of Alberta, not only supported the project but provided seminal feedback on the text. And Dr. Maryam Razavy, a former student of mine and collaborator on several projects, contributed excellent editorial skills. Without these three individuals, this book would not have been completed.

Others need special note: Khalid Tarrabain, current president of Al Rashid's board of directors, shared his extensive knowledge of finances, key players, and the currents within the community. Richard Awid, who in his retirement has done much to document the early community, provided great assistance. Salwa Kadri has been of immense help, providing materials and arranging meetings. No one can speak of Al Rashid without noting the extraordinary Hamdon family, beginning with the amazing Hilwie. What a treasure she would have been for a historian in her time. Many are the moments I mourned not being able to chat with her! Karen Hamdon was most generous in providing perspectives. Sine Chadi, Sameeh Salama, Jawdah Jorf, Yousef Chebli, Issam Saleh, and retired Judge Edward Saddy read and provided helpful additional materials on Al Rashid and the Arabian Muslim Association. Mike Drewoth's daughter, Peggy Nelson, sketched the history of Mike's contribution to the early mosque. Several people contributed to Appendix I and the profiles of creativity among the mosque members, including Dalia Saafan, Adnan Elladen, Omar Mouallem, Waleed Elsafadi, and Anwar Elsafadi. I wish also to recognize the assistance of Mr. Clare Peters from the Arts Resource Centre at the

University of Alberta for recording equipment and his technical expertise. Scores of community members have spoken with me over the years, and while time has dimmed who they were, the impression has remained, and this work is largely the result of what they said. Forty years ago, when I was a young scholar in Islamic studies at the University of Alberta, Al Rashid's Muslims welcomed my queries, tolerated my ignorance, and joyfully opened their homes and their hearts. They have graciously suggested that this writing would make a fitting bookend to my career; obviously, they continue to be generous, since they have many options for such a work. I am humbled by their confidence, and think it a fine denouement for our long relationship. Naturally, I am solely responsible for the interpretation of this story.

Al Rashid is an impressive Canadian story; it is my hope that this book sufficiently celebrates a community's amazing contribution to our collective lives.

Finally, a heartfelt thanks to editor Joanne Muzak, and to Peter Midgley and the wonderful staff at the University of Alberta Press.

Earle Waugh
Edmonton

ACKNOWLEDGEMENTS
FROM THE COMMUNITY

THIS BOOK WAS MADE TO HONOUR all people who came together and made Al Rashid Mosque a reality. May Allah (God) reward all those who aided this establishment and continue to support the Canadian Muslim community.

First and foremost, we thank Allah for guiding and blessing us with an Islamic community that has established a prominent place in Canada. We would like to express gratitude for all the pioneer families, who laid the foundations of the mosque and a place to call home. Special thanks go to the Muslim generations that followed, especially the Ladies Association for their efforts, ambitious vision, and tireless perseverance that made the mosque, once a dream, a reality. The generosity and support of these generations made Al Rashid what it is today. All of this would not have happened if not for the dedication of the governing board members, Al Rashid staff, and volunteers, for whom we owe the utmost respect. The vision and dedication you provided made Al Rashid Mosque what it is today and ensured that it fulfills the needs of the Canadian Muslim community.

We would like to take this opportunity to express our gratitude to the federal, provincial, and municipal governments for their efforts in paving the way to build an establishment that will always serve the Muslim community and integrate Muslims into the Canadian fabric. We would like to highlight the efforts of former mayor John Wesley Fry, who believed in our cause, provided the land, and facilitated the process of making Al Rashid a reality. All our years of success would not have been possible without the devotion and support we received from the interfaith community, including our friends from the Jewish and Christian communities.

We extend our thanks and appreciation to Dr. Earle Waugh for his endless commitment towards understanding, researching, and educating the public about minority groups, especially the Muslim community. His dedication has earned him our community's utmost respect. We also wish to thank the University of Alberta for providing an environment that supports research that is vital to sharing knowledge about different cultures and faiths.

We would like to acknowledge the help of all the people involved in this project, including the reviewers who read the earlier versions of the manuscript, and Al Rashid staff who provided the documentation to make this work complete. Without their support, this book could not have been completed. There are so many people who contributed to the Al Rashid's success to date, and to each of them we send our utmost gratitude. There are not enough pages for us to list them all.

We are especially grateful to the following people for their wonderful support over the years:

- Canadian leaders and political connections from both the federal and provincial governments for their support from day one
- The City of Edmonton for being supportive, beginning with Mayor Fry and continuing to today, providing land for us, adjusting the bylaws, and making it easy for our community to move forward

- The board of directors and leadership of Al Rashid for having a solid vision and commitment, for being cohesive, embracing, and open
- Other faith groups, both Jewish and Christian, for their welcoming and helpful attitude over our many years together
- The pioneer families such as the Tarrabains, the Hamdons, and others for their commitment
- Community members, especially the women, beginning with Hilwie Hamdon, right to today
- A special thanks to the board of Al Rashid and Al Rashid staff, along with the volunteers for helping put this history together
- Dr. Earle Waugh and the University of Alberta Press for their work on this history.

Subhana allah
Khalid Ahmed Tarrabain
President, Arabian Muslim Association,
Board of Directors, Al Rashid Mosque

The homelands.

LEAVING FOR RIHLA

The Homeland Situation and the Travelling Identity

1850s–1930s

SCOTTISH CONVERTS WERE THE FIRST MUSLIMS IN CANADA. According to some reports, the Love family from Scotland were the first registered Muslims in Canada in 1863, followed by the Simons in 1871, who came from England via the United States (Hamdani 1997). As Daood Hamdani (2013) notes, the Hunts— Eliza and Henry—were a very prominent family of "Gaelic-speaking Highlanders," who were most probably born in and arrived from Scotland. Perhaps their being Scottish made acceptance in Canada easier, given the country's history of Scottish immigration. Also, the similarity of social and cultural values between Scotland and England and Canada may well have made adjustments for these Muslim families less difficult. Later, Bosnian Muslims arrived in Ontario. They were the first trickle of what would become a steady stream of Muslims from throughout the Muslim world after the Second World War.

It always has been fashionable in the heartland of Islam to appropriate the known world, by either travel or commercial gain.

In classical Islam, the word *rihla*, purposeful movement, defined this kind of travel. Ibn Battuta, the Moroccan scholar known for extensive travels throughout the medieval world, was only one of many Islamic travellers who exemplify this characteristic. Today, with millions of people displaced or in refugee camps, it seems facetious to speak of such purposive travel as "Islamic." Yet it is instructive to acknowledge that there was a Muslim confidence that the world was Allah's and could be embraced no matter how far afield one went. To this has to be added a propensity on the part of "Phoenician"/Lebanese people to be seafarers, as Abu-Laban points out in the documentary film *Al Rashid: The Story of Canada's First Mosque* (Reel Girls Media 2010). Hence, the legacy continued to have some purchase in the eastern Syrian territory of Sham. Indeed, some apparently embraced the travelling identity as their own.

For those who founded Al Rashid, their homeland had been unsettled for at least a century, and, like the milieu of the first rihla traveller, the Prophet Muhammad, movement appeared to offer a more productive and peaceful option than staying. It is helpful, then, to rehearse some of the more critical background issues and motivations that brought about the founding of Al Rashid Mosque in Edmonton in the mid-twentieth century and to relate them to the age-old urge to travel that is implicit in early Islam.

LOOKING OUTWARD FOR A PLACE OF HOPE

Why would Middle Easterners even think of coming to the new lands in the West, especially to those as cold as Canada? How could youngsters in a tiny village in Sham even dream of going this far west? The answer is partly told by the growth of Western colonialism and the development of the new republic of America. Even to today, Middle Easterners do not distinguish between the United States of America and Canada—we are all just America. This lack of distinction is usually taken to indicate a lack of sophistication in geographical knowledge, but North America is more resolutely perceived as a singular place of opportunity for a better life "across the great sea." Effectively, Middle Easterners long ago found America a beacon of hope for a better life. The current hostility towards America arose later, as a post–Second World War phenomenon.

As early as 1777, the fledgling United States of America had a friendship treaty with Morocco to protect American naval vessels docking at Tangiers; this gesture of mutual support has stood the test of time. By 1840, the Sultan of Oman had sent a diplomat to the United States after a treaty of commercial and political peace was signed between the two countries in 1833. These are only the most evident of many elements that connect these two important regions of the world. These ties reflect a growing awareness of the New World and its potential among residents in the Mediterranean region; they paved the way for perceptions of a new and better life in a distant land. The perception of America as a place of hope can be sampled in the articles published in *AramcoWorld*, the Saudi oil magazine, which are replete with rags-to-riches memories. These articles sum up the prevailing views of immigrants from Arab countries—America fulfilled their dream of a peaceful and profitable place to settle and be successful.

Canada was part of this vision. A sizable group of people of Arab heritage filtered into this country from around 1882. By the time of the 1931 census, there were 10,700 people of Arab back-ground, with 645 of them identifying as Muslims (Husaini 1999, 16.) Almost all of them remained in Toronto and Montreal, but a few went to Manitoba. By the late 1920s, Larry Shaban recalled, there were only a handful of Muslims in Alberta, and his "grandfather knew every one of them!" (Lorenz 1998). This slow movement west was typical of migration patterns among the Arabs, who tended to prefer the metropolitan areas where jobs were more plentiful than the tough homesteading life on the Prairies. We will explore some of the reasons for this perception later.

The Middle East, 1830–1920

1833	Syria control to Mohamet Ali of Egypt
	Ottoman Empire in decline
1888	Beirut Vilayet established from Syria, included Sham
1902–1932	Conflicts to establish Saudi Arabia
1914–1918	Eastern Mediterranean in First World War
1916–1921	Middle East areas under British protectorate via the secret Sykes–Picot Agreement

Syria has often been on the receiving end of various political and military invasions. From time immemorial, its geographic location guaranteed the attraction of controlling regimes. In the period leading up to the Arabs coming to Canada, Syria experienced occupying forces—Byzantine, Turkic Mamluk, Ottoman, and later French and British. It was not extraordinary for Sham businessmen to speak several languages and to have dealings with agents from many far-flung places. In the late 1700s, the Ottoman Empire's power was waning, and a new corporate identity based on the Arab foundations of Islam and the widespread use of Arabic was being fostered among tribal groups and the peoples of the Levant.

The catalyst for this change from the 1700s on was the decay at the centre of the Ottoman Empire; that empire controlled most political and financial aspects of life in Syria. The Ottomans showed signs of growing soft, the sultans inept and their viziers corrupt. The communities were occupied by troops under Istanbul's heavy hand, troops that despised them as "lazy Arabs" and as military failures—who cared little for their suffering in seasons of drought or during natural or military disasters. Poor governance thrived, taxes rose. Even when the Ottomans formed an Arab contingent, they were the poorest in training and last in possession of modern weapons. A range of negative experiences promoted an inward turn, a turn expressed against the Turks. It fomented a new "national" spirit where none had existed before. Shaped around the

Arabic language and Muslim culture, the result was an Arab nationalism born in the Mashriq, east of Egypt, but that soon migrated to
nearby regions. This new nationalism was driven by a renaissance
articulated by Arab writers (Tamari 2000), but it was spurred on by
the longstanding results of colonialism (Lewis 2010).

In North America, as the term *Arab* became more and more
associated with *Muslim*, early Arab Christian migrants opted for
the ancient designation of coastal Lebanon *Phoenicia*, to imply a
separate geographical identity from Muslims. The identity blending
of Islam and Arab began a trend that has continued apace around
the world today, even though Arabs do not form the largest group
of Muslims. Indeed, there is a certain sense of responsibility for
Islamic greatness attached to Muslims of Arab heritage, and along
with it the burden of ownership and caring for the health of the
Muslim faith around the globe. This sentiment was certainly felt
among early Muslim families in Alberta.

With internal discipline faltering in Turkey, chaos ensued.
Istanbul, facing the inability to raise large sums of money to run
its far-flung empire, decided to cut costs by downloading security
and military demands onto local governments and contingents.
Rather than pay for its expensive Janissary corps to guard the
Levant, it opted to let local chiefs construct their own armies and
to give them the power to conscript young Arabs into their armies.
Ill-equipped and poorly paid, the young Arabs chafed under the
attitude of their Ottoman commanders, who, though Muslim,
treated them like outsiders and second-class citizens. Syrian
families in Sham worried about the validity of their sons serving
in such a system, and they cast about for other options. America
looked very promising.

Another ingredient that aided Arab nationalist development
has become legendary among Westerners: the saga of Lawrence
of Arabia. For most people in America in the nineteenth and early
twentieth centuries, and indeed even in Europe, Syria belonged to
Asia; it was veiled with a certain Eastern mystique. That mystique was
further enshrined in the word *Orient*. The mythology of Lawrence

solidified this mystique for the ordinary European American. For migrants, these outsider perceptions impacted their perceived identity abroad in several ways: they were surely not European; they came from an inscrutable culture; their values and religions were "different." Some of this mystique continues to shape public perceptions of Middle Eastern immigrants in the West. The turn-of-the-century youth who came to western Canada could hardly have been expected to know the cultural hurdles they faced. In reality, they may have just escaped the Ottoman destruction, but they now had to deal with a ready-made image of who they were that was not compatible with their real lives—a disconnect that continues today.

Nineteenth-Century Changes in the Islamic Heartland

Most early Arab immigrants had dealt with dramatic political change in the homeland, which continued later in the Middle East with the presence of Britain and France as colonial powers. But the dominance of foreign commercial and political representatives also heralded another kind of challenge: the quandary of how Islam, which Muslims believed was God's final religion, could now appear as relegated to a secondary position historically in God's plan for the world's peoples. To have representatives of the earlier theological traditions—that is, Judaism and Christianity—now dominate the world required Muslims to undertake considerable ideological adjustment.

The situation in the Islamic heartland spurred a number of responses, many of which are still with us today. For example, it is important to note that the shift brought about by the West in the Middle Eastern power structures awakened Muslims to the potential of moving west as the next great direction of emigration. The lure of careers within the vortex of colonial powers offered much to the struggling youngsters of Sham. Some of the pragmatists among them saw opportunity awaiting them in the West.

This was not, however, the only reason for going west. Britain, France, and America appeared to offer a way of life that fit with the modern temper of the times. All around them, voices were calling for various degrees of reform and accommodation to new models coming from these centres of political power. Those intent on quick reform, as youth are wont to espouse, found the pace of change in the Islamic heartland too miniscule and full of contention.

It is critical to note that many immigrants left the heartland of Islam precisely at a time of great religious upheaval there. They were often directly affected by these reforms. The most long-lasting of the period's reform movements is undoubtedly that deriving from the military and religious activities of Ibn Saud and Muhammad Ibn Abd al-Wahhab during the mid- to late 1700s. Two significant movements arose from these activities: one called Salafism, the other widely known as Wahhabism. The first was rapidly exported throughout the Muslim world, when Muslims attended the *hajj*. Salafism advocated a return to the basic principles of Islam as represented by the activities of the pious founders, the *salaf*; doing so meant a jettisoning of much of classical Islamic development and embracing the time of the Prophet as normative.

The Wahhabi tradition, on the other hand, argued for a purging of the social and tribal life of Arab Muslims, with a strict adherence to the doctrines derived exclusively from the Qur'an. Sharia, conservatively conceived, was the ultimate law. That ideology became the official doctrine of the new Saudi Arabian state, particularly after 1901 when military hegemony was established by Abdulaziz Ibn Saud. Yet both Salafi and Wahhabi movements were anti-modernist and anti-democratic. Those who were restive under these movements must have viewed migration to the West and to America as a shift away from antiquity and towards the modern, in contrast to the influences they saw emanating from the central cities of Mecca and Medina. The religious attitudes behind immigration, therefore, were complicated; not all motivations can be captured by the rihla theme.

The very development of these Islamic reformist movements meant that people could harbour sharply divergent views about what was going on at "home." On the one hand, it was obvious that migrants could not establish a replica of the community they had left, since that community itself was in the throes of change. On the other hand, they all were aware of the critique of Islam by Westerners; British and French governments of the time, for example, adamantly held that Islam could not be reformed—it was too buried in medieval sophistry to be able to adapt to the New World. Some Islamic reformers argued that this was simply not true, and sought to prove it. They picked up the gauntlet. The result was not always edifying.

How many left homelands because they disagreed with the reformists is not known, but it seems clear that the early settlers felt they were not just building an outpost for ancient Islamic doctrines in Canada; rather, they were looking to establish a socially cohesive group that would enlist others to help define the community of Muslims here. The desire to shift from tribal and traditional cultures to creating a more cohesive Muslim community abroad was a significant one.

Furthermore, it seems clear that Muslim culture abroad was not concerned with mimicking the fundamentalism of the Salafis. For example, energy was building among Muslim women. Turkey, the Levant, Egypt, and North Africa were all being shaken by another movement that was to have a profound impact: the Islamic feminist movement. While initially it took a strong stance against the dictums of the theologians on the role and rights of women, the movement actually grew from the trend to return to the Qur'an for Islam's values, a leaf from Salafi ideology. When they returned to the holy book itself, they saw clearly that Muslim governments had overwhelmingly embraced patriarchal views, even extending those notions into the sharia. The results are still being felt in Muslim environments.

Certainly, the women who migrated to Canada believed in their inherent rights as defined by the Qur'an, and their actions in Canada indicate that they fully believed in their equality. Some women even dared to come west on their own. Sheila McDonough and Sajida Alvi (2002) document a young Muslim widow named Amina from the Beqaa Valley who arrived in Canada with one of her two daughters, Rikia. Historians traced their arrival to Calgary and then to Edmonton, where the stronger Muslim community was forming. According to Camilla Gibb and Celia Rothenberg (2000) in their examination of Turkish and Palestinian Muslim women in the diaspora in Canada, the recorded number of Muslims in Canada in 1871 was thirteen. Amina and her daughter may have been two of them.

SYRIAN ADAPTABILITY AND THE SHAM MIGRANTS

The application of the term *Arab* to migrants from Syria was not universally embraced by the earliest immigrants—and for good reason. No unified collective government comprised "the Arabs," so, geographically, the term was ambivalent, and the designation of who belonged to the term was problematic. Many, such as the earliest immigrants to Alberta—Sam Jomha, Mike Tarrabain, and Ahmed Awid—had their "Arab" identity filtered through cultural dimensions of their own backgrounds. They came from small communities clustered in Sham, a territory in the eastern part of Syria in what is known as the Beqaa Valley; it was a fertile region often overrun in history by invaders with whom they naturally disagreed; their ancestors were often disenfranchised. They possessed Ottoman passports but these were not always useful—a certain suspicion was attached to them. They were small farmers or businessmen and unaccustomed to large cities or big-city ways; they dealt with customs officials who said that Americans didn't like Muslims, so they should change their names. Their most valued networks were not the polyglot of immigrants like themselves but their families or surrogate families—that is, their language and faith communities.

These surrogate families formed social networks much like they had back home. There they had been knit together around a common religious culture defined by the headman or sheikh whose religion was more or less that espoused by most others in the community. The model applied to both Christians and Muslims. Furthermore, there was no strong divide religiously between the members of these communities abroad; in fact, they usually celebrated each other's festivities and enjoyed holidays together. They were aware that the most numerous early migrants from Sham were Christians, some of whom had settled in South America or eastern Canada. Since they shared common social values across religious boundaries—the people they knew became a huge asset abroad—Muslims had no difficulty in seeking perspectives from Christians on life in America. This social attitude was to contribute in a major way to settlement in Alberta and in Canada.

One cohesive Sham community, called Kerbet Rouha, whose claim to fame was the tallest minaret in the land, espoused Sunni law and doctrine, yet its residents practiced various faiths while sharing certain social values and living peacefully within it. Many early settlers to Canada came from that village, as well as the neighbouring village of Lala. The fertile Beqaa Valley had many small communities of people from various religious backgrounds—Marionite and Melikite Christian, Eastern Orthodox Christian, Druze, and even Shia. They had existed within the Ottoman Empire as identifiable communities, *wilayats*, with their own law courts, cultural traditions, and doctrines. While their outward identity fragmented along religious lines, they had key aspects of their lives in common—language for one, a dialect of Arabic—and they all existed within an umbrella of Islamicate cultural cohesion, meaning a shared value system that featured an appreciation of tolerant Islamic social life, an acceptance of Islamic moral and artistic traditions, and an adherence to an Islamic business framework. Most important perhaps, the various religious groups had a history of living peacefully together for centuries.

The conclusion to be drawn from this background is that there was a strong internal cohesion among the early migrants deriving from two directions: the close-knit social order of village life and the unifying nature of an Islamo-Arab cultural network. As we shall see, these features of their original civic situation continued to shape public life in Canada, and helped foster an internal integrity to the growing community. However, village life was not simply transferred to Canada, since the urban environment in which Al Rashid developed brought influences far more complex than that, but the community never lost sight of its Sham roots. Moreover, the social dimension, steeped as it was in Islamic hospitality values and Arab linguistic commonalities, motivated the pioneers to construct the mosque as both a place for Sunni prayer and (in the basement) a place for social gatherings that reached beyond any sectarian division. These features were to have a profound effect on community life with Al Rashid at its centre as it matured in Canada.

RATIONALES FOR MIGRATION

Both oral and published sources describe a variety of personal reasons for migration. As mentioned above, families were concerned about sons being conscripted into a Turkish army, and explored emigration as a means to protect family stability and growth (Awid 2010). Some of the movement was to escape from the violence of war. However, most of the early pioneers were entrepreneurs. They often developed businesses. Some, such as Ali Abouchadi or Peter Baker, started as fur buyers and peddlers (see Baker 1976). Others—namely, Sam Jomha and Ali Awid Amcrey—began as goods suppliers, and others still—including Ali Ahmed Abouchadi and Bedouin Ferran—opened general stores. These early entrepreneurs developed an extensive network of customers throughout Canada's north. They partnered with locals who had cultural or religious commonalities. They maintained linkages to the old country by favouring companies that had roots in Middle Eastern culture, including Kouri Wholesale Grocer, established in Montreal in 1898, and Tabah Cousins Ltd., a dry goods dealer founded in Montreal in 1900. They were also subject to the snowball network effect, where mail exchanged by early Canadian pioneers and Middle Easterners fostered community and created perceptions of successful business opportunities and good living conditions. Invitations to migrate then became the basis of a personal network that linked would-be migrants with those already established in Canada.

This network characteristic is reflected in the leapfrog nature of early development—the northern movement of immigration had to deal with the lack of rail transportation to northern Alberta, which meant that Winnipeg and Brandon, Manitoba, were early stopovers for pioneers. The Fahlman family, for example, moved from Brandon to Edmonton, and Sam Jomha walked over 1,100 kilometres from Brandon to Fort Saskatchewan in Alberta, selling goods along the way. It took a lot of determination to undertake such treks!

There is an untold story of how these hardy pioneers linked up with Indigenous peoples. Often they dealt with Cree-speaking communities that were scattered in irregular patterns across the north. Some of the Muslim newcomers, like Abouchadi, learned some Cree and used it in business. According to Mahmoud Tarrabain (1981), some peddlers even invented new Cree words to describe the pots and pans they sold. They learned the value of cultivating relationships with Indigenous customers in the wilderness, for they could stay with them during an evening rather than venturing on in the cold, dark night. In effect, Indigenous communities became partners in a far-flung peddler's circuit in the north country. Certainly, the success of the Muslim enterprises was founded on Indigenous hospitality throughout the northwest.

This Muslim group had different motivations than other newcomers to Canada around this time. They did not come primarily as homesteaders or farmers such as brought floods of Ukrainians to Alberta in the 1900s; nor did they come as besieged groups seeking relief from persecution as Russian, German Mennonites, Amish, or Doukhobors often did. Nor did they come as adventurers or explorers, as so many from Scotland and England had in earlier times. In short, the early Muslim community was constructed around those who looked to the New World as a place to foster a successful life, mostly in business, but they were certainly adaptable to whatever opportunities the new land would afford. Much of Al Rashid's success has flowered from these kinds of expectations that brought its members to Canada.

Rihla as Motivation

One aspect of Muslim motivation for migration is not usually found in studies; migration really originated in a travel ideology, usually for business, but also for pleasure. In fact, travel was considered of great significance for the expansion of Islam in its early days. While the dominant perception holds that Islam expanded by conquest, business travel motivated much of the religion's early growth. During the rise of classical Islamic civilization, its citizens established an impressive tradition of writing about travel, journeys, and foreign places for business. The inspiration for such travel, in part, has religious roots: the most paradigmatic journey of all was the Prophet's, who moved to Medina to escape the plots against him in Mecca. The journey's importance was reinforced by the once-in-a-lifetime requirement for the believer to journey to Mecca for the pilgrimage. The result is an impressive history of travel writing and documentation, ranging from a description of trips to and from the *hajj*, to letters to business associates about cultural activities in foreign capitals. Generally, this writing is grouped under the term *rihla*. It is somewhat surprising that this rich vein of Islamicate productivity has not been probed by historians and other scholars; although some accounts have attracted enough attention to be translated, they really only serve to signal the vastness of the storehouse of memoirs in personal libraries throughout the world (Broadhurst 1952; Dunn 1986).

Certainly, the Orientalist tradition in Middle Eastern studies in the West has been slow to recognize the significance of this prodigious output, to examine its importance in the development of Islamicate culture, and, for that matter, to give it much attention as a genre within Islamic history. In our day, postcolonial analysts have often examined the writings of migrants and exiles, with an implicit or explicit intent, usually to indicate the unfortunate result of colonialism, but they have not searched this material to determine the relevance of earlier models, such as the joys of discovering and inhabiting a new place (Vassanji 1985, 63–67).

In *Muslim Travellers: Pilgrimage, Migration, and the Religious Imagination*, however, editors Dale Eickelman and

James Piscatori (1990) bring together articles that survey the scope of this travel literature. What emerges is a far more complicated picture of the relationship of religion to the genre than one might have supposed. Their research shows that the rihla genre encompasses *hijra* (emigration), *hajj* (pilgrimage), *rihla* (travel for learning and business), and *ziyāra* (visits to shrines and holy places), all of which are practiced under some degree of purposive *religious* intent. Yet the literature that this travel generated and the motivations it endorses reflect "pervasive intricacy and even ambiguity" (Eickelman and Piscatori 1990, xii).

Travellers' writings shift back and forth between the religious and what we would call the secular, as migration for business or pleasure sometimes carried with it the need to establish the community wherever Muslims put down roots, a quasi-cultural as well as religious motive. It would seem, then, that even the most secular of motivations might also entail covert religious intentions, and the writers are quite capable of shifting their self-understanding between several different cultural and personal agendas, apparently without discomfort. Reflecting the elasticity of rihla, the boundaries continually shift: religious concerns may be expressed in business or educational forms, and private matters may be garbed in religious language. In short, ambiguities born out of identity differentiations, whether racial, historical, political, or ethnic, appear to be part of the genre, not necessarily generated by recent experience (Malak 1993). Rihla could also take on a missionizing dimension. This dimension was most often associated with the travel of a Sufi leader who would take up residence in another part of the world where his spiritual vision appealed to adepts. But rihla was not a tool of crusading or conversion, at least as it came to be expressed in some forms of Christianity. Islamic culture was far more embracing of religious diversity.

Given its historical significance, the rihla genre helps us understand why the early Sham migrants came to Alberta and why they thought it critical enough to establish a mosque. It was not enough to find a place for prayer, which, after all, could have been accommodated in schools or even church basements. Building a mosque is one of the themes of travel and establishment rooted in the rihla genre. It is a way of marking the Muslim community's existence in another environment. It is a basic way of belonging— one sanctioned by the very life of the Prophet himself.

EARLY MUSLIMS AND EMERGING CANADIAN VALUES

What kind of social and cultural values did the early Muslims come to in Canada? What ideological foundation did they find? George-Étienne Cartier, one of the Fathers of Confederation, expressed the basis of religion for Canadian history as a unity of diversity: "If we unite we will form a political nationality independent of the national origin and religion of individuals. As to the objection that we cannot form a great nation because Lower Canada is chiefly French and Catholic, Upper Canada English and Protestant, and the Maritime provinces mixed, it is completely futile...In our confederation there will be Catholics and Protestants, English and French, Irish and Scotch, and each by its efforts and success will add to the prosperity, the might, and the glory of the new federation" (Boyd 1971, 222–23). The fruit of this policy was the acceptance of religion as a formative element in Canadian identity. The Canadian Charter of Rights and Freedoms notes that Canada exists *under God*. Yet it ignored the potential conflicts in the prioritizing tendencies of religious commitment; for example, the Charter says nothing about disagreements on the religious foundations of social and ethical norms.

The Canadian west, however, was defined by the missionizing and colonial impetus of the Christian tradition. Indeed, the nature of Canadian immigration in total has been directly influenced by the national churches: in the early days, the majority of immigrants came to Canada through these church organizations. As a result, the number of immigrants with little church or religious affiliation was small. Especially when the prairies opened up and the flood of movement onto the land in the west began, arrangements for migrants who respected certain "values" allowed churches to sanction the movements of whole communities onto the land. The Mennonites are one example. In turn, a significant number of churches built both a national and ethnic consciousness. This feature is important for Muslims, because, while Islam is religious and claims no ethnic content, in effect Canadian culture has consciously assisted ethnic Muslims in retaining and affirming their national and ethnic identities by insisting on an "ethnic" character to migration—hence the early emphasis on Al Rashid being established by the Arabian Muslim Association (1934), just as the Jewish congregation had done in 1906 when they formed the Edmonton Hebrew Association to build Beth Israel Synagogue.

The policy of migration via church organizations was carried out through the active participation of the governments of central Canada for their own reasons. It was, on the one hand, a colonization policy, designed to enact a Canadian national destiny by peopling the prairies with a "socially acceptable" population. Part of this was motivated by a concern that if Canada did not populate the west, the United States would. Immigrants were part of national establishment policy. In addition, the prospect of a western Canada that required the manufacturing capabilities of eastern Canada was attractive to Toronto and Montreal. But there was also a Canadian ideology behind this move: a vast unpopulated land lay open to developing British conceptions of law, justice, and, ultimately, a distinctive sense of freedom.

Immigrant ethnic and religious diversity was the price the eastern English-speaking governments were willing to pay, since it not only offset the dreams of the French Catholics but also guaranteed a grateful and submissive foreign contingent. All this change took place in a remarkably short period, between 1870 and 1920, which also made cultural continuity all the more important. It was precisely this era that brought Muslims west.

All was not rosy for immigrants to the west; Canada had instituted a policy of incarcerating "enemy aliens" during the First

World War—mostly, Ukrainians or Germans with connections to the war territories in Europe, but there were also a few Arabs among them, especially those with direct links to Ottoman territories and conflicts. While this policy had little impact on Arab migration to the Canadian west, it did throw a pall over Canada as a destination.

While the ideological balance of religious forces might have provided Canada with positive elements for discourse across diversity in the early decades, that conversation did not occur. In fact, from the early days, a tone of rancour and competition prevailed, and played a role in the mission enterprises and reactions of the churches in the developing west. Protestants looked to western lands as arenas to extend the Reformation heritage, and Catholics saw them as grounds for the logical extension of the Church in Quebec. The French hierarchy supported the French language and culture as a means of maintaining the hegemony of the Catholic vision in Canada, while Protestant groups laboured vigorously so that their dreams would not take second place. The one positive result, not immediately evident, was that settlement on the prairies was intimately tied to the notion of developing a cohesive national church in Canada, in direct contrast with the situation in the United States, where individuals and sects migrated to the west in pursuit of religious and personal freedom. Therefore, organized religion asserted far more than a voluntary role in the shaping of the Canadian experience. It also infused a kind of nationalism into the religious enterprise in Canada. We see this role played out in the dominance of the perception of Muslims in the West as "Arab," even though many early Arabs were Christian.

Pluralism also triumphed through a cluster of ideological concerns that had religious dimensions. Some of these concerns were connected with the mission of the Church to the masses of immigrants. More than one Church official saw the Christianizing of the nation as a necessary ingredient in civilizing it. The Church, whether Catholic or Protestant, developed energetic mission programs, at the heart of which was the conviction that moral fibre and strong character were essential in building up the kingdom of God. This mission blossomed mightily during the nineteenth century, when Catholic orders and Protestant mission groups set their sights on continuing the great values of Christian tradition in the new nation of Canada. These two religious orientations differed significantly in the definition of the mission—the ultramontanists of Quebec would look to a strong hierarchy, almost medieval in ideal, from the local parish through the archbishops to the Holy Father in Rome, while the most aggressive Protestants, the Methodists and the Baptists, would brandish millennial visions and actively fight against alcohol and other social vices in their effort to bring about the morally upright Canada of their hopes. Yet both Catholics and Protestants wanted legislation to reflect their concepts, and in many cases it did. Government was shaped by their concerns. Ultimately, social activism embodied in legislation was to secularize the mission legacy of the churches, giving Canadian governments the appearance of both liberalism and community sensitivity. Especially among Protestants, the moral responsibility built into missions would translate into the material and cultural development of the nation when the original message had withered and died. Muslims and Jews were grafted on to this sense of moral responsibility, as we shall see in the establishment of religion-based schools, notably the Edmonton Islamic Academy.

This focus on community over the individual has made the Canadian experience far less schismatic and particularist than the American experience; Canada's Wild West was very dull indeed compared with that of its southern neighbour. The North-West Mounted Police, established in 1873, were already in the west before most settlers arrived, and the sense of extending tradition in a hostile environment applied not only to religion but also to law. Since some of the greatest conflicts were between groups within a religious tradition, the law mediated for them. Because law was held to embody the moral dimensions of society, it transmuted into a kind of supra value system for all. Respect for law remains one of the chief traits on which Canadians pride themselves. This loyalty to a hereditary law would eventually clash with notions of freedom of religion in Ontario's confrontation with the establishment of sharia courts, a critical issue that is explored later in this book as it impacted Al Rashid.

Loyalties to community and law have had their impact in turn on Canadian religious life. The impacts of these loyalties affected the Al Rashid community in two ways: first, the impact of the unification movement in Protestant groups countered fragmentation on ideological bases; and second, the Canadian resistance to the adoption of schismatic religious organizations required adherence to a majoritarian viewpoint. In the first, just as the community was organizing itself around a mosque project in the early 1930s, the Presbyterian, Methodist, and Congregational churches decided they could not singly meet the needs of the Protestant population with the few resources they had. In 1925, they amalgamated as the United Church of Canada. This move was important for the mosque project because the failure of these churches to sustain their original congregations meant that Christianity might not be as universal in Canada as had been thought; it meant there was room for other traditions. It also meant that, in the post-unification years, a new vigour seized the Protestant churches. Muslims realized that organizational structure was necessary in Canada if they were to retain their beliefs and pass them on.

The second fact—Canadians' reluctance to adopt schismatic religious organizations—points to early efforts to convert Canadians to Islam, which were always low key and individually oriented, and generally unsuccessful. The strength of the Christian tradition was too strong, so that even attempts to convert Indigenous people, as evidenced by the growing Baha'i movement, had very little success. The fact is that no authentically Canadian religious group has sprung up in Canada. No equivalent to the black Muslim movement in the United States has evolved in Canada. A number of movements and revivals have influenced the whole, but no new group has appeared as a genuinely Canadian religion. Canada's best-known evangelist, Aimee Semple McPherson, did not remain in her homeland but found her greatest success in Los Angeles in the 1920s and 1930s. Individual religious initiatives always seemed to run counter to the prevailing spirit of the country, and, as a result, Canada is lauded for its stability and conservatism while being chastised for its reluctance to risk and its resistance to difference. Conversion to a new group is not massively salable in Canada—only sixty-one groups are noted in a 2001 census of identifiable Christians; in contrast, the United States has several hundred (Waugh 2010). Even converts to the new jihadist ideology connect to ISIS or al-Qaeda abroad: creating religious difference is not a Canadian social phenomenon, and it is not linked to any Canadian Muslim institutional organization. In fact, Islam has followed well-worn patterns in putting down roots in Canada. And the way it has been established follows furrows of Canadian making. Awareness of this reality slowly convinced the earliest Muslim newcomers that they needed to establish their own tradition from abroad to serve their own people according to the perceived Canadian pattern.

The Muslim families of the pioneer era, approximately 1900 to 1914, often describe the problematic of keeping Islamic values and cultural traditions alive. They highlight a simple lack of technological and travel capabilities, the dominant Christian social and cultural fabric to which they had to adjust, different political structures, and the lack of an international Muslim support system as barriers to cultivating Islamic values. Hamdani (1997) underscores the lack of religious and societal institutions within Canada during the pioneer era to support Muslim individual and familial identities; during this time, and in the absence of other Muslims, "religious identity depended upon the extent of one's own determination…Retaining religious identity would have been difficult enough, transmitting it even harder" (3). Constructing Edmonton's mosque was, in part, a reaction to that felt lacuna.

Hamdani (1997) also notes that, in contrast to the European immigrants of the earlier generation, the 1900 to 1914 era was marked by non-European Arab Muslim migrants. It is true that the earlier European migrants had had no social or religious institutional support, but they at least came from a known political culture. Unlike them, non-European Arab Muslim migrants found

that everything, including cultural values, were very different.
Moreover, the countries from which they arrived were under
Ottoman colonial rule, which, in effect, had a completely different
political structure. In contrast to the earliest Scottish Muslims, their
knowledge of the English language was next to nil. Furthermore,
the migrants from the Arab Muslim countries did not arrive as
families; instead, they came as young single men primarily for
economic reasons (Abu-Laban 1983, 76). Indeed, at the time, historians determined that the largest settlement of these new Canadian
Muslims was in the Prairie provinces of Alberta and Saskatchewan.
The third-largest province of settlement was British Columbia.
Young Arab male migrants of this time were well suited for life in
the Prairies; they were in their late teens and early twenties and
were hard-working agriculturalists (Hamdani 2013). According
to scholars, interfaith marriage was common during this period,
and therefore mainstreaming and carrying religious values on into
their children became a major issue. Apparently, families developed
rapidly. Camilla Gibb and Celia Rothenberg (2000) state that the
population of Canadian Muslims in 1901 grew to between three and
four hundred, comprising equal numbers of Turks and Syrians.

EDMONTON, A RIHLA COMMUNITY'S STOPPING PLACE

Edmonton's historic role as meeting place, as well as its importance
in the fur trade and the long tradition of trade among Indigenous
peoples, gave it a sense of permanence that few other cities offered
in Alberta at the turn of the century. Rail lines, North-West
Mounted Police staging grounds, and courts reflected its growing
position in Canada's west. Educational opportunities were rapidly
expanding. A growing population indicated the city's increasingly
influential role in the development of Alberta. Recent migrants
to Edmonton could sense its future. Reworking the old proverb,
they had travelled, now they had to vanquish the wilderness and
make it home. At least five dimensions of Edmonton of the period
might have drawn Muslims to it: the formation of an Arab/Muslim

social community; the emphasis on educational resources for a
growing younger generation; the city's connection to business
opportunities in the North; the felt need to root the community
physically in Alberta; and a cast of charismatic leaders who shaped
the community's future in Edmonton.

Edmonton's Growth, 1894–1940s

1894   Settlement beyond walls of Fort Edmonton

1904   City of Edmonton (pop. 5,000) established

1905   Edmonton named capital city of Alberta

1912   Amalgamation with the City of Strathcona extends
the city south of the North Saskatchewan River

1914   Rapid population growth (72,000)

1929   Blatchford Field, first licensed airfield in Canada, opens in
Edmonton; Edmonton recognized as Gateway to the North

1947   First major oil strike made in nearby Leduc

The Formation of a Muslim Social Community

With Edmonton's rise as the province's capital and the focal point
for northern destinations, and mindful of the resources that were
building in the city, Muslims were attracted to it. By 1904, there were
only two or three families living within the city, but that encouraged
a nucleus that banded together for social and religious support.

The emphasis on a social community is evident from the name
of the sustaining organization: it was not the Mosque Construction
Society, but the Arabian Muslim Association. The social focus was
paramount, perhaps a reflection of the city's willingness to accept
the need for a compatible social meeting place for those who spoke
Arabic, just as there were already meeting places for the Ukrainians,
Poles, Germans, and French. As the community moved towards
integration, the Arab nature of the group was dominant, as can be
gleaned from the eleven main families whose surnames appeared on
the incorporation papers in 1934. The eighteen members who signed
the documents constituted the early community.

Al Rashid Mosque charter members, 1960s.

Arab Families of the Early Community

Ahmed	Mahmoud Sa'id, Rikia Mahmoud Sa'id, Vira Samuel
Al-Hadjar	Najjib Ali, Margaret Ali
Amerey	Ali Awid, Sa'id
Awid	Ahmed, Ali Alex, Richard, Lila
Chadi	Mohamed Ali Mostafa, Sine Mohamed
Darwish	Mahmoud, Omer, Mimi
Halat	Kasim, Mohamed, Nabiha
Hamdon	Ali, Hilwie, Mohamed Ali, Faye, Mahmoud, Mojamed Monier
Jomha	Ali, Sam Mohamed, Mohamed "Rony"
Tarrabain	Sa'id, Ali, Esmil, Ahmed, Mohamed
Teha	Darwish, Mohamed, Miriam, Eva

(Awid 2010, with additions by the author)

Beyond the usual propensities of a city, though, Edmonton had other attractions for these migrants: it was a city made up of small communities. Unlike some urban centres where growth can be measured as a radius from a civic nuclei to clustering appendages around the inner circle, Edmonton was formed by the regular addition of self-defining communities with historical or personal roots—Strathcona, Garneau, Windsor Park, Bonnie Doon, and so on, all uniquely identifiable geographically and all (now) part of a master organization of community leagues, each community with their own club house and social programs. In effect, the city was made up of villages. While it is unlikely the early Muslims consciously responded to this village culture, it is worth pondering whether the Sham migrants felt at home because they had moved from a Sham village to an Edmonton village. This idea is given more credence when the centre of their life in Edmonton was the village of Central McDougall, a community stretching north from Jasper Avenue and connecting with the growing community taking shape east of 97 Street, which was home to many flourishing churches. This was a settled community with which the early sojourners could identify.

Interestingly, it was the women who helped bring integration both with the community at large and the Muslim *ummah* itself. Community dinners attracted many friends and associates. It is not hyperbole to say Edmontonians loved the women's cooking. Community dinners were always well-attended affairs. Until the Muslim community had its own place, it had to use someone's parlour or a schoolroom for dinners, but people came.

As the community began to flourish, it picked up a tradition from the Ukrainians and Poles: the box lunch. Girls and young women bought and decorated their own baskets, and filled them with homemade goodies. The boxes went to the highest bidder, and the funds went into the mosque fund. Needless to say, the young men carefully bid on their favourite girls' handiwork. It was great fun and gave rise to all kinds of speculation! These box lunch auctions also developed a sense of community that could not be bought at any price.

Educational Resources for a Growing Generation

Muslim families who lived in the hinterland could survive there when the children were young, but once they grew, parents were aware that they needed social contact with like-minded people if they were to maintain their heritage. Thus, moving to the city, even in the name of education for children, has a large element of seeking social context to maintain the Arab/Muslim belief system beyond the first generation. Moreover, Canada's policy on filling the prairies with immigrants meant that the country could hardly turn around and deny immigrants their religious identity. The wide variety of churches was testimony of the success of embracing all kinds of diversity in order to people the land with immigrants from abroad.

By 1907, Alberta's first premier, A.C. Rutherford, had prevailed upon the government to support his plan for a university, a place that would uphold the common good, or as the University of Alberta's first president, Henry Marshall Tory, said, "Uplift the whole people" (Corbett 1992). Muslims would see that as another sign of the viability of calling Edmonton home, for now they could foresee their children excelling in scholarship that they could never have dreamed of back home. The potential for education for their children must have made the city a solid choice, given the long history of Islamic education, a history that led all the way back to the world's first university, Al-Azhar in Cairo. It must have been a heady outcome for these migrants, many of whom could scarcely speak English, to look forward to the day when their children could attend university.

The community had another educational issue: no one had been trained in Islamic theology. Indeed, other than an awareness of prayers and special activities such as Ramadan, few had any particular insights into how sharia should apply or if it did in Canada. In Sunni tradition, no spiritual role was theologically assigned to mosque personnel, such as the imam. The most honoured and eldest of the male believers led the prayer, but no priestly significance attended that function. Yet the fledgling community in Canada could see that the heads of religion around them acted in many ways for the community. Moreover, just advice on how to handle moral issues with other Canadians needed a seasoned viewpoint.

The community needed someone to be involved in the education of their children. They needed someone to teach the community proper prayer etiquette and to be a leader in a whole range of activities related to Islamic life: studying and reciting the Qur'an in Arabic, interpreting sharia, overseeing and performing marriages, providing advice on Muslim divorce, preaching the sermon after the Friday noon prayers, conducting funerals, assisting immigrants with government documents, and so on. (Parenthetically, we can note that the development of such services signals a dramatically different role for the imam in Canada than what the immigrants had been used to abroad.)

All of these requirements suggest an institutional setting dedicated to their provision. The perception of a building to house these service specialties was quite in line with other religious organizations in Canada and the community responded in the same way that other immigrant groups had when they encountered the need: they built a building dedicated to those purposes.

Business Opportunities in the North

Edmonton's claim to fame in the early 1900s stemmed from its long association with the fur trade. Trappers, fur buyers, and mink ranchers continued to send their pelts through the city when the first Muslims arrived. Indeed, some of the earliest arrivals, such as Bedouin Ferran, established themselves in the fur trading business to compete with the Hudson's Bay Company. Others became mink farmers in places like Lac La Biche. The city didn't lose its frontier connection to furs until the twentieth century.

The ability to adapt was key. As those businesses dwindled, supplies for coal mining, forestry and lumber, and farm equipment blossomed. Muslims adapted easily to this new sphere of growth. Peddlers had connected communities in the north early on through theirs treks with pots and pans, trinkets, and toys. They gradually moved into dry goods as families drove demand for clothes. As soon as the population grew, groceries became the principal commodity. Muslim businessmen launched stores and shipping enterprises. As

Soraya Zaki Hafez (2014) noted, "The early Muslim founders first of all embraced Canada as place of economic accomplishment: they began on foot, then moved to horse, then on to carriage and then to the built store and a sedentary lifestyle—a picture of the evolution of success."

As the north gradually opened, both rail and air transport linked the capital to the developing territory. In 1919, following the First World War, returning pilot Wilfrid Reid "Wop" May built a barnstorming company to provide supplies and health services to northern communities. Although the company failed, he eventually founded a viable service in the north (Allan 1966). Thereafter, Edmonton became the centre of a supply network to remote areas in northern Alberta, and the city became known as the Gateway to the North.

The Need to Physically Root the Community

The motivation for building mosques, Islamic schools, and cultural centres is closely tied to an Islamic sense of appropriating space. As Barbara Metcalf (1996) points out in *Making Muslim Space in North America and Europe*, a number of variables come into play when Islam is established outside of identifiable Islamic territory, and these variables shape the community.

Traditionally, the mosque has never played the role as the focus of Muslim identity, even though Muslim governments and caliphs built mosques as expressions of their piety or for political purposes. Technically, Muslims can pray anywhere, so long as they orient themselves towards Mecca; a sacred environment is not a prerequisite for that prayer to be effective. Friday noon prayer is the only time when Muslims are abjured to gather together for prayer as a group, and then only men usually congregate. The result is that the mosque functions as only one indicator that Muslims live in a region; no measure of Muslim religiosity can be gleaned by checking regular attendance.

The fact that Alberta's Muslim immigrants formed an organization to build the second purpose-built mosque in North America in Edmonton, during a severe economic depression even, signals a distinctive feature for these believers; that is, they held Muslim identity to be tied into the creation of a sacred space. In effect, they came to hold that a definite physical presence in the Canadian landscape was necessary to accommodate their spiritual develop-ment. Thus, a mosque, as building, becomes a central affirming element of Muslim permanence in Canada. Like the twenty-three brethren churches nearby, the mosque was both an Edmonton and a Muslim creation, reflecting a way of announcing a presence in the larger community and yet following the model well recognized by newcomers with different religious ideas: one needs a group-owned structure to declare permanence. It indicates equality of claim in a land so given to movement and impermanence. In fact, one of the attractions of the city was its religious diversity: one could find just about any group one wished somewhere in the city's environs. Indeed, the area around which the mosque was initially built was known as Church Street. One of the strengths of Edmonton from a Muslim point of view was this very diversity. The case could easily be made that with such variety, a Muslim house of prayer fit right in.

A Cast of Charismatic Leaders

Just how much do we owe the building of this community to the personality of its people? In many Al Rashid publications, there is almost an implicit belief that the community was constructed by the indomitable Arab/Lebanese spirit of the eleven leading families. This view is a natural outgrowth of the predominant Syrian origin of the community's principal early migrants. But we owe the building to far more than this. Other communities across Canada have had predominantly Syrian migrants, but they neither developed a mosque nor fostered a mosque culture. Even the substratum of Arabness cannot explain both the depth and success of Edmonton's Al Rashid community. So, while this history acknowledges the role of leading personalities, allocating singular credit to them is not quite appropriate. At the very least, as it was established, the Muslim community received important input from the experience of other faith communities, as well as instruction from Christian Arabs and Jews on crafting a viable working community. For example, the early history of the mosque community shows a great deal of flexibility in adherence to doctrine; people could end up Christian or Muslim merely if their parents were convinced that it mattered. Otherwise, many norms (about marrying outside the faith, or drinking alcohol, for example) were ascribed to on the basis of a slow maturing of the community. We suspect that somewhat the same process was at work in shaping the community. Family names and family traditions slowly rose to the surface and came to define the mosque community. In keeping with the idea that leading families played a significant role in shaping the community, a few key people are profiled below. There is not space to describe everyone who contributed to the myriad elements that went into building a mosque community, but these folks—Najjib Ali al-Hadjar (James) Ailley, Ali Hamdon, Hilwie Teha Jomha Hamdon, and John Wesley Fry—had key roles in building the Al Rashid Mosque.

Najjib Ali al-Hadjar (James) Ailley

Najjib Ali al-Hadjar (James) Ailley was a businessman and Al Rashid's first imam. Najjib immigrated to Canada in 1904, first settling in Ontario's farming belt, and then moving to Cut Knife, Saskatchewan, to homestead his own farm. He later moved to Winnipeg, where he met the woman who would become his wife, Margaret, at a dance. He established himself in the confectionary business. After the couple was married, they decided to move to Edmonton in 1937 to explore the growing opportunities from the north. They bought and expanded Waverly apartments and rooming houses, and Margaret worked in stores around town. Najjib was a natural leader, and he quickly gained popularity within the community and became its spokesman. He enthusiastically supported developing a mosque and became its driving force. The community opened its arms to the couple, and Najjib became the imam, leading prayers on days when he was free. Najjib established an important

Imam Najjib Ailley from Lebanon was the first imam of the Al Rashid Mosque, a position he held from 1938 to 1959.

rule for spiritual leadership in the mosque: the imam was not to be an employee, he was just a member of the congregation, just the leader of prayer. This norm differed significantly from leadership in both Christian and Jewish houses of worship.

Ali Hamdon

Ali Hamdon, born in 1873, arrived in Canada in 1900, and then moved to Brandon, Manitoba, where he had heard of a community of Arabs. He began peddling from Manitoba into Saskatchewan. By 1907, attracted by the tales of the opening of the north, he came to Edmonton. He and his first cousin Sine Alley (Hussein Ali Abougosh, who was born in 1891 in Lala and whose name was changed by an immigration officer to Sine Alley) established a partnership, and together they travelled north—to Fort Edmonton and then on to Fort Chipewyan where they set up a fur trading post. He returned to Lala in the Beqaa Valley to marry Hilwie Taha Jomha, and he took her north to Fort Chipewyan. The Hamdon home became a centre of social life in Fort Chip. From Fort Chip, Ali moved his family to Edmonton in the 1930s so that his children could go to school, and he commuted between Edmonton and his business in Fort Chip until it was sold in the 1940s.

Hilwie Hamdon was one of the key members behind building Canada's first mosque.

Hilwie Teha Jomha Hamdon

Hilwie Hamdon was born in Lala, Lebanon, in 1899. She arrived at Fort Chipewyan in 1915, and she and Ali set up their home there. Eventually, a Jewish family moved to Fort Chipewyan and the two families became friendly. The women would visit and compare notes about the challenges of keeping halal and kosher and bringing up their children in their respective faiths. The Hamdon family moved to Edmonton for schooling. Dr. Lila Fahlman, well-known community leader, recalls how Hilwie, whose vibrant personality "could win anyone over," catalyzed the community. Early in 1937, Hilwie and her friends decided to approach the city's mayor, John Wesley Fry, for a plot of land. "You don't have any money to build a mosque," he pointed out (Wikipedia 2015.) "We'll get the money," they replied. Little realizing the women's determination, he agreed to give them the land if they could come up with the funds. They needed five thousand dollars—a hefty sum during the Great Depression. They went from shop to shop along Jasper Avenue, the city's main street. Whether shop owners were Jewish, Christian, or Muslim, the women approached them all. "It was a very co-operative community then," recalls Sydney Hamdon (2015). In the end, Canada's first mosque was built with contributions from members of all three faiths, and Hilwie had a significant role in making that happen.

John Wesley Fry

John Wesley Fry was mayor of Edmonton from November 10, 1937 to November 7, 1945. He hailed from Woodstock, Ontario, and he travelled west to become a schoolteacher. In 1897, he attended Normal School in Regina, and after being certified, he taught in Saskatchewan until he married and moved to a homestead near Lloydminster, Alberta. In 1911, he gave up farming and moved to Edmonton to be a real estate broker and contractor (Wikipedia 2017). His eight years as mayor were the longest in Edmonton's history at that point. Fry's expertise in real estate helped the Arabian Muslim Association. In his view, the city had too much property and he wanted to sell some of it off and put the money to other uses. When Darwish Mohamed (Joe) Teha, the president of the association, approached him he agreed to sell them two lots at the corner of 108 Avenue and 102 Street, providing they would guarantee that they would build on them. The city sold the land for $550. The plans, described by James Ailley to the *Edmonton Journal*, had a cost of $4,850 for a brick building and an overall budget of $6,000 with furnishings. Local contractor Louis Buray was to build the mosque. Fry was on hand for the opening of the mosque on December 11, 1938, where, as recorded by the *Edmonton Journal* that day, he reminded those assembled that "many faiths sitting friendly together…couldn't happen in many lands, but was in Canada."

In hindsight, these founders share certain characteristics. They were all active members of the community, most of them successful businessmen. The Islam they presented was adaptable and activist, with a Canadian complexion. Their business acumen propelled them into the heart of the Edmonton community. There was nothing radical or antagonistic in their attitudes towards other religious groups; they all were part of a larger religious history. They stressed working within the cultural context where they lived, rather than insisting on imposing rules from abroad upon the community. They all learned how to build coalitions and partnerships in business and they used the same tactics in furthering Islam. Rather than difference, they insisted on similarity. Symbolically, this attitude was incorporated into the construction of the mosque building itself.

CONCLUSION

The Muslim community was tiny. Most of its resources were tied up with survival and family development; its connections with wealthy individuals in the Middle East were tenuous at best. Furthermore, by the time the community had grown enough to establish a mosque, Canada was deep in the Depression of the 1930s. Yet the will was there to build the mosque in Edmonton. What social assets did the community have to create a mosque? Mayor Fry was dubious, and he was not the only naysayer. More than one person said it: eleven struggling families cannot build such a building! Five thousand dollars in a recession? Impossible!

What to do? Enter a dynamo named Hilwie and a strategy tried and true in Sham: call on all your friends and neighbours, and get them to help you! The coalition idea was central. Ignoring the supposed antipathy to Islam in Europe's history, and affirming that Canada was a new place with everyone in the same boat and all working together to help each other grow, Hilwie and her determined band of Muslim women went door to door, to all their business acquaintances and contacts in the diverse community. Forming partnerships, planning dinners, selling baked goods, making handicrafts, offering a wide variety of the fruit of their skilled hands, and inviting their Christian and Jewish friends to help them, these women laid the groundwork for a partnering vision. They planned for a new addition to Church Street—their own mosque!

On the one hand, they were applying a social strategy derived from Islam's longstanding cultural value system: the People of the Book were actually fellow travellers in God's world and hence partners in expressing a tolerant, integrated community. If any needed evidence, the women could point to Muslim Spain, where Jews, Christians, and Muslims built one of the most progressive and culturally sophisticated societies in the world. No one in Edmonton could refute that argument, so they all came, ate great food, and donated to the project. On the other hand, Hilwie and company took a page out of the Canadian pioneer script. They worked long and hard, and they did not expect fellow Edmontonians to cough up money for their religious building as if they deserved special treatment. They used community tools, friendships, and networks in the same way their Ukrainian and Polish friends did when they had a special project they wanted help with; at a community barn-raising, everyone chipped in regardless of viewpoint.

In sum, the Muslim strategy of community building drew some strength from Islamic culture, some from the can-do attitude of the early Sham immigrants, some from Edmonton's unique village structure, and some from the extraordinary personality of Hilwie and her band of women volunteers. The merging of these elements provided the foundation for Al Rashid's future vision, and bore delightful fruit in the social and cultural life of Edmonton and Canada, including the remarkable institution of the Al Rashid Mosque. To its development we turn now.

2

THE FOUNDATIONS OF AL RASHID

Creating a Social and Cultural Place

1930–1970

TODAY, THE ORIGINAL ICONIC AL RASHID MOSQUE, first opened in 1938, rests in a verdant field in Fort Edmonton Park, among a collage of buildings and structures that go back over one hundred years to fur trading days. On most days, the mosque is tended by long-time unofficial custodian of Arab life in Edmonton, Richard Awid. Despite its currently benign presence, the history of the mosque is a complicated one, and Awid explains to visitors the background of such an unusual appearance in such an unusual place. Yet its story reflects the depth of Muslim roots in Alberta and in North America, and calls for the elucidation of the cultural foundations of such a startling occurrence.

Two small towns in Lebanon contributed to the growth of the Al Rashid community, Lala and Kherbet Rouha. Muhammad Deeb (1994), former professor of comparative literature at the University of Alberta, often remarked that the Muslim community evolved from small-town Lebanon, and that many of the values from that environment shaped the construction of the mosque community in Edmonton. Indeed, personal connections were the earmark of the early Edmonton community, and both businesses and social life were built around an Arab identity, a common commitment to helping each other, and a common sense of values deriving from an Islamic milieu.

Equally important is that these values fit well with the contours of a developing Edmonton. People flooded to the city in the early 1900s, and developing a strategy to help them get housed and fed was a major concern. In 1920, successful Whyte Avenue businessman Thomas P. Malone proposed the creation of community leagues. As the city grew, various vicinities were given names that provided focal points for cultivating commun-ity spirit, and in each neighbourhood a community league was established to develop social and recreational opportunities and infrastructure and advocate for community members' civic needs (Edmonton Federation of Community Leagues [EFCL] 2017). Each community league had a designated building, open to everyone. Nine community leagues existed in Edmonton by 1920, providing local community action and giving people a sense of village life (EFCL 2017). The city, thus, developed as a series of communities, knit together by joint programs reaching across communities, not as a conglomerate with an inchoate centre. In effect, Edmonton's structure was reminiscent of small-town culture, much like Lala and Kherbet Rouha.

Furthermore, the modus operandi of the distinctive structure operating in Edmonton made it clear that ethnicity was the key element in moving forward, since the city was firmly identified culturally that way. The unofficial history of the place has several distinguishing groups dominate: the Cree, the Scots, the French, the Métis, the English, the Ukrainian, and the Scandinavian all had solid connections to the city and gave it a particular character. All of them still maintained a clear vitality. As a consequence, the Jews used an ethnic identifier when they had developed their first synagogue in 1906 under the rubric of the Edmonton Hebrew Association, and it was the way that groups as distinctive as the

Russian Orthodox Church (St. Vladimir's, 1934) and the Ukrainian Catholic Church of Canada (St. Josaphat Cathedral, designed 1938) had been distinguished within society (Reel Girls 2010). Very often, religious organizations provided community centres that could be used in good times and bad—for festivals and in crises, for example. Public support for religious institutions, then, implied this community dimension, and ethnicity and religious identity blended easily in 1930s Edmonton, which meant that using the public purse to assist religious organizations was not considered problematic. Moreover, such blending created a sense of community beyond religious affiliation. The city's growing population saw community value in working together to help each other out quite apart from the government.

It was this cultural matrix that made Al Rashid possible. When Darwish Teha and James Ailley approached Mayor Fry for a piece of land, his first response was not that they did not warrant it under Canada or Edmonton law, or that a mosque "didn't fit," but that they could not afford to build on that piece of land; it was, after all, the Dirty Thirties. But Edmonton's religious public policy was a welcoming one in Fry's Edmonton. He was forever the businessman, and the sale of land for a religious building was as good as any. He sold the land at the same price he did to Christians and Jews or companies. It was all good business and money for the city.

Besides, he looked at the building committee they had formed—all highly respectable businessmen in town: Darwish Teha, president of the Arabian Muslim Association (AMA) and owner of a successful rooming house on 98 Street; Mike (Mohamed Saaid) Tarrabain, secretary of the AMA and northern pioneer in trade; James Ailley, treasurer of the AMA and Waverly real estate owner and imam of the congregation; Sam (Mohammad Ahmed) Assiff, treasurer of the AMA, who owned a successful store and had contracts with the Alberta government to look after homeless folks in his rooming house. Added to this were people Fry had worked with in town: Lee "Pop" Sheddy, a popular grandfather figure long known for his work in the city; Ali Hamdon, well-known

Honouring the founders of Edmonton Islamic Academy, 2012.
SEATED, LEFT TO RIGHT: Abdul Ghafoor Rana, Mohamed (Rony) Jomha, Mohamed (Mickey) Jomha, Mahmoud (Bill) Tarrabain, and Hamdan Hamdan.
STANDING, LEFT: Sine Chadi.
STANDING, RIGHT: Khalid Tarrabain.

businessman and fur trader from Fort Chipewyan; E.M.M. Hassann, an importer and businessman; and Milton Saul, taxi owner and Edmonton businessman. Whatever antipathy there was in society was vitiated by the social affirmation of a distinctive ethnic identity moderated by diversity. Fry was aware that Canada was vast and that people needed to have a sustaining identity in a developing Edmonton. The positive impact of the group in the community meant that there was little overt rejection of the idea—he and just about everyone else had attended one of the Arab ladies' famous dinners. His only concern was that they have the funds to complete the structure. So financial legitimacy was the issue that initially brought the AMA into being.

The governing structures of mosques are diverse: some are comprised of longstanding members whose positions came from the veneration of age; some are elected by a special meeting where dominant members are nominated; some are ad hoc—made up of willing workers who agree to band together to run things. They are uniformly male. So, indeed was Al Rashid's board. The early board, the original signatories to the AMA, was a group of willing members who agreed to take on active roles in developing the mosque and to make policy decisions for the community. But as their vision now included a building, the community needed the legal affirmation of the City and the Alberta government. Although the mayor agreed to give them a piece of land for their mosque cum social centre, he would only do it if they had a viable way of raising the minimum needed to construct a decent building, which, as we have seen, he deemed, five thousand dollars. The way forward was through formal registration with the provincial government as a charitable organization. The AMA was that charitable organization, and we will return to the story of its founding later in this chapter.

ORIGINS OF THE AL RASHID NAME

How did the mosque come to be called *Al Rashid*? There are several explanations for the name, including both doctrinal and cultural possibilities. The notion of *rashid* has considerable doctrinal depth. Deriving from the Arabic root form of *ra-sha-da*, the word reflects a sophisticated conceptual ancestry—one derived from notions of following the correct path, justice, integrity, proper training, true belief, and intelligent guidance. It is found in the Qur'an in *Surah al-Hud* (11:78). Al Rashid is articulated by the "ancestor" Lot. Lot is concerned with the precarious state that Prophets faced among human society. Additionally, he loathed the despicable way humans lived. He cries out, "Is there not among you a single rightly-guided man?" (11:78). This story represents the treatment of all Prophets by a sinful society on the one hand, and a measure of how debased humanity had become on the other. True belief rose above it all.

The term *rashid* also has implications for Sunni belief, for the four first caliphs or leaders of the fledgling Islamic empire were designated by the epithet "Rightly Guided" (*al-khulafa al rashidun*, derived from *rashada/rashid*); that is, they had received direction directly from the Prophet Muhammad himself while he was alive. The epithet sets them apart from the dissenters who came to be known as Shi'i—who came to their positions through secret, sacred sources of authority. The use of *Al Rashid*, then, fixed the mosque within a Sunni orbit.

That interpretative source, however, might have played a lesser role than the political and intellectual sources. The designation of Al Rashid is most famously associated with Harun Al Rashid (ca. 763–809), the Abbasid caliph who ruled from Damascus over a wide swath of the Middle East and who is credited with establishing détente with Charlemagne or Charles the Great. His reign was known for its wealth but also for the relative autonomy granted to various regions of his empire, an issue of some significance to Sham's peoples and their many Christian communities. He also brought his court to the zenith of Arab greatness when he instituted the famous Bayt al-Hikma or House of Wisdom in which a rich translation tradition of texts from Greek into Arabic became the norm. The result was an important link in providing texts to the West when its own scholarship floundered during the Dark Ages, as well as a positive model of Islamic and Christian relationships. For Syrian people, the Damascus of Harun Al Rashid's time represents a glorious moment in Islamic history.

But perhaps neither the doctrinal nor the political and intellectual were sufficient reasons for the designation. Rather, it may be that the popular conception of the Golden Age of Islamic culture in Al Rashid's court is the foundation: it was and is the source of the famous *A Thousand and One Nights*. These tales, which first appeared in manuscript form and were first translated in 1706 by Galliard of Paris, had a long and profound impact on Western perceptions of Islamic society. The power of their imagery inspired British Arab linguist, Sir Richard Francis Burton, to provide another interpretation (he also added some stories he created

Abdullah Yusuf Ali, the prominent translator of popular English Qur'an, attended the opening of Al Rashid Mosque in 1938.

himself) in 1888. His version was transported to the Americas, where it took hold of the imagination of New Yorkers and others at the same time as the early immigrants were coming to these new shores. The stories were embraced as a true expression of the exotic east, all in a very positive sense. Syrian culture was different but richly accessible. Harun Al Rashid's magical caliphate attested to what can be learned from another culture, and how much one's own life can benefit from it. It may well have been this element of intercultural exchange that fixed the name of the mosque—an awareness that was congruent with the "fit-in" and commonality culture adopted by Edmonton's first Muslims vis-à-vis Christians and Jews, but also offered a connection to the relatively recent perception of Syrian cultural greatness.

Finally, there is some evidence within the oral tradition of Al Rashid that the mosque was named by Abdullah Yusuf Ali, the Pakistani Shi'i translator of the Qur'an. In which case, Ali must have meditated on all the options and accepted *Al Rashid* as the proper name. The current oral tradition suggests that the constituent members of AMA ratified that name. Thereafter, the members of the AMA became the operating board of Al Rashid Mosque.

RITUAL REQUIREMENTS AND MOSQUE ARCHITECTURE

The ritual requirements of Islam determine mosque architecture, and the original mosque design attempted to construct a building that would adhere to these demands. A Sunni mosque is not organized around the same principles as a Jewish synagogue or a Christian church, and consequently the shape of the building has to be configured differently. The only life-course event that takes place in the mosque is prayers before burial; there are no children's christenings, no marriage ceremonies, no coming-of-age celebrations like bar and bat mitzvahs, no dedications for special service such as raising someone into the priesthood. While the mosque is a place where the Qur'an is recited, the reciting is only part of the sacredness of the place. Indeed, a mosque is primarily a house for prayers, which are ritually required five times per day. Even then, a mosque is not required. One can pray anywhere. So long as the prayer is directed towards Mecca and is in the prescribed form for the time of day, it will be deemed acceptable. Yet the mosque has been the central feature of Muslim piety right from the time of the Prophet, and it continues to carry significant socio-religious weight. It sets up a decidedly sacred space, one that touches many aspects of community and personal life. We'll take a moment to highlight some of these aspects because they provide important context for understanding how ideas about the architecture of the Al Rashid Mosque and its purposes developed.

Muslim tradition requires people to pray, but they cannot pray, at least not legitimately, if they are unclean. When one enters a mosque, one must remove one's shoes because they represent the profane environment outside the mosque and are regarded as unclean. Further, the mosque must provide a place for *wudu*—ritual washing of the hands, face, feet, and, in some cases, the privates— before entering the mosque to pray. In essence, the washing is a preparation for one's spirit, since performing the ablutions are a way of entering into a relationship of purity before Allah. The washing, then, is not to "clean" spiritually, but a ritual form that prepares the soul to enter the presence of God in prayer. In the

A Sunday gathering at the Al Rashid Mosque, 1953.

original Al Rashid, all washing facilities were downstairs, an unusual place compared to some of the earliest mosques in Islam that had running water fountains at the entrances of the precincts, but nevertheless a common place in many mosques where privacy has greater emphasis.

It is also the case that the dead must be washed before entering the mosque proper. In Al Rashid, family members or board members attended to this at a funeral. Women family members attend the female deceased.

Prayers are typically led by the most esteemed Muslim in the group or, if there is one, an imam who stands at the head of all believers in facing Mecca. It is he (women do not normally lead public prayers in Islam) who articulates the elements of prayer and all follow his lead. Architecturally, then, the building must contain the recognized direction for prayer in the form of a qibla. The qibla need not be elaborate, but it must effectively demark directionality. In early Islam, the faithful were called to prayer from a minaret, a tower that allowed the human voice to carry. While unnecessary

Men's learning circle at Al Rashid Mosque, 1953.

today, minarets have become a feature of Islamic architecture. The 1930s Al Rashid had two purported minarets, a style derived from historical architectural design rather than practicality.

The only other element necessary in a mosque is the *minbar*, the place from which the imam or prayer leader reads the Qur'an and preaches sermons. The *minbar* can be very plain and really only provides a few steps up for the imam so that all members seated on the floor can see him. Traditionally, the *minbar* was often gifted by a wealthy practitioner. Highly political mosques might also have special rooms for dignitaries and guests. While all members are regarded equal in prayer, enclosures secured privacy for controversial members whose policies might render the mass of people less than intent on prayer. An interesting feature of Al Rashid is that the direction of prayer was changed when it moved to the site near the Royal Alexandra Hospital; the qibla was moved from front of the mosque to the northeast corner because that direction was the shortest distance to Mecca.

Imam Najjib Ailley delivering the Friday sermon during the 1950s.

City of Edmonton Archives EA-600-3690i

The place of prayer for women is also a consideration in mosque architecture. Traditionally, women might have their own prayer space behind men or in an enclosed space much like dignitaries. Historically, women seldom attended the Friday noon prayer, but prayed at home. However, when they did come to the mosque to pray, they formed lines behind the men or in adjacent areas of the mosque.

As is well known, Ramadan is an important sacred time in the life of Muslim believers, and it also has certain implications for the mosque structure itself. During the month-long fast, when most Muslims wish to attend prayers in the mosque, the mosque may be overcrowded, which motivated the construction of a larger prayer space. Ramadan also has food constraints and celebrations, and Al Rashid had to be designed with the later in mind, since during that religious rite, providing alms to those in need was one of the occasions Al Rashid reached out to the larger city community. At those times, the mosque often provided food for the area's poor. Food raises the important issue of providing halal meat, an issue that Muslims shared with Jewish believers in the city. Because Al Rashid did not have a kitchen or storage facilities, food had to be brought in by members. Since there was no halal slaughterhouse in Edmonton, it is known that many disregarded the halal requirements in their families because it was often impossible to procure properly blessed meat. Hence meals served in the mosque reflected the limitations of the larger society, such as the absence of properly killed animals.

Other ritual requirements shaped the architecture of mosques. For example, powerful or highly esteemed believers might have their tomb placed within the mosque to show that, in death, they are forever at prayer for the community. In addition, lamps and carpets became a brilliant part of the décor of great mosques as did *mashrabiya* (arabesque screens) and illustrative Arabic writing from the Qur'an. As mosques developed, they provided rooms for the officials of the mosque, particularly the imam, to change in and out of the distinctive garb he wore for leading prayers. The original Al Rashid had a small room at the back of the prayer hall for this purpose. Circumcision for boys was not carried out in the mosque environs as is sometimes done in Muslim communities in developing nations; those who were circumcised relied on doctors in hospitals.

Although we have no record of whether these issues were formally addressed, knowing that the mosque was being built to uphold Muslim values and traditions, it's safe to assume that there was at least some discussion of how the architecture of the building would meet the ritual requirements of Islam. There must have also been conversation about the architecture of Edmonton's other religious institutions and how the Al Rashid Mosque would compare to the grandeur of some of these buildings. For example, the McDougall Methodist Church, a fine Renaissance-style church, was first built circa 1909; by the 1930s, the most recent version had been built by H.A. Magoon, a well-known local architect, at a hefty cost of $85,000. But then, it could seat up to 2,500 people. After the mosque was opened, *Edmonton Journal* articles published in November 1938 described its luxurious nature, and especially noted its floor-to-ceiling rounded window. Magoon had established a tradition of replication among Edmonton churches, but it's not immediately clear which replica the mosque was to reflect.

The claim is often made that the mosque design reflects a Ukrainian character, and popular sentiment has it that Mike Drewoth, the contractor, built it as an expression of his own Ukrainian roots. If replication was a norm for religious building design at the time and popular notions since then, it seems reasonable that Drewoth's Ukrainian Catholic background could have provided it. However, such a theory is questionable. At the very least, it is worth examining this perception.

AL RASHID'S ARCHITECTURAL DESIGN

The building that originally stood in a lot at 101 Street and 108 Avenue was of simple but firm design. (It had to be, because it was moved twice: once to a lot near the Royal Alexandra Hospital and then finally to Fort Edmonton Park!) Architecturally it was very much like the earliest model of a church building in Edmonton: the plain Methodist Church. That building was constructed as a single-storey rectangular hall without any interior adornments or physical modifications. Al Rashid was similarly constructed, except that it had a small partitioned room at the rear and a staircase to the basement and outside access door. The door at the front entranceway opened into a small foyer that stood on the right side of the building. It was here that shoes were deposited upon entering, as is customary in Muslim mosques. Design-wise, none of the overall construction details of the building set it aside from a standard community hall.

Still, we must keep in mind that the design of the mosque had to elicit appreciation of it as a place for religious activities—it had to impress as a religious building. If the rectangular structure of Al Rashid was more congruent with Methodism than Ukrainian Catholic or, for that matter, Orthodox tradition, what are we to make of the extraneous elements that point beyond that? It does

Al Rashid Mosque after the move from its original site at 101 Street and 108 Avenue to the nearby Royal Alexandra Hospital site, 1946.

City of Edmonton Archives A98-55

have four distinctive elements reminiscent of a Ukrainian church: a small central dome over the front part of the building; two domed towers on each side of the front of the building; distinctive rounded and elongated windows reminiscent of Orthodox or Turkish architecture; and an open, non-seated interior, quite in keeping with Ukrainian Orthodox tradition (where congregants stand). None of these are necessarily Ukrainian Catholic in architecture. On closer examination, however, some of these elements begin to set the mosque in a different architectural context and to point to influences other than Drewoth's perceived background.

The most noticeable element of the mosque's construction is the twin towers on each side of the entranceway. Towers such as these can be connected to the longstanding tradition within Islam of the minaret, that tall tower from which originally the muezzin called the faithful to prayer. Over time, the minaret became stabilized into a spire or spires, by which the building was identified as a house for prayer even if the muezzin no longer climbed to the top

In 1938, Ukrainian-Canadian Mike Drewoth was hired as the contractor for the historic undertaking of constructing the first mosque built in Canada.

to issue the call. That explanation could justify one of the towers, but why two? It is here that the influence of architectural norms from Edmonton can be seen. The use of twin towers on each side of the entranceway was present in the 1909 McDougall Methodist (now United) Church. By this time, however, that feature adorned other notable religious buildings, including, most notably, the First Scots Presbyterian Church in Charleston, South Carolina, which was built in 1814. It has the same twin towers (and, incidentally, the same stylized windows said to be Ukrainian in design) as found in Al Rashid. By utilizing two stylized towers in this way, the community was signalling that this was a religious building standing within the same architectural tradition as a very dominant church in the city and one well known throughout North America.

In the original mosque of 1938, a large dome stood over front part of the roof. Later, when the mosque was moved to the Royal Alexandra site, the dome was removed. Oral tradition says it was trucked to Lac La Biche when they constructed their first mosque there, but I have been unable to confirm this. At any rate, the large dome and the two smaller domes on the twin towers might suggest these had been inspired by Ukrainian architecture. Domes are conventionally found in Ukrainian religious buildings. Many have a central dome, elongated windows, and a high tower. Yet in none of them can be found twin towers.

The first use of the single dome in Islamic civilization came with the Dome of the Rock, built in 691 in Jerusalem, which had been inherited from the Romans. Thereafter, domes appeared regularly in mosques, but most particularly from the sixteenth to the eighteenth centuries in Turkish culture. Initially justified to allow light into the interior, the dome also had a theological purpose. For some Muslim designers, the inner side of the dome reflected the same notion of expansion of the heavens associated with deity as is found in Eastern Orthodox and Eastern Catholic tradition. It was designed to reflect the control of God over the world. So its use in Edmonton is a reflection of a very old tradition in Islam.

Why was the single dome over the front of the building not preserved when it moved? Neither the Royal Alexandra reconstructed mosque nor the one transported to Fort Edmonton had a single dome. The simple answer might be that, unlike many Orthodox churches in the west, it does not have a hipped roof, a structural feature evident in many versions throughout Alberta and Canada. The original dome of Al Rashid could not be seen inside the building.

Additionally, Al Rashid does not follow the construction design of an Orthodox church, which traditionally has a narthex, nave, iconostasis, and sanctuary. Orthodoxy designs a worship area around the idea of the Jewish temple with zones deemed to reflect a more sacred power and served by official authorities. The faithful stand in strictly allocated areas. The dome over the nave has special paintings, representing the notion that God is present in His heaven and is present to worshippers in the building, so the dome serves as a fixture with theological intent. The structure of the building is tied to that symbolism.

If then, it does not really track an Orthodox model, what of the Ukrainian Catholic? Catholic churches usually have an apse where the priest performs the ceremony of the mass. It is most often smaller than the building itself and sits at the front of the church, directly opposite to the entranceway. This is where the sacristy is placed and towards which worshippers face. In some constructions, a Catholic church will have a hipped roof that gives it a decidedly Ukrainian character. None of theses features are present in Al Rashid because the theological system underlying the design is different.

The mosque will have a direction (usually regarded as the front) towards which prayers will be focused, but it does not have a sanctuary—only a *qibla* set in the direction of Mecca to which prayers are addressed. Therefore, Al Rashid does not have the distinctive Ukrainian addition of an apse, a small rounded enclosure at the front of the church where mass is held. Nor do all the windows have the rounded tops of the mosque, so the elongated window of Al Rashid is not necessarily Ukrainian in style. It is reasonable to suggest that without the towers and the dome, the building could be taken as a Methodist or Baptist building. No dome is required for those. What seems present in Al Rashid is the gabled roofline, one that fits the inclement weather and snow of the Prairie provinces, and that roof was originally adorned by a distinctive set of domes. If one wishes to see domes of similar design, one must go to Wishart, Saskatchewan, where St. Michael's Ukrainian Catholic Church has small domes shaped very much like those on the twin towers, along with a similar sized drum. Yet there is no record of Drewoth or any of the members being familiar with that building. Beyond that, similar designed drums can be seen in mosques and religious buildings throughout Turkey, Bosnia, and even in the Middle East.

We conclude that while it is tempting to see the mosque design as shaped by Ukrainian contractor Mike Drewoth, it is more complicated than that. The mosque appears to reflect an amalgam of stylistic elements that speak of the mosque being at home and even together with other houses of religion rather than being one distinctive among them. As a building, Al Rashid is much more eclectic than a decidedly Ukrainian Catholic or Russo-Greek or Ukrainian Orthodox church. It also could be construed as an old Methodist or Presbyterian church with an admixture of Ukrainian and Orthodox elements. The message is that the mosque was at home within the religious amalgam of Edmonton in the mid-1930s. That message was surely powerful—here was a mosque rooted within a diverse culture. Islam was quite at home in this environment!

THE FUNDING AND CONSTRUCTION OF AL RASHID

Although it's not entirely clear who was responsible for the design of the 1938 mosque, there is no doubt that Mike Drewoth built it. Information provided by his daughter, Peggy Nelson, during interviews with the author, provides a few missing details. In newspaper and mosque publications, Drewoth is heralded as both architect and builder. The facts are somewhat different. According to Ms. Nelson, the original contractor commissioned by the AMA board was Louis Buray, a general contractor who began digging the foundation shortly after the board received approval for the mosque from the city. According to published information (Awid 2010) and community members, the deal with Mayor Fry was finalized because a group of individuals, including the indomitable Hilwie Hamdon, convinced the mayor that they could raise the funds necessary to build a mosque. From what we know of this group, they were small businessmen, former farmers, or ordinary workers. None of them could be said to be wealthy. Ali Hamdon had been in Fort Chipewyan as a fur trader, and still commanded solid connections with that business. The Ailley family, the Chadi family, the Haymour family, the Amereys, Tehas, Assiffs, and Awids all had local business connections and knew many people in Edmonton and beyond. But they could not pay for the mosque by taxing themselves. A permit to begin construction was issued on

May 15, 1938 by the City of Edmonton (see the City of Edmonton Archives). Clearly, someone had guaranteed that the funds would be there. Perhaps it was members who guaranteed the funding so that the basement could be dug and footings poured. Louis Buray did that early work.

The story goes that Hilwie and the ladies' group went door to door on Jasper Avenue asking shopkeepers and businessmen to help them build the mosque. Apparently, they were successful, but what seems likely is that Arab businessmen in the community prevailed upon the authorities to allow the preliminaries to go ahead, to get the foundation of the mosque in the ground. They likely guaranteed that much. Board president Darwish Teha had his rooming house near 101 Street and 108 Avenue, the site of the mosque, and he was tasked with checking on whether the workers were doing what they were supposed to be doing during construction (Nelson 2015). By September, the money that the women had raised had dried up. Buray refused to go on. Construction ceased. According to Peggy Nelson, he and Darwish Teha had a major disagreement. Teha fired Buray. There were fireworks from that row. Mayor Fry, himself a contractor, may have called his Arab friends to account over the action. Yet we can surmise that he did not want a foundation left in the ground that could not be used for anything.

The businessmen had to act; their reputations were at stake. The mosque board decided on a more co-operative, business-like approach. They decided they had to canvas other businesses and people beyond their local connections, and to offer them some-thing in return: a charitable donation receipt. They travelled Alberta, Saskatchewan, and Manitoba to ask donors to help them reach their goal. To register as a charitable organization in Alberta (which would allow them to ask for major donations from funders and to issue receipts for tax-deductible donations), they had to establish the Arabian Muslim Association and draw up a charter and constitution for the group. The charter, signed by eighteen members of the eleven families listed in Chapter 1, became the signatories of the new association. They received official charity registration on September 12, 1938. In effect, the community took their place within a larger provincial family of charitable organizations, including the major churches and social service groups in Alberta at the time. The community had grown beyond the bake sales and community dinners that had undergirded the ladies' early fundraising.

From then on, Al Rashid activities took an increasingly business-like approach to organizing and development, whether it was in relation to the mosque or, later, a school. This shift was crucial for another important lesson learned early on: business people are necessary in building a community. They provide the financial know-how that makes things work. Al Rashid has been heavily business-oriented from early on, when the AMA was established. This is not to say that they relied exclusively on themselves. As their travels through Alberta, Saskatchewan, and Manitoba in search of major funding for the mosque suggest, they built crucial partnerships.

With Buray out, the AMA needed someone to complete the construction. Before his work on the mosque, Drewoth had been living in Calgary. He was working in a cabinetmaker's shop, designing and constructing the fixtures for the new Woodward's department store. He was known as Metric Mike for his caustic remarks about measuring things in metric; he would build nothing if it were not in imperial measurement. According to Peggy Nelson, he was born in Manitoba, where his father had homesteaded. His father married a Russian woman named Glubish, who spoke only Russian, and if the family had any religion it was not evident—it certainly was not Ukrainian Catholic. Nor did Mike Drewoth himself have any religious interests until he joined the Baptist Church in the 1950s. Therefore, arguments that Mike Drewoth designed the mosque from his own loyalties to Ukrainian Catholic or Orthodox churches are misplaced. In fact, Mike's original surname was Drewot; because he had applied for land in Manitoba, he could not do so in Alberta, so he added the *h* to be eligible to homestead in Alberta.

When Mike was in his early teens, his father and neighbours decided to pick up stakes and move to Alberta. His mother died on that trek and was buried on the way. The group all settled in the Thorsby area, where they attended the Union Church, a precursor to the United Church of Canada. Mike spoke only Ukrainian. He had been sent to school as a lad, but his English was hardly workable. Nelson said he chronically underbid on contracts, perhaps because of the language issue. On the day in 1938 when Buray was fired, Mike was in Edmonton to find work. He walked up to Darwish Teha and asked him if there was work on the project. Darwish turned to him and responded, "Yes, you can built the mosque...Buray is gone!" How much Mike was paid has not been recorded, but we do know that, once the mosque was completed, he went to work for Hayward Lumber for 33.3 cents an hour! It appears that the AMA board said, "We have 'x' dollars. Build us a place to pray," and left it at that (Nelson 2015). Those were the kind of agreements Mike was known for.

So the outcome of Mike Drewoth wandering onto the building site of the mosque was that he had to finish it. It was Mike's first big construction project. He went on to be a very successful general contractor, constructing many homes and buildings throughout Edmonton and Alberta. If there were architectural plans, they must have been drawn up by the board and the former contractor. Mike hired Sidney Parsons as bricklayer. (A bricklayer by trade, Parsons would also serve as mayor after Fry.) Mike was able to get lumber from Hayward Lumber, and he coaxed Lupul movers to use their trucks to bring it. He may have been without a full architect's drawing, but, as his daughter said, Mike had a wonderfully creative eye for making things work. Obviously, he must have had, since he apparently created the cupolas without plans.

All did not go swimmingly between Mike and Darwish, however. According to Peggy Nelson, Mike remembered ordering the workers to take their shoes off when they went inside the building, even if it wasn't finished. Mike thought that was unnecessary. Mike also had to adapt in constructing inside décor.

The *Edmonton Journal* report on the funeral of Ali Tarrabain, a Muslim pioneer who immigrated to Canada at the turn of the century. His funeral was the first to be conducted at Al Rashid Mosque in November 1938.

He had no say in how the building was placed on the lot; that decision had already been made by Buray and the mosque board before he came on the scene, but the building was placed almost directly north–south, which meant that prayers would be held along the east side of the building. (The rule is that worshippers are meant to be as close to Mecca as possible, and the earliest notions were that straight east was correct.) That already places the *qibla* on the east side of the building, while the shape of the building meant that lines for prayer would be long and narrow. Mike had no control over the fact that people would remove their shoes in a front porch that was really too small for all those who might attend—an evident design flaw that spilled over into the prayer area. Besides, worshippers then had to proceed downstairs to perform *wudu* in their stocking feet, which was another problem. Furthermore, since Darwish had control over funds, Mike had to defer to him about the kinds of materials he used, and where he placed them. Despite all the contention, the mosque was completed in time for the funeral of Ali Tarrabain in late November. It officially opened on December 11, 1938. *Edmonton Journal* reports from the time set the final cost at six thousand dollars.

The opening was an extraordinary event. The ladies had set up tables in the basement laden with home-baked food. The aroma

THIS DAY IN JOURNAL HISTORY

Abdullah Yusuf Ali, visiting Islamic authority, presents the keys of the mosque to D.M. Teha, president of the Arabian Moslem Association.

Dec. 11, 1938: Edmonton's Al-Rashid Mosque first of its kind built in Canada

Edmonton Journal

When the Al-Rashid Mosque opened in Central McDougall, bystanders couldn't help but notice it resembled a Russian Orthodox church.

"It is significant that people of many faiths are sitting friendly together," Mayor John Fry noted at the opening ceremony, which featured more than 100 people.

The building, next to the Royal Alexandra Hospital at 102nd Street and 108th Avenue, was the first of its kind in Canada.

The mosque was dedicated by the visiting Abdulla Yusuf Ali, a renowned Islamic authority and Pakistani interpreter of the Qu'ran.

"There is nothing mysterious, nothing everyone cannot understand about a religion

such as ours or this mosque," Ali said at the ceremony.

Pointing to a niche in the southeast corner, he declared all followers of the faith worshipped in the direction of Mecca.

"No matter where the followers of this faith are, they all turn toward Mecca, a symbol of unity among every brother."

The project came about in 1931 when the Muslim community spoke to Fry about purchasing land to construct the mosque.

At the time, Islam was practised by about 700 people in Canada, 150 of them in Edmonton, and many believed the city would become the country's spiritual headquarters of Islam.

To come up with the $5,000 needed for construction,

volunteers went from shop to shop along Jasper Avenue, soliciting Muslims, Christians and Jews alike. "It was a very co-operative community then," said Lila Fahlman, founder of the Canadian Council of Muslim Women.

No builder in the area had seen a mosque, let alone built one, according to the Muslim women's website WomanCan Edmonton.

"Nonetheless, the women chose a Ukrainian-Canadian builder named Mike Drewoth and told him, 'We want a place to pray.' After some discussion, Drewoth set about building the best mosque he could: one main room, lofty arched windows, two little rooms for ablutions, an insulated basement for social gatherings and two hexagonal minarets, each with an onion-shaped silver dome

topped with a crescent moon. Although it clearly resembled a Russian Orthodox church, the community was elated with its new mosque and members enthusiastically donated carpets and lamps."

The mosque was expected to be the first of its kind in North America, but that honour went to Mother Mosque of America in Cedar Rapids, Iowa.

By the 1980s, Edmonton's Muslim population had grown to more than 16,000, but the Al-Rashid Mosque had fallen into disrepair and the city pondered demolition. But in 1992, the restored mosque was moved to Fort Edmonton Park at a cost of $75,000.

To read more stories from the series This Day in Journal History, go to edmontonjournal.com/history

A 2012 *Edmonton Journal* article recalls the formal opening of Al Rashid. The 1938 photo caption reads, "Abdullah Yusuf Ali [right], visiting Islamic authority, presents the keys of the mosque to D.M. Teha, president of the Arabian Moslem Association."

drifted upstairs during the proceedings. Dignitaries included the mayor of Hanna, Ira F. Shakir, a Christian Arab. The speaker of honour was the brilliant translator of the Qur'an and the one to officially name the mosque, Abdullah Yusuf Ali. As recorded in an *Edmonton Journal* report of the day's events, Mayor Fry remarked, "It is significant that peoples of many faiths are sitting friendly together." It was not a platitude: Edmonton had been the scene of a Ku Klux Klan gathering just four years earlier, which caused great trepidation among Jews and Arabs. A few years before that, in 1930, local police had violently dispersed disgruntled farmers who were protesting the government's lack of action during the Depression in a massive march on the Legislature Building. Fry must have found this neighbourly assembly of Ukrainians, Scots, English, Poles, Jews, and Arabs to have been one of the city's more civilized social events! Indeed, the pleasant scene, with people from all parts of town and various religions sampling the succulent cooking of Hilwie and company, was enough to make 1938 a banner year in Edmonton.

THE SOCIAL ROLE OF THE MOSQUE

In today's world, religious buildings have a kind of sacredness to them that militates against free social intercourse. Such was not the case with Al Rashid. The mosque upstairs was indeed a sacred place, free from food, drink, and non-religious activity. However, the basement of the mosque had intentionally been designed for social activities: tables covered with colourful oilcloth and kitchen chairs filled part of the space. Eventually, a piano found its way down there, and a floor for entertainment of various kinds was kept clear. Lebanese celebrations fostered the *dubke* (Middle Eastern dance), and the basement was happy to encompass the community's joy that way. The youngsters were taught down there; there were periodic classes in Arabic and the Qur'an, along with a mosque equivalent of Sunday school.

At the same time, the community decided that it would foster social cohesion by keeping the Arab youngsters together, which was a common social dimension of churches and synagogues at the time, and a way of encouraging intermarriage within their respective communities. The Al Rashid community had no problem celebrating with their Christian neighbours—Christmas, Easter, and other religious-type holidays that had a secular side. Christmas trees and gifts for the poor, Easter eggs, and Valentine's Day

Charter members of the Al Rashid Mosque, 1953.

parties all found a place in the social side of the basement of the mosque. These social events always included some fundraising for the practical operation of the mosque: heat, electricity, snow removal, caretaking, landscaping, payment for special speakers, and buying and distributing Qur'ans. In each case, the ladies' group cooked impressive foods that attracted a wide range of Edmonton's population. Al Rashid community gatherings gained a reputation for wonderful and affordable food, pleasantly served in a jovial atmosphere.

The basement of the mosque also became the scene of marriage celebrations. Here it is evident that the usual strictures so often heard in relationships between men and women in mosque communities today seldom applied. The mingling led to intermarriage. Muslims married Christians, and Christian married Muslims. Women who married Muslim men sometimes converted, but there was no hard and fast rule. Some Muslim men were not too concerned if children were raised in the mosque and the church, since they saw nothing sinister in people enjoying both traditions.

Photograph taken in the Al Rashid Mosque, after Jumaa prayer during the visit of his Eminence Muhammad Abdul Aleem Siddique, 1950.

While Christian men might undergo conversion to marry within, as was the norm back home, a few were comfortable attending both religious environments. Indeed, some families maintained both Muslim and Christian festival days. Cross-religious social connections were cemented. Mike Drewoth and his wife, Thelma, for example, remained long, loyal friends with Dr. Lila Fahlman and her husband. The public perception was that the mosque community was very progressive and outgoing, strongly committed to living fully in the Edmonton community.

Some lines of demarcation still held; there was little intermarriage between Druze, Shia, and the Arab Sunnis. The divisions among Muslims were not emphasized, however, and no great doctrinal debates arose among the immigrants. Obviously, all Arab-speakers did not pray together. Nevertheless, the mosque oriented itself among Muslims and other Middle Easterners in a decidedly Sunni manner, a stance that became more dominant as time went on. But Sunnism was never an overt marker of belonging, since, in Canada, the lines seemed even more remote and irrelevant, and distinctions between various sects within Islam hardly seemed worth emphasizing. Indeed, sometimes the power of language and culture played a more dramatic role than religion in bringing people together.

Al Rashid quickly became central to Edmonton. In the early days of the mosque's life, it became integrated into the community in a very positive way, with none of the apparent secrecy and isolation that accompanies many mosque projects today. Edmonton welcomed the mosque as indicative of the city's sophistication, and the public embraced it as the home of a pleasant group of people who shared their cultural lives in a lively Canadian way. People of all religious commitments—and none— contributed to the mosque community through social events it hosted. It is a remarkable achievement that, in such a short time, Muslims should be so proudly and importantly a part of this urban Canadian environment.

THE IMPACTS OF THE SECOND WORLD WAR AND THE ESTABLISHMENT OF ISRAEL

It cannot have been lost on the fledgling community that many among them had once fled from war only now to land in a situation in which Canadians were at war with Germany. The mosque had barely become a fixture on the street in Edmonton before the call came for young men to sign up for war. There is little in the City of Edmonton Archives about Muslim response to the Second World War, and whether or not any men from the community enlisted. During the First World War, Muslims and Arab Christians who were deemed "Ottoman" were placed in work camps, but during the Second World War, although there were significant battles in North Africa such as the Siege of Tobruk, there was no singular campaign to round up Arabs as was undertaken against the Canadian Japanese.

The most fearful aspect of the war effort for Muslims with sons was whether there would be mandatory conscription, but, because that did not come about, families did not have to find ways to escape the war. Since the mosque community was regarded as small and still developing, no public call came for them to provide soldiers. They sat within the public conscience much like Jews. Those who wished to go were lauded, but there was no compulsion to sign up. So far as we know, very few in Canada and none in Edmonton signed up: no Edmonton Muslims gave their lives for Canada during the Second World War.

Other more troubling issues that were to have a long-term impact on the community were afoot. After Zionism was born in Europe, the Al Rashid community, like most Canadians, saw it of little consequence. But the local Arabs were less convinced of the innocence of the British Mandate, which basically took over rule in Syria and Palestine. The later provoked the famous Arab revolt in Palestine (1936–1939), and the Jews in the region willingly joined the British forces as they faced an invasion from Rommel in 1941. The Arab forces in Palestine were vastly outnumbered by the Jewish brigades, and the result was that the British favoured the fledgling Jewish nationalist movement in Palestine.

By the time the mosque was in place in Edmonton, attitudes towards what was happening in the Middle East were beginning to have an effect. Some welcomed the overthrow of British rule in the region and argued for it on Arab identity grounds. Others believed that if Rommel was successful in taking Palestine, no one who was Semitic would be spared, including the Arabs, who had lived all their lives with Jewish neighbours in an amicable relationship. They also were filled with trepidation about what the Germans would do once in charge. The Edmonton community accepted the sympathy that fellow Canadian had for the Jews, assuming that an equitable view would win out for their friends and relatives in Palestine. Consequently, they supported the Canadian government's position on the British maintaining control in the Middle East until all parties could work out the details of independent countries after the war. Most were suspicious of British motives, especially in Palestine.

Internally, the community moved away from public engagement as it became clear that the Second World War had changed many things. When immigration policy at the end of the war moved very little beyond the restrictions on Asians and people of colour, many community people despaired. Visiting folks back home became the only hope of seeing them throughout the war years; even postwar, the chances of returning to the home- land were slim, while the potential to bring relatives seemed increasingly remote. The community had no other recourse than to band together and establish a deeply held loyalty to each other and Al Rashid. So the scars of war and Middle East politics shifted the community from enthusiastic participant in the growth of Edmonton to a cautious community concerned to shape its own inner identity. Out of that came a much more dedicated vision of a distinctive Muslim community.

September 2, 1945 was more than the end of the war: it was a release from the restrictions and limitations that were imposed on all Canadians. The end of the war had a liberating effect on the Al Rashid's community. The group looked to grow, as Edmonton grew, and with the discovery of oil in Leduc, the region seemed poised to make major advances. The businessmen who made up the bulk of the male members of the community had come through the war unscathed, so families did not have to start over, as was the experience of countless Canadian families whose sons and husbands had perished abroad. The businessmen of Al Rashid faced the future with confidence because they now had deep connections to many of the most important people in the wider community. Many Muslim families had been successful during the war years. Since many were in service industries—clothing, real estate, food, automotive—they quickly saw that there was ample room for financial expansion. The next generation had taken advantage of education during the war years and were ready to take leading positions in education, law, engineering, and medicine. The community's future looked bright.

Yet change had come to the mosque. The City was looking to expand Victoria Composite High School, a school dedicated to the arts. The school needed more space for a theatre and other offices, and Al Rashid sat squarely on the required land. After prolonged negotiations, the City of Edmonton approved the transfer of a parcel of land on 111 Avenue and 102 Street, which wasn't far from the mosque's current location but still necessitated uprooting the mosque and moving it to a new location. With funds obtained from the sale of the land to the City, plus the allocation of the land at the new site donated, the community accepted that there was no financial reason why the shift could not be made. So the mosque had its first move in 1946.

The dome in the middle of the mosque's roof was removed, and the decision was made not to replace it. The basement, once the scene of community gatherings, now had a more restrictive purpose; it was no longer deemed acceptable to make it the centre of the community's social life. Dances ceased, the piano was not replaced, tables stayed but now served only the community for Eid celebrations, Ramadan gatherings, and other expressly religious occasions. Much more serious intent was placed on training the younger generation in the necessities of Islamic learning and Qur'anic study. The basement was still social but in a much more confined manner. Fewer outsiders were welcomed there, and the multi-religious complexion shifted to a more focused Muslim environment. A sobering set in.

The initial reason for this shift was an issue quite beyond the Muslim community's control. They had to deal with a major cultural and political event: the establishment of the State of Israel in 1948 in the heart of Islamic territory. Throughout most of the Arab families' sojourn on Earth, they had lived in peace with people of other religions: Muslims, Jews, and Christians had lived and worked together for centuries in the Middle East. Most drew their identity first and foremost from their families and their culture, of which Islamic and Middle Eastern values were a significant part. The nineteenth century had added nationalism to the agenda, but village life had little in common with the new awareness. It was with some surprise, then, that Zionism advocated a national Jewish identity and sought to associate that directly with the land of Palestine.

The Jewish national movement, while it had begun in 1882, did not appeal to the Jews in Palestine, for their attachment to the land was religious rather than political. The Jews of Zionism were largely secular and clearly not in kinship with the complex Ottoman culture.

Following the First World War, the British Mandate policy of promising independence to Palestinians while encouraging Jewish settlement lead to clashes, eventually to war, and the immense disruption of Palestinian life. Between 1947 and 1949, over 700,000 Palestinians were forced into refugee camps, and many more fled their homes in the face of violence and Jewish military campaigns. Now, as many as 5.6 million people live in this region (Beinin and Hajjar 2014, 5), and another 1.5 million reside in refugee camps (UNRWA 2017). In 1948, the new State of Israel was announced, and the Arab populations, many of whom were Muslim, faced a bleak and stateless future. Some of the more fortunate were able to get to Canada where they began a new life.

The event sent a shock wave through the families in the Al Rashid, some of whom had relatives or acquaintances in Palestine. Attitudes were polarized; relationships with Jewish neighbours, strained. The subsequent wars with the Arabs only exacerbated the trauma, as one after another group of Arab combatants was defeated by a superior military force. The fear of difference became more marked and more remarked upon by outsiders. The once-vaunted Arab identity became somehow less glorious, and community spirit retreated, becoming less robust.

There were a number of other reasons for this change as well. First, the generation that had endured sparse community numbers in the beginning was now aging, and while they still controlled the mosque organization, they responded to their own aging and to trends of conservatism abroad. Second, the emphasis on sustaining mosque rituals required a more professional attitude towards the hiring of an imam. It was no longer acceptable to have someone who could not speak both Arabic and English, for example. They also saw that an Islamic education was necessary for the new generation. Third, the community had to confront the triumph of Israel in the late 1940s and the disruption it provoked among those who saw this as an intrusion into Muslim lands; it made many in the community feel helpless. As they observed the wars and triumphs of Israel, and perceived the support for Israel among many churches and institutions that had not shown such support earlier, the older generation turned inward. They spent their time maintaining an Islam that fit within the Canadian context, even as they noted the rise of Salafism, Islamism, and the Wahhabi doctrine within their former homelands. Fourth, new immigrants, many suffering from displacement, such as the Palestinians, or financial loss, like the Pakistanis, did not look upon Canadians with the same set of eyes that the original immigrants had. Fifth, the nature of the congregation had changed. With the relocation of the mosque, a shift took place in the community's perception of itself. Many regarded the mosque as *the* representative of Islam in the city, and the members felt they were part of the city's establishment groups. The younger members wanted the mosque leadership to represent them in the city, and to have Muslims leaders represent them with sophistication. Finally, the community realized its limitations. Attitudes had changed within Canada and Edmonton, and old animosities crept into relationships. Contentions over women's place in the community isolated some who had enjoyed earlier freedoms, and the move towards looking after their own people meant a shift away from connecting with other Edmontonians. Their distinctiveness now had public freight of a different kind.

SPIRITUAL LEADERSHIP AND NEW MUSLIM POPULATIONS, 1950–1970

The Muslim population in Canada grew slowing during the 1950s and 1960s. By the early 1970s, the Muslim population had reached about 33,000 (Husaini 1999). Families had grown and prospered, the founding generation gave way to the second, and the vigorous pursuit of place and recognition pushed the Muslim community into the broader community. But no one was prepared for what would happen from the 1970s through to the turn of the millennium: Canada would welcome close to four times as many Muslims as it had up to that point. There were urgent calls from some public sectors, such as social agencies and schools, to provide Muslim services for a growing population.

The central issue in the mosque was its spiritual leadership. When the community needed a public persona, it called upon Ameen Ganam, who regularly taught Arabic in the mosque to youngsters. In a 2008 article in *The Walrus*, Guy Saddy describes Ganam teaching the generation before his: "When my father was taught his prayers in Arabic every Sunday, it was often by Ameen 'King' Ganam, a Saskatchewan-born farm kid who played fiddle with Tommy Hunter and had his own CBC radio show." As we have noted, in the early years, Najjib (James) Ailley fulfilled the role of imam. Though not a trained imam, he spoke confidently in Arabic in front of those he knew well. Ailley served from 1938 until his death in 1959. His career as imam bridged two distinct periods in Al Rashid's history: from founding to establishment. As Guy Saddy (2008) recounts, "the first imported imam to preside over Al Rashid, Hammudah Abd Al-Ati (born and trained in Egypt), was a clean-shaven sophisticate. He eventually left his flock for Princeton, where he completed a PhD in sociology." This contrast between Ailley and Al-Ati exemplifies the shift from founding to establishment.

As we have indicated, one problem was that by the 1960s, the community had become fairly sophisticated. Muslims were part of the professional class in Alberta and Canada. Again, Guy Saddy's (2008) description of his father's generation at Al Rashid is illustrative: "Over time, the community spawned its share of businessmen, academics, and sundry other pillars. My father's brother, Edward Saddy, was the first Muslim judge in Canada. Another uncle (by marriage, to my father's sister), Larry Shaban, was Alberta's minister of economic development and trade—the first Muslim in Canada to hold a provincial cabinet position. One of my father's sisters married Muhammad Ali Bogora, from 1953 to

1955 the prime minister of (then united) East and West Pakistan." The Edmonton community had achieved a place in the pantheon of established religious institutions, but its growing population of young people, many of whom did not speak Arabic, were looking for someone who could relate to them.

The board decided to contact Al-Azhar University, the oldest university in the world, where there was an ongoing training program for imams. Al-Azhar indicated that one of their best, Hammudah Abd Al-Ati, was already in Canada, at McGill University in Montreal. The board contacted him and offered him the position of imam. Hammudah Abd Al-Ati only remained for two years (1961–1962), but Al Rashid had a lasting impact upon him, as he notes in his several Islamic publications.

The community increasingly needed articulate spokespeople to present the claims of the Muslim tradition in newspapers, on television and radio, and in the courts of business and law. Much as clergy in churches and synagogues handled a myriad of issues among their parishioners, the imam was called upon to support Muslim newcomers, youth, and established community members in understanding Canadian ways: how to obtain marriage licences, navigate the trials of divorce, apply for supporting relatives to come to Canada, access health care and housing in a tight Edmonton market, find an appropriate school for children—the list is endless. Naturally, imams who were trained abroad had no idea where to start with these kinds of issues, let alone provide concrete recommendations. The community learned, then, that the spiritual leader in Canada played a far more complex role than just leading prayers. The board was at a loss as to how to fill this distinctly Canadian need, since those properly trained in Islamic theology had no understanding of Canadian culture. The only answer seemed to seek out someone who was trained abroad but had a solid understanding of Canadian culture. The board soon discovered how much the role of imam had changed in Canada and how difficult finding the right person for the job could be.

The very nature of the Islamic community was about to change even more dramatically, however. Many from a Muslim community quite different than the Arab Sunnis had lived in peace and prosperity in East Africa for three generations. On August 5, 1972, Idi Amin, president of Uganda, gave all Asian people ninety days to leave the country. The head of the community, the Imam Aga Khan, sought out Prime Minister Pierre Elliott Trudeau with a plea for Canada to receive these refugees. With some one hundred thousand people in need of a place to go, Khan brokered their immigration to Canada. They left millions of dollars in assets behind, and settled in communities in Vancouver, Calgary, Edmonton, and Toronto. Their arrival posed a new challenge for the Sunni establishment.

In the first place, their Canadian counterparts now learned that the term *Muslim* covered religious variations of which they were not aware. Furthermore, they realized that not all Muslims believed the same thing, that the tradition was fragmented, just like Christianity. They also became aware that there were considerable differences arising out of culture, which not everyone believed was part of religion. Additionally, the Muslims who Canadians knew best were largely Arab. With the newcomers, *Arab* and *Muslim* had to be separated. While many may have intellectually understood this distinction, they had never encountered such diversity. All of these factors posed possible distress in the Canadian population.

For some in the Al Rashid community, the Ismaili Muslims should not even be regarded as Muslims. For starters, they did not speak Arabic. But old theological issues also boiled to the surface. The Ismailis belong to the Shia tradition, the second Muslim group in the world, which represents some 15 per cent of all Muslims. Even then, the Aga Khan's group was a minority within a minority. The issues were complicated because Ismailis have had a different response to their position in the world and hence have distinctive practices that do not easily mesh with the larger Shi'ism group, the Twelvers, let alone with Sunnism. In Edmonton, the Muslim community suddenly almost doubled, but the newcomers weren't the same kind of Muslims as those who established Al Rashid. The mosque community, too, was somewhat bewildered by this influx.

Despite having to leave Uganda without their assets, the Ismailis were a very resilient and innovative group. The Aga Khan worked with the federal government to help them adapt to life in Canada through training and other programs. Most of them spoke English, so they had no language problem. Many of them were highly trained professionals. They immediately set to work and, within a decade, became thoroughly embedded in Canadian culture. But they were not the only Muslims who came to Canada during this period: Pakistani Muslims, Ahmadiyya believers (contentions abounded as to whether they were Muslim or not by both major Muslim groups), Druze from Syria (an offshoot of Islamic culture in the Middle East), and major Shia populations from Iran also arrived. The Arab Muslim character of the pioneer mosque community was called into question. How was the mosque to adapt to these changes?

The community faced this deluge of newcomers unevenly. In some cases, they provided office space for alternative groups; with others, they debated theological issues. For the more doctrinally inclined among Al Rashid's members, the diversity was a challenge. For those folks, there was only one way to react: become more Sunni. By becoming even more exclusively Sunni, and by turning to those seeking a Sunni Islam community to offer training, comfort, ritual precision, and doctrinal edification, Al Rashid's Sunni background moved to the fore. Where the early pioneers had embraced a flexible Islam, and had deliberately blurred the lines of doctrine and cultural difference, by the mid-1970s, a new orientation came into being—one dedicated to maintaining the legitimacy of Islam's largest and longstanding religious tradition. We might say the community was forced onto an ideological terrain that its history had not shaped it for, and for which the future seemed much more cloudy. At the same time, however, the demographics were changing, and the mosque community was growing by leaps and bounds.

3

THE EVOLUTION OF A CANADIAN MOSQUE TRADITION

The New Al Rashid

1975–2005

AL RASHID ENTERED A CRITICAL PHASE of its development in the 1970s. Where the previous phases had focused on nurturing the local Muslim community and providing it with worship space and a social environment, Al Rashid now had to adapt itself to a wholly different situation. Indeed, it is not stretching the truth to say that Al Rashid, as an institution, could have faltered during this period of intense change. This chapter tells the story of how Al Rashid addressed the stresses and strains of the thirty years from about 1975 to 2005. While the community had its difficulties, it also engaged in the momentous building of a new Al Rashid—the one story that eventually was the best remembered.

GEOPOLITICAL CHANGES

The community responded to several background issues that set the tone for Al Rashid's development. These issues were to elicit various responses from members. For example, the post–Second World War period had ushered in the oil boom in Alberta, which meant that politicians provided visions of continuous development and growth. Expectations were high, and they did not always pan out. Al Rashid faced strains that the founders could hardly have envisioned. Where the early founders had remained in contact with the "heartland territories" (Lebanon, Palestine, Syria, Iraq, Jordan, Egypt, Saudi Arabia) by slow-moving mail or irregular wires, this period ushered in proximity to "home" that they could not have imagined. News of the homelands could arrive nightly on radio or television. Dramatic changes were underway in the Middle East that paled the experiences of earlier generations: oil, independence struggles, wars, social movements, socialism, political shifts, even religious dynamics could not be predicted from one decade to the next. Never had connections to the homeland had such immediate significance for Arab Muslims.

This period is bracketed by two disasters that generated much introspection from members: the Yom Kippur War (October 1973, also known as the 1973 Arab–Israeli War) and the Second Intifada (September 2000–Februrary 2005). These conflicts indicated a cycle of violence and dislocation. The heartland experience stood in marked contrast to the dramatic economic development in Alberta and Canada, and raised issues within the community and between generations. The entire region seemed to be descending into chaos and destruction, and the trauma of immigrants was an issue that the Al Rashid community had to deal with. The Al Rashid community wrestled with whether a public stand had to be taken about these affairs: those with relatives back home were torn between remaining neutral to protect the mosque community from criticism and the concern for their loved ones. They were also mindful of the almost universal lack of concern among their Canadian neighbours on the problem of justice for the Palestinian people. At the same time, they wondered about their relative prosperity while their next of kin were suffering so greatly. Handling this mix of emotions was draining.

In the Heartland, 1973–2000

1973	Oil embargo
	Yom Kippur War (also known as the 1973 Arab–Israeli War)
1978	Egyptian President Anwar El Sadat and Israeli Prime Minister Menachem Begin author *A Framework for Peace in the Middle East*
1979	Islamic Revolution in Iran
1981	Sadat assassinated
1982–1987	Israel invades Lebanon
1990	Persian Gulf War
1996	Taliban capture Kabul
1999	Arafat/Peres/Rabin awarded Nobel Peace Prize
2000–2005	Second Intifada

The cultural distance had changed. The early migrants never had to deal with the traumas of political and cultural conflicts immediately and so directly. The fallout from earlier conflicts occurred several months after the fact, via a letter, for example. Now, the effects were felt straightaway. Within a day or two of an event, phone calls and voice messages, though expensive, kept everyone abreast of what was happening in the heartland.

Alberta culture had changed as well. The Arabs were not the only ones who suddenly lived in a smaller world. Alberta could not concentrate solely on itself. The Second World War had made everyone aware that what happened abroad had an instant and sometimes deadly impact on local people. While few Arabs had joined the war effort, they were more than a little concerned with the ongoing crises in the Middle East. These crises didn't remain exclusively "over there." The Al Rashid community became aware of a range of attitudes and outcomes that they could not escape: for many Canadians, the Arab Muslims were on the "wrong side" of the Arab–Israeli conflict. The conflicts in the Middle East were almost always reported as "Arab" or "Muslim," so each new situation forced members to deal with local criticism, whether or not ethnicity or religion had anything to do with it. More often than not, Edmonton Muslims were forced into a defensive position—a far cry from the spirited interaction that had built the community in the earlier decades of the century.

Suddenly, geopolitical issues muddied what Alberta and Canada thought they knew about Muslims, including the Al Rashid community and its history. Likewise, the mention of "Islam" conjured a range of half-articulated ideas that Canadians were now using to (mis)understand the concept; the believers could no longer be a simple Arab Muslim group integrating into the larger society through social norms. Moreover, many Canadians began stereotyping and demonizing those who followed the Prophet Muhammad.

CHANGING ATTITUDES TOWARDS ISLAM AND THE WEST

If it ever was, it was no longer a simple exercise to articulate what Islam had become in the West. Several intersecting contexts—all of them contentious—characterized this field of study. The massive migration of Muslims to the West, the rise of Islamism (Islamic fundamentalism), the evolution of Islamophobia, the rise of militant jihadists, and the attacks of 9/11 have directly impacted the comprehension of Islam outside the Muslim world. Where it was once sufficient to speak of classical Islam as understood by scholars, mediated somewhat by modernization and mixed with notions of adaptation and integration, the model no longer held by the mid-1970s. In short, there are now several Islams in the West, and Muslims who live within any of them react to each other and to several Islams within their home countries. These perceptions are interconnected with what is represented as "Islam" and "the West." For Al Rashid, the crucial questions became, just what kind of Islam was the mosque community developing in Edmonton?

In point of fact, young Muslims raised in Al Rashid from the mid-1970s through to the turn of the century may never have lived

The Al Rashid Youth and Sport Club participating
in the Run for the Cure cancer fundraiser.

under "traditional Islamic culture." Rather, they received their
Islam through a variety of modes: memories of their parents,
missionaries of various stripes (some under the influence of
conservative or Wahhabist doctrine), evangelical sheikhs on
television, youth clubs dedicated to an idealized Islam, or even,
perhaps, through the phrasings of radical Islamic rap. They had to
negotiate their special religious vision without the support of an
embracing cultural matrix, even within the mosque community,
which was undergoing dramatic cultural changes.

The Al Rashid Youth Hockey Team, 2012.

Similarly, opinion-shapers within Muslim communities
abroad often constructed a negative image of "the West" to contrast
it to a righteous Islam they wanted people to embrace. Many
Muslims in the Al Rashid community were uncomfortable with this
kind of characterization. After all, they had been very successful in
the West, and so they often felt a dissonance with these types
of discussions.

The consequence of all this was an interesting contrast: if
one could not talk about "Islam" as if it were one kind of entity,
now one could also not speak with any confidence of a single
meaning of "the West." Al Rashid Muslims were successful
Westerners, and they were successful Muslims. They found that

these words defined themselves precisely by the way in which they intersected with each other. Indeed, we might even suggest that they needed each other to maintain some deeper sense of identity.

This is not the place to examine these issues, except to point out their relevance to the cultural growth of Al Rashid. We restrict our discussion to only the most evident of these intersecting constellations during this time. Muslims in Edmonton demonstrated that they responded well to the process of hybridization, meaning that Muslim cultural values assimilated to and were modified by the diverse cultural contexts within which they exist. Indeed, one can still say on the basis of the Al Rashid experience that Islam as a religious system is highly adaptable and profoundly sensitive to its surroundings. It is an activist religious system and, as such, is fully congruent with other world religions that are increasingly restive today.

Islam remains a civic religion—especially in iconic Al Rashid. There is the perception among most Muslims of shared values across religious boundaries and a dedication to the common civic good wherever they live and with whomever they reside. We note, too, that the public context of Islam has changed dramatically since the 1960s. The religion of the Prophet Muhammad has shifted from being invisible in many regions of the world to a religion that is tracked with care by media and intelligence services on a daily basis around the world. Eccentric Muslim behaviour in some remote corner of the worldwide *ummah* gets aired and evaluated in the *New York Times* and on television as if to demonstrate some hidden character of the Islamic tradition. The driver of this kind of attention is not just the thirst for knowledge or the rise of social media: it is part of a cultural suspicion that has arisen following recent historical events. Furthermore, contemporary Muslim communities have a profound impact wherever they take root. These larger trajectories in turn play a role in shaping the several constellations of meaning circling Al Rashid.

AL RASHID'S RESPONSES TO CULTURAL CHANGES

When events from the heartland appeared daily in the newspapers, and neighbours asked, "What do you think of...?" it was obvious that it was not business as usual at Al Rashid. Take the political stance towards Israel, for example. While Edmonton Jews and Arabs continued their business relationships without rancour, the secular side of the Jewish community fully supported the geographical goals of Israel. Each failure was attributed to some character defect in the Arabs. The ground for discussion and healthy disagreement was slowly being vacated. Personal friendships waned.

The Al Rashid community closed around the ideology that technically they supported their brethren abroad, but they could not abandon the solid support they had for their own goals by concentrating solely on the problems abroad. Thus, some members wanted a more forthright, public stance on Israel. Some refused to support the mosque because of its apparently pacifist position. Many were outraged with the Israeli invasion of Lebanon. In the end, however, Al Rashid articulated that its policy was to build a resilient community in Edmonton, not to be the spokesperson for the complicated situation in the Middle East. The community did what it could to support Red Crescent and Red Cross assistance, and members supported people on the ground in Palestine with funding if they could. Al Rashid deeply felt the effects of the Israel–Palestine conflict, but, as a community, Al Rashid steadfastly remained committed to Edmonton's growing Muslim community. Nonetheless, this conflict was not the only example of how Al Rashid was forced to respond in one way or another to attitudinal changes affected by political conflicts around the world.

As discussed in Chapter 2, the influx of Muslims from Africa and South Asia during the 1970s affected a change in the general function and ethnicity of Al Rashid; the mosque community shifted from engagement with the larger Edmonton community towards engagement with other Muslims, and deliberately attempted to be the resident Sunni Muslim establishment. Al Rashid continued to seek to represent an acceptable and doctrinally secure form of

Islam, but it was no longer explicitly Arab. Which form of Islam would best present the values and beliefs that this new group of people identified with as Muslims? What of their Arab identity? Their public identity more and more foregrounded religion, which generated a concern on several fronts. The validity of the imams who represented various phases of the tradition publicly, for example, became a concern. These cultural changes also meant that Al Rashid had to take seriously when a community member represented his views as belonging to the mosque. The members of the board remained primarily Arab Lebanese, so the inner direction of the mosque—its ideology, if you will— remained in tune with a moderate, non-activist Islamic stance. Even when the majority of the worshippers on any given day hailed from places far removed from Lebanon, the centre of the mosque culture held. Yet something had shifted significantly. Public perception of the mosque quietly shifted from a collection of Arab friends to a cohesive group dedicated to a religion few understood. For some it was a troublesome shift.

Events in the Middle East clouded Al Rashid's attempt to remain neutral. The case in point: the Iranian Revolution, also known as the Islamic Revolution or the 1979 Revolution. Mohammad Reza Shah Pahlavi, autocratic ruler of Iran, who largely retained his position with aid from the United States and European nations, was overthrown by the religious establishment in Iran headed by Ayatollah Khomeini. The intent of the revolution was to construct a nation more in tune with Iran's Shia roots and to return power to the Iranian people and not to foreign influence. Many hoped that the strength and resolve of the revolutionaries in Iran would inspire the whole Muslim world. Many Muslims voiced support for Khomeini, even among the Sunni populations, perhaps because Arab peoples had had meagre positive outcomes to identify for their youngsters. Some thought the Iranian Revolution would be the catalyst for democratic expansion in other countries. At the same time, Edmontonians wondered privately whether the local Muslim populations would remain loyal to Canada if international events transpired to put them at cross purposes to Canadian policies. Al Rashid businessmen especially were highly sensitive to these nuances, as several conversations with Mahmoud Tarrabain and others during these three decades indicated.

Engaging Public Discourse on the Middle East

While some members of Al Rashid preferred to turn inward, away from the marches and public demonstrations that many Canadians exhibited in the 1970s, others saw Canadian freedom of expression as a means to articulate a different stance. Important leadership in the mosque—namely, Saleem Ganam and Yousef Chebli—helped with this latter engagement.

Saleem Ganam was born in Sheho, Saskatchewan, in 1911, the son of Sied and Chelsea Ganam. His brother later became known as Ameen "King" Ganam, Canada's king of the fiddle. Saleem was educated in Swift Current, Saskatchewan, and Edmonton. He learned his Arabic from his father and his Islamic knowledge from a variety of teachers and imams. He had strong connections to community development individuals within the city and was instrumental in moving Al Rashid into engagement with the interfaith community. His sister, Lila, eventually became a teacher in the Edmonton public school system and founder of the Arabic program, which is discussed below. Saleem was esteemed by his teaching colleagues when he acted as Muslim chaplain at the university and was liked by all those with whom he worked. During the later part of his career, he was sponsored by the World Islamic Call Society (WICS), a Libyan-supported initiative to spread Islam around the world, as a means to further his work on Islam in Alberta and Canada, funding that allowed him to develop a more visible Islamic presence on the University of Alberta campus.

A second important leader of the period was Imam Yousef Chebli. Chebli grew up in al-Karawi (near Lala) in Lebanon, which is now known as al-Karoun in the Beqaa Valley. He attended high school there, went on to college, and then taught locally after 1959 in Lebanon. He decided to become a religious leader and imam, and studied Al-Azhar University in Egypt, graduating in 1965. While there, he came into contact with the Saudi Arabian–held Muslim World League (MWL).

That league had been formed by major Sunni nations in 1962 in Saudi Arabia with the intent to regulate the expansion of Islam throughout the world, to articulate what was deemed correct Islamic doctrine, and to provide orthodox leadership in the form of properly trained imams for the rapidly growing Muslim community around the world. Several Sunni nations contributed to the MWL funding. Chebli was one of those who had been accepted by the MWL as properly trained.

He then returned to Lebanon, where he took up a position as imam under the sponsorship of the MWL. In 1970, Chebli came to Edmonton in response to Al Rashid's call to Al-Azhar for an imam. Chebli held the position at Al Rashid for thirteen years, until 1983. He was widely respected for his recitation of the Qur'an and his abilities in Arabic and English. In 1979, after meeting with Dr. Muhammad Sherif at a MWL meeting in Tripoli, Chebli received sponsorship from WICS (Jamiat al-Dawah Islamiya). He has remained closely associated with that organization ever since.

Saleem Ganam and Yousef Chebli both were what one might call engaged activists. Taking a cue from marches and civil demonstrations across Canada and the anti–Vietnam War movement in the United States, they joined university teach-ins, along with students from the University of Alberta, and participated in marches in the city. By 1984, they were openly involved in the anti-war march against Iraq for its use of poison gas and other weapons against Iran. In a dramatic expression of cohesion with Shias, Chebli and the Shia Imam Ali Naqvi marched arm and arm down Jasper Avenue, advocating a boycott of trade with Iraq. This in the oil capital of Canada! Canadians had never seen such images before.

Some members of Al Rashid were wary of such public disclosure and worried about backlash, which caused them to move away from this kind of political engagement with the community at large in favour of a more inward thrust—namely, the support and nurturing of Muslims in the mosque community alone. In the 1970s and 1980s, several statesmen within the community, including Mahmoud Tarrabain and Mohamed (Mickey) Jomha expressed concern with the popular activist mindset (1977, 1981). They cited the danger to the mosque community: publicity of a virulent kind could unleash reprisals on an unwitting community in the form of confrontations on the streets, in shops, and at schools. The tendency by Canadians to lump all Muslims into one community, reinforced by the Islamic notion of *ummah*, could lead to vandalism and destruction of the physical mosque and perhaps even to threats and violence against its members. Stories of mosques being attacked in Canada and the United States circulated and added a sense of impending disaster. Many in the Al Rashid community sensed that there were movements afoot that were larger than they comprehended, and many felt helpless to address these issues. The difficulty was that the Muslim *ummah* as a whole had no operative strategy to handle these unforeseen circumstances. And they had no obvious public voice to express their concerns.

Outreach and Engaging New Muslims

While, on the one hand, this period of political change saw Al Rashid turn inward, on the other hand, this period, marked by the influx of new Muslims, also saw considerable growth in the mosque's outreach activities among both Canadians and other Muslim minority groups. The mosque had to address, for example, the number of converts who, through marriage, wished to join the community, as well as other social needs that came with a growing population of Muslim families. More specifically, as a result of the Iranian Revolution, Al Rashid had to address the Twelver Shia in Edmonton.

Initially, the Iranian Revolution gave Arab Muslims great hope. They saw the possibility of the rise of a genuinely humane traditional Islam in the heartland areas. The rejection of the Shah gave many hope that within their homelands new movements would stir among Muslims and a new order would break through. For many, for a few months, it was a heady time. Some in Canada saw it as an opportunity for Islam to deal respectfully with old wounds and finally put the split between Sunni and Shia aside. Others saw it as the birth of a legitimate Islamic state that would point the way for other countries to honour their Muslim beliefs in a political manner.

While initially there was some resistance to accommodating the Shia by offering them the mosque for prayers, the revolution dulled the antagonism. Some of the contention rose from the inter-faith orientation of the imam. Some rose though Sufi/Shia adherent Buff Perry, who had an office in the mosque for several months during the 1980s, and led a group of Twelver Shia in the mosque while their own building was under construction. Perry (2015) recounted some of his memories of this time:

> I was very involved with Al Rashid on many levels, starting in 1984: First, I was part of the inclusion process of having the Shia community attend every *salat al-jum'ah* (Friday prayer) at Al Rashid. Second, I'd bring in anywhere from five to ten Indigenous people who would first gather at Anne Anderson's Native Heritage and Cultural Centre every Friday to attend *salat al-jum'ah*, and this group included Anne Anderson, Harold Cardinal, and other well-known Cree, Stoney, Métis, and other First Nations folk. Third, I co-ordinated the flight and itinerary of people like Bob Small of Ermineskin First Nation and Maskwacis Cultural College, Daryl "Bilal" Agecoute of Okanese First Nation in Saskatchewan, and others I brought with me to Libya, and specifically to the offices of Jamiat al-Dawah Islamiya in Tripoli.

Ganam and Chebli also reached out to other religions in a number of ways during the 1970s and 1980s, and interreligious dialogue increased considerably. Both men worked actively with the Interfaith Council, which represents a variety of religious groups in Edmonton. As part of that group, they sent between one hundred and two hundred letters of invitation to all the chiefs of First Nations bands in Alberta, urging them to join with the inter-faith community. By virtue of their representation of Islam as a welcoming religion, they demonstrated a principle of multicultural solidarity that was valued by most Canadians. In this way, they sustained the strong social connection that the founders had with the larger community.

Ganam and Chebli also made connection with two environments scarcely addressed by local imams in the homeland: universities and the prison system. At the time, the University of Alberta was expanding exponentially; new programs and services were springing up almost daily. The student body reflected wide-spread disaffection with traditional religions and a new era of exploration of religious possibilities, as the establishment of the Department of Religious Studies at the university demonstrated. Likewise, the cultural presence of various gurus from meditation traditions in India (e.g., Hare Krishna, Tantric Yoga) and widespread interest in Buddhism in Canada pointed to expanding religious possibilities. The 1970s also witnessed the vigorous exploration of cults and sects in North America, with some very violent ends (e.g., Jonestown, Branch Davidian).

Al Rashid was very conscious that they could not rely on the university to develop Arabic and other courses without some impetus from the Muslim community. As a consequence, in 1980, a group from Al Rashid, headed by businessman Mohamed H. Assaf, presented a cheque to the University of Alberta to cover the costs of establishing an introductory Arabic course. In 1984, an additional $14,700 was donated towards a trust fund for the study of the Arab peoples (Awid 2010). This funding eventually attracted other funding, including singularly critical finances from the Kuwaiti government to support graduate studies in Arab areas of interest.

Ganam and the university students responded well to each other. In his rather fatherly way, he was able to present Islam in a reasoned manner, without the usual hysteria of the new religious movements or those on television. His work at the University of Alberta as Muslim chaplain had a lasting impact. This period saw an increasing acceptance of Islam as a viable religious option on campus, with special places being set aside for prayers and counselling. University authorities realized that there was a growing population of Muslims on campus, and a new awareness of Islamic values took shape. Ganam was undoubtedly part of the reason for that development.

Aware of the growing need to assist the prison population, both Ganam and Chebli asked for and received clearance to visit local jails. They even prayed with inmates in the maximum-security wing. Such an outreach placed their activity much closer to the pastoral or the chaplaincy than exists in Muslim countries, so in a very real way they broke new ground in ministering to this population. Ganam and Chebli played key roles in Al Rashid abandoning an inward stance and adopting an engagement strategy. They set the parameters for community engagement that more recent imams and leaders have had to address.

Unfortunately, the Iranian Revolution soon turned violent, fomenting problems beyond its borders and pouring money into oppositional groups in Lebanon and Palestine. Praise for the Iranian Mullahs morphed into anger and resentment. Many in the community felt that the great possibilities had been somehow squandered or hijacked. Despite the fact that Imam Chebli visited Tehran several times to significant accolades from Tehran, and Saleem Ganam was invited to walk with the funeral bier of Ayatollah Khomeini himself, the rapprochement that many had hoped would come from the change fizzled. Yet the goodwill born of the period continued between Al Rashid and the Shia populations in Edmonton, and continues in muted form even today.

Finally, the rise of the number of Muslims in the city also resulted in an increased demand for social and personal services.

Families felt these needs directly. They had sons and daughters of marriageable age, but where were they to find good partners for their children? Each option had problems. Some went "back home," as the old timers had done, to arrange for a marriage partner, usually under the watchful eye of a relative; spouses were not always happy in the radically different Canadian culture. Some allowed daughters to marry Canadians who converted, even though many within the community were not happy about such choices, and were skeptical about how committed such converts were (an issue addressed by the Bill Tarrabain family in the film *Giving up and Holding on*, set in Lac La Biche in 1990). Some, such as Harriet and Abdullah (Ed) Shaben, elected to invest a great deal every year and take their children to Eid celebrations in Chicago and other centres in the United States where they could meet eligible potential mates. Both Ganam and Chebli spent considerable time counselling young people on proper marriage partners, and even kept an eye out for potential matches; they both were known to have introduced future spouses.

At the other end of the life cycle, the needs of older Muslims also increased during this period. Slowly, the community came to recognize an expanding cohort of geriatric Muslims who were often isolated by illness and affected as younger members of the community moved out of the city for work. This population grew slowly and became more significant in the next period, but, as early as the mid-1970s, the older Muslim population had already stirred discussions about exactly what young families' responsibilities were to aging parents. The first migrants had not faced this issue, although it did have some impact on mate choice for children, especially for young women. For them, leaving relatives back home meant that they simply could not care for elderly parents. When the government relaxed immigration rules, particularly to unite family members, many brought aging parents to Canada—unfortunately, not always happily. Not only did imams spend more time visiting hospitals and seniors' homes, they also became quite deft at handling touchy immigration requirements—a development that few could have foreseen as a prerequisite of imam training.

Official Multiculturalism and the Significance
of Financial Investment

A number of federal policy and government moves during this period impacted the growing mosque community. The Trudeau era, 1968 to 1979, ushered in some long-lasting policies, one of which had a direct impact on the mosque community: the Canadian Multiculturalism Act of 1971. The act set forth a doctrine of openness towards cultural values that not only tolerated difference but valued it. In effect, diversity was at the heart of the Canadian ideal. The policy was controversial, and remains so, but there is no doubt that it empowered groups such as the Al Rashid Mosque community to celebrate their religious difference and to embrace the notion that their difference was good for Canada. The policy had a number of salutary results but its financial effects are often overlooked: the Muslim community was confident enough that it invested heavily in infrastructure throughout Alberta through to the end of the century. An unofficial tally of building dollars spent on Alberta Muslim structures is staggering: Edmonton and district Sunni investment (Al Rashid, Islamic School, Markaz, University mosque, Sahaba, Quba mosques) totalled $9.75 million; Calgary Sunni (East Mosque and school, Southwest), $3.89 million; Red Deer, $900,000; Lac La Biche, $900,000; Slave Lake, $1 million. These figures do not include Shia, Ismaili, or Ahmadiya investment, which are likely to be considerable. Overt investment on Sunni infrastructure alone exceeded $1.5 billion in the 1990s (Waugh 2002)—a far cry from the timid $5,000 required for the first Al Rashid. This financial investment is a measurement of the community's self-confidence and its sense of permanence in Canada.

The federal policy of multiculturalism provided a great deal of comfort for Muslims in Alberta and laid the groundwork for a period of growth and development. The ramifications of their confidence and investment cannot be undermined by the critics of the Multiculturalism Act or by studies that doubt the significance of multiculturalism. It is to Al Rashid's response to a positive cultural environment that we turn next.

TOWARDS THE NEW AL RASHID BUILDING

The new Al Rashid building, which officially opened in 1982, would likely not have been built were it not for three broad sets of factors: Canadian and provincial population growth, federal immigration policy, and local cultural change. While these first two factors take us back to before the central period of concern in this chapter, they nonetheless provide important context for the new Al Rashid building and the reinvention of one of Edmonton's prominent cultural and religious institutions.

Population Growth

Muslim migration to Canada took place in four major waves: from the second half of the nineteenth century through till the Second World War; from the postwar period to roughly 1967; from 1967 until about 1990; and finally from about 1990 onward (Abu-Laban and McIrvin Abu-Laban 1999). Directly before and after the Second World War, the growth of the Muslim community was the result of more births than deaths. After 1951, however, the increase in the Muslim population was mostly the result of immigration. Around 1951, the Muslim population in Canada is estimated to have been between 2,000 and 3,000. By 1971, this number had increased dramatically to an estimated 33,370, and by 1981, the population again tripled to roughly 98,160 (Waugh, Razavy, and Sheikh 2011). After the civil war erupted in Lebanon in 1985, Edmonton saw a large number of new families, as people struggled to bring over relatives who were caught in the war. Between 1981 and 1991, the Muslim population in Canada grew 158 per cent to 253,260. Those identifying as Muslim had the largest increase from 1991 to 579,600 in 2001, representing 2 per cent of the Canadian population (Statistics Canada 2003).

From about 1975 to 2005, Muslims came to Canada from virtually every country in the world. Like most other immigrants, they came for a variety of reasons, including education, employment, and family, but others, such as refugees from the civil war in Lebanon, came to escape political and social unrest, particularly during the 1980s. At least in terms of language, this group fit well with the Al Rashid community. Al Rashid members suggest that hundreds of families came to Edmonton in the mid-1980s. As well, during the 1990s, Canada saw a substantial influx of Somali Muslims who were fleeing the Somali Civil War (Statistics Canada 2015). These international influences have played a significant role in Islamic growth processes in Canadian cities, and directly impacted the resources and services of Al Rashid. According Government of Canada statistics, by 2001, there were 19,580 Muslims in Edmonton, and they constituted 2.1 per cent of the population (Strategic Research and Statistics 2005).

As we've already seen, Canada and its multiculturalism policy also had a direct impact on the migration of another minority Muslim group: the Ismailis, who were expelled from Uganda by Idi Amin. They were soon to challenge the iconic position of Al Rashid, and in a way spurred the Sunnis towards a more aggressive development model. The Ismailis are one of the smallest minorities within the complex of Muslim groups. The group traces its ancestry to the events following the death of Ja'far al-Sadiq (d. 765), the fifth Ismaili imam, when the group disagreed with the succession of the larger Shia group, which came to be known as Ithna'Asharis or Twelvers, from the number of imams they recognize following the death of the Prophet. The Khoja Nizari Ismailis split from the larger Nizari group following the death of the Fatimid imam, Caliph al-Mustansir bi'llah in the eighth century, but it was several centuries before they took up abode in India. Once there, the tradition had considerable success in converting members of the Lohana caste, one of the higher caste groups who were usually addressed as "lord" (khwaja), from which derives the term Khojas.

The Khojas migrated to East Africa during the seventeenth century, largely to take advantage of business opportunities, and as a group they were very successful. Many Ismailis helped found important medical, educational, and governmental institutions in Uganda, and generally they were well educated and held important positions throughout the country. In 1972, perhaps to lay the blame for the country's poor economic growth upon someone, Idi Amin ordered all Khoja Nizari Ismailis to leave the country. An arrangement between Prime Minister Pierre Trudeau and the Aga Khan allowed the disenfranchised group to come to Canada as refugees. Given their business and institutional predilections, they all migrated immediately to urban areas in Canada, where they almost as quickly made a considerable mark. The resulting flood brought a new dimension to Islam in Canada, and today they have been joined by others from Africa, the Middle East, Afghanistan, and Iran. Current estimates are that Ismailis number about one hundred thousand in Canada (Canadian Heritage 2017; Ladha 2008).

The Ismaili influx had little overt impact on Al Rashid. After all, the Khoja were from the Shia tradition, and thus largely incompatible with the Sunni point of view. Al Rashid was impacted because, up to this period, Canadians thought all Muslims were Arabs. It took some time for Canadians generally to realize that there were significant divisions within Islam and that not all Muslims believe the same thing. The Al Rashid community was divided on how to deal religiously with this group, and they were suddenly aware that they had a powerful group in their midst that would contend for another definition of Islam; and the Ismailis were both activist and politically savvy.

Immigration Policy

The immigration of all Muslims could not have taken place in Canada without two policy moves on the part of the Liberal Party of Canada. The Liberal Party espoused that people from the Middle East were not Asians, and hence immigrants from that part of the world were not subject to exclusions under the Asian category. The adoption of this policy had an immediate impact on Quebec, where immigrants, especially those who were Christian and French-speaking, found a welcome environment.

Trudeau's government undertook a study of immigration policy and decided that much of it was based on biased, even racist, categories. In 1966, an internal white paper proposed a new set of rules, which were eventually ushered in by the Canadian Multiculturalism Act of 1971. In 1982, Trudeau's signature piece, the Canadian Charter of Rights and Freedoms was enacted. The charter guaranteed the validity of religion under the constitution without regard to its definition or origins. This not only made diversity a theme in immigration but established the position that the deeply held religious and cultural views of immigrants would be regarded as a strength of the people: immigrants to Canada need not give up their deepest values to be a Canadian. Rather, immigrants were to deepen Canadians' understanding of civilization by adding their values to the collection.

A number of other issues involving Canada and the heartland areas required the community to respond. Muslims felt for their relatives and friends as America waged the Gulf War. A resistant Prime Minister Jean Chrétien kept Canada from joining the invasion of Iraq on the supposed presence of weapons of mass destruction. Arabs in Edmonton were outraged earlier when then Prime Minister Joe Clark proposed moving the Canadian embassy in Israel to Jerusalem, which would in effect recognize Israel's hegemony over that sacred city. Marked backlash from Arab constituents and behind-the-scenes politicking from other countries shelved the plan. But it put the Al Rashid community on alert that policy made in Ottawa was not neutral: it could damage relatives overseas and uproot relationships in the community. Canadian politics could not be ignored. The community had to become engaged in Canada's government if they were to maintain their position.

Local Cultural Change

The growth of the Muslim population and changes in its composition had material effects at the city level as well, which also affected the direction Al Rashid took during the 1970s and 1980s. The community made some major shifts, both physically in terms of its building and psychologically in terms of shaping a new place in Canadian consciousness. As it had done before, Al Rashid experienced a process of negotiation with its cultural environment—accepting hybridization, adjusting to new expectations, and accommodating itself to some new norms and not to others. This flexibility was its modus operandi for thriving in a major Canadian city.

In the 1970s, Edmonton was experiencing a boom, during which newcomers eagerly established businesses. New areas were being developed, and Edmonton's major urban sprawl began. Those years were marked by events such as the 1978 Commonwealth Games, which saw the city construct new facilities and earn a reputation for organizational skill. Volunteers from the city set a new standard for their selfless work, as writers from all over the world noted. The strength of Edmonton as a community-centred sports city also attracted international attention, particularly in 1979 when the Edmonton Oilers hockey franchise (including a young Wayne Gretzky) joined the NHL. The demand for a new Al Rashid arose in this context, partly out of a period of vivid financial and real estate growth in Edmonton.

Population growth, immigration policy, and Edmonton's boom meant that the mosque—the original 1938 building that had been moved in 1946—could now scarcely hold all worshippers for Friday prayers. The foyer was generally loaded with a great disarray of shoes. The *wudu* facilities were woefully inadequate for an overflow crowd, so much so that most performed the ceremony at home before coming to the mosque. It was also discovered that the shortest distance to Mecca was not due east, as the founders had thought, but northeast, over the pole. In that respect, the old Al Rashid Mosque was incorrectly placed for its primary purpose for the community—prayer.

The vision for the new mosque, then, was informed by the momentum of the 1970s and 1980s, nationally and locally. Furthermore, at least four of the board members at the time had experience in the property market and were cognizant of the benefits of building in a period of high demand. Several had skills in negotiating real estate sales. The City's offer to consider several sites for the new mosque came to a board that was not only aware of property values but also familiar with land swaps and areas of development in the city. It was a fortuitous mix of business skill and city momentum.

Most of the negotiations with the City of Edmonton for a new location were made under Mayor William Hawrelak. Hawrelak was known to be a wheeler-dealer, and his deals were not always above suspicion. Nevertheless, it was under Hawrelak that the city administration proposed that the Al Rashid board look at several possible sites to see which might fit the purposes of building a new Al Rashid when the old one closed.

The City of Edmonton and Al Rashid, 1976–1986

1976–1977	City begins negotiations for land for Royal Alexandra Hospital
1977	Land swap plus finances for 113 Street and 127 Avenue property
1978	First plans drawn for new Al Rashid
1980	Funding raises $1 million; in light of shortfalls, leadership makes visits abroad
1981	Mosque completed and opened in fall
1984	National energy oil collapse
	City of Edmonton in major decline
	Arabic classes sponsored at the University of Alberta
	Financial partnership between WICS and Al Rashid on funding formula for apartment building
1986	Larry Shaban becomes first Muslim cabinet minister in Canada

A NEW BUILDING SITE AND FUNDRAISING EFFORTS

Early in 1976, the City indicated that it wished to explore the purchase of the property on which Al Rashid Mosque stood. The local hospital, the Royal Alexandra, required more space for parking and expansion. Al Rashid stood on important ground. As part of the negotiations, the City suggested several pieces of property around Edmonton. As Edward Saddy (2015) explained, steps had been taken earlier to address a new building but it had never materialized:

> The association purchased a parcel of land on 148th Street, south of 87th Avenue in the early 1970s when land in the area became open for development as a residential subdivision with areas set aside for community services. The property was held for several years but there was little enthusiasm to build on this site as a majority of the Muslim community lived in the northwest and northeast quadrants of the city. Some years later, the land was sold at a substantial profit, and...The City's request for our site created the basis for proceeding to plan a new mosque, though not one anywhere near as large as it ultimately became.

The AMA board wanted the mosque built by Muslims. Moe Mansour became the engineer and project manager for the new mosque building. He had worked with an architect named Khan at Colt Engineering, a local firm. Mansour (2015) explained how the connections that helped make the new mosque a reality came about:

> I worked for MONENCO, a holding company of forty different firms across Canada at the time with head office in Montreal. I had come to Edmonton to the University of Alberta in 1976 to study for my master's degree in engineering. I worked for six months at

Colt Engineering, then elected to leave the company and start my own firm. I knew Saleem Ganam, and he and I were good friends. He came to my office because he believed the committee needed someone to handle the big technical dimensions of the project. I have a deep respect for Saleem...There would have been no mosque without Saleem as far as I'm concerned. It was his spirit that created it. He was a good role model...a Canadian with flair! He could talk to the prime minster or to the ordinary Joe. He was able to convey to the people his vision of how Muslims should respond to the building. He said, if we start building, then people will contribute...If they see a real mosque rising, they will rally around!

The board worked with the three-acre lot on 113 Street, north of 130 Avenue. Mansour recalled the deal with the city:

The city actually offered us a deal we couldn't refuse. They offered to exchange the property for a three-acre residential site worth about $400,000 to the city. There was some reluctance to accept the deal, but Saleem sold it to the community. Ed Saddy was in charge of negotiations, Saleem sold it to the community, and Mahmoud Tarrabain was what you might call a good public relations man, not a strategist. Alex Awid was part of the committee...He had been critical in raising funds for Hawrelak as mayor...This team basically smoothed the path out. The whole thing was delivered in four or five months.

Mansour hired a Pakistani architect named Atta H. Hai Khan, who was an official at Public Works Canada, and "a great structural engineer," for the project; the board established a project committee consisting of Mickey Jomha, Edward Saddy, and Khan, who began drawing up plans. They worked with the 113 Street site. There was plenty of room for a mosque; it was near many of the Arab populations in the city's north end, and it had space for more parking and development. The committee negotiated a land swap with the city and paid $100,000 for the new lot, a trifle in the market of the day. The understanding was that the community would no longer use the old mosque once the new one was built. If it wished to save the mosque, the community would need to cover all costs to move it. The building, in its last hours, looked forlorn.

By December 1978, Jomha, Saddy, and Khan had completed preliminary drawings for a new Al Rashid Mosque, which would be built on the north end of the new property. The project committee was dismayed because they had been telling the community that the costs would be a little over $1 million, but their projections were clearly far too low. After the board rejected the first proposed design, the committee returned with some nine or ten options, according to Mansour, but they found problems with all of them. Finally, the committee went to Ottawa to view a mosque that had just been built there, hoping to find some inspiration and solutions to their design problems at the Scott Street mosque.

One central concern was the ablution arrangements—how to construct individual places of ablution so that splashing wouldn't occur as the person moved away from the tank; how to make sure the water was an acceptable temperature, a technical problem at the time. Furthermore, how to design the dome was problematic, and even in a pleasant climate it was never an easy exercise, but this one was complicated by Edmonton's temperature extremes. All of these issues had been addressed in Ottawa, and the board was impressed. Khan, who designed the dome as a shell design, also had to have a plan to have it lifted in place. Mansour continued,

> We found the Ottawa trip to be very valuable. First of all, we took pictures of the mosque and it gave people as visual reference. Then, we needed to have some way of covering the mosque's dome with copper without

having it buckle or warp...Khan demonstrated an overlapping system...We had to put shingles underneath because we didn't think it could be welded. We also obtained from them different ratios, so we could transition their measurements to our mosque, and this improved our thinking of technical details. We also had to decide about related buildings...We could not just construct a mosque with no place for programs, so we had to push a gymnasium as a community centre, with a youth focus. Then we had to add the multiple usages of that space...weddings, parties, funerals...a space that could be leased to the larger community for moneymaking ventures. This meant we had to have commercial kitchens, commercial-sized bathrooms, and fixtures that were [up to] code. Once we elected to add the gymnasium, we had to address the problem of noise...You couldn't have prayer upstairs and weddings below! So we had to have Hambro joists with resistant topping—a kind of rubber rumbler protector between floors to muffle noise. Since the community wanted to have a school in the basement, we had to incorporate that into the design...Obviously we had to deal with the prayer hall...It had to be built in an octagonal shape to accommodate the lot size and the direction of prayer, and we needed a model...We found it in Al-Aqsa Mosque in Jerusalem...It had a similar shape. Before we finished drawings, I went to Ottawa to check out our design and discovered that we needed a foyer...a place for socializing after prayers. So we had to add that in. These things were not all acceptable to others, but I said that's it, this has to be in there. Building Al Rashid was a very complicated process!

Everyone knew the building would be expensive but, until all the plans were approved, no one knew just how expensive. The

Members of the Fundraising Committee for the
new Al Rashid Mosque, 1980.

board was really worried how they were going to sell the project.
On the day of the congregation meeting, it was evident the price
was double the original $1.5 million estimates! The architect was
adamant: "If you guys want to build, build for fifty years. Build a
centre! You don't need just a mosque, you need a gym, you need
to grow big." The message, *don't build for today, build for tomorrow*,
resonated with the community (Mansour 2015). They could see
the wisdom of building larger, since the community was growing
by leaps and bounds, and the Al Rashid community approved
the project.

Appropriate groups were formed to make the building
happen: a fundraising committee was established to find the
money; the AMA board and community elders played the political
role of interpreting the community's building issues; and a technical committee, with Mansour as project manager, was set up.
Mindful of the board's requirements, Mansour hired Tahir Ayas, an
Afghani as structural engineer, and he engaged a Pakistani, whose

The Al Rashid Fundraising Committee in 1980.
LEFT TO RIGHT: Khalil Rahime, Ibrahim Rabu,
Imam Yousef Chebli, and Mahmoud Ali Tarrabain.

name is not recorded, from Nask Engineering to handle all electrical engineering issues.

While the groups had specific roles, there was overlap in some areas. For example, the board often had to deal with the difficult issue of fundraising once the preliminary preparations of the land were complete. The 1979 approach to fundraising was similar to the 1938 approach: counting about 2,000 families in the active database, the fundraising committee calculated that they needed between $500 and $700 from each family; strategically, they requested $800 from each family to raise their target of $1.5 million.

The AMA board contracted with Norco Contractors, headed by Bill Katerenchuk, and construction began early in 1979. Whether they could generate the necessary money, they did not know. They all realized that with one misstep Al Rashid could be dead! The community was distraught. People were wringing their hands, muttering to each other, panicking. Meanwhile, the project committee had no money in the bank. Worse still, the board did not have a commitment from a single person to help with the funds that had to be obtained.

The early fundraising among members, led by some seventy individuals, had been sufficient to get the project off the ground, but everyone knew they did not have funds to complete it. Late in 1979, the contractor threatened to withdraw from the project because, as he argued, it had taken the fundraising committee some eight months to get financial commitments from the community for preliminaries at the site. Katerenchuk pointed out that the money from the initial fundraising had been spent, and he warned that he would go no further without the necessary funds.

Faced with a stalled project, the board met several times on the issue. Finally, they created two committees: one committee for community fundraising in Edmonton, led by Ali Alex Awid; and the other to go abroad for funding, led by Mahmoud Ali Tarrabain. Alex swung into action. He brought ten well-known business people together and said to them, "I want each one of you to sign a line of credit guarantee of $100,000, and I will sign one for $500,000!" As Khalid Tarrabain (2014) explained, "In the 1980s a guy who says I will put down $500,000 and ten others laying down $100,000— those are not rich guys, they are not multi-millionaires. Yes, they are business people, but a hundred grand is a lot, and that is the story to be told." Obviously, they also all had willing bankers and an impressive credit history. Alex collected all these letters for credit, which amounted to $1.5 million, and presented them to Katerenchuk.

Fundraising in the Middle East

That $1.5 million would get the outside of the mosque built was likely, but the project committee reckoned they still would have to find another $1.5 million to complete landscaping and paving, so Mahmoud Tarrabain took the foreign fundraising group—Yousef Chebli, Saleem Ganam, and himself—to visit the heartland of Arab Muslims: the Middle East. Early in 1980, they went to Saudi Arabia. They had planned to spend a week there, but ended up staying for twenty-one days, visiting many people and enjoying the hospitality. Though Saudi Arabia was funding many sites abroad, including many mosques in the United States through the Muslim World League, nothing came from King Khalid or the head of the Saudi government. The group was disheartened. Chebli, long a loyal recipient of Saudi largess, was amazed and dismayed.

Saudi Prince Sulayman thought they deserved something, and persuaded the Dawla al-Arabiya in Jeddah to give them $20,000. They did not receive anything close to the necessary $1.5 million. They went to the Islamic Conference in the United Arab Emirates, which gave them $10,000. They went to Kuwait and likewise received nothing towards the mosque. Frustration boiled among the delegates. Chebli, known for his forthrightness, went on television and condemned the Kuwaiti government for not heeding their call for help. It did no good.

They flew to Jordan where they met King Hussain, who gave them just five hundred dinars (about C$100) and some books. Mahmoud Tarrabain, completely frustrated, went to the airport to go home. Meanwhile, Chebli and Ganam continued to speak with the associates of the king. Unable to get flight connections, Tarrabain went back into town, where he met up with an old friend from his younger days. His friend, now in the government, had some useful advice, as Chebli (2015) recalled: "Look," his friend said, "If you really need money, the only place that gives you that amount upfront is Libya. And there is an association called World Islamic Call Society [WICS]—it's an organization led by Dr. Mohammed Sherif. And he is a very good gentleman."

So, his friend contacted an official in Jordan who called Dr. Sherif and informed him that he knew these people very well, and they needed his help. Off they all flew to Tripoli, where they met with Rahim Rabo and Muqtar Della of WICS. They were warmly received and invited to stay on an empty cruise ship in the harbour, which was reserved for pilgrims to Mecca, while they waited for Dr. Sherif, who was away on business. On the second day of their sojourn there, Dr. Sherif arrived on the boat and welcomed the delegates from Canada. Dr. Sherif recognized their desperation; he looked at the history of the Muslim community in Edmonton and then checked on the record of Al Rashid Mosque, the first mosque in Canada. According to Chebli (2015), Dr. Sherif's response was this: "For this community, that planted the seed of Islam in North America, a million and half dollars for them is not a problem."

Mahmoud Tarrabain had to leave for Canada, but there was still work to be done. The committee debated the matter, and, after some negotiation, it was agreed that WICS would provide Al Rashid $1.5 million—$750,000 would be an outright gift, and $750,000 would be paid back a little every year. The entire complex would be called the Canadian Islamic Centre, and ownership would be shared equally between WICS and the Arabian Muslim Association. The mosque itself would remain Al Rashid. Dr. Sherif arranged to transfer the funds through the Libyan Embassy in London. He insisted that WICS should be the only name associated with the gift, and he declined to allow the names of specific WICS committee members to be broadcast. He insisted that the gift was not from the government but from *zakat* and *waqf*—gifts from the Libyan people. "I am flying now to Surinam," he said, "but on my way back I will come through Edmonton to see how the construction is going in a few weeks' time. As for you gentleman, you are welcome here at any time!" (Chebli 2015). The delegation headed home, along with the promise that the imam's and the caretaker's salaries should be paid from an additional $50,000 per year gift sent from WICS.

But then, there was a major crisis: Dr. Sherif could not visit Canada without a visa. Judge Edward Saddy had for many years been well known to Pierre Trudeau. After he called the Prime Minister's Office and talked to Trudeau's personal assistant (a friend of Saddy's) to ask that Dr. Sherif be given a quick visa to visit Edmonton, the visa was granted within twenty-four hours. The community arranged for Dr. Sherif to stay at the Westin Hotel and to travel around the Edmonton area. He visited the site and was pleased with the project. He made a call to insist that the funds that had been held up in London be transferred immediately. In fact, Dr. Sherif was very much impressed with the businessmen who were running the mosque board. In particular, he came to appreciate Mahmoud Tarrabain, whom he thought had an excellent business sense. Sherif used to say, "As long as Mahmoud Ali Tarrabain is in Edmonton, whatever he says to do will go" (Mansour 2015).

By 1981, the mosque was slowly appearing out of the ground, but the façade posed another problem: pricing for the white brick was expensive—$400,000! Around the mosque, depression prevailed. At an emergency fall meeting, everything seemed bleak. The community was financially and emotionally exhausted. The general consensus was that they couldn't afford this building; there were simply no resources left. People insisted, "We must reduce our expectations; we just can't afford this construction." Enter Saleem: "Do you believe in God? Well then, God will build it!" (Mansour 2015).

Sherif had kept track of building progress. Pleased by how rapidly the mosque was rising, he indicated that the entire amount from Libya would be considered a gift rather than a loan. There was rejoicing all around town at that announcement. Once the builders knew that funding was available, they changed the design for the façade. The oversight committee decided to do precast, a new technology at the time. The committee arranged with the project engineer to have precast made with embedded marble chips, which would give the mosque a distinctive, rich exterior. They also upgraded the kitchen, fitted the lecture hall with sloping screens, and arranged to add a sleeping unit for the imam, which raised the ire of city officials at the time. Plans for a library were also incorporated, and added touches were made to floor and plaster configurations. Finally, they added a minaret. The watchword changed: it went from "What can we cut to reduce spending?" to "How can we make this building great?"

With the backing of Libya, builders were able to move ahead month by month with construction. Mansour (2015) explained, "The key people at this time were Alex and Mickey Awid.

Construction of the new Al Rashid Mosque in 1980.

Bill Tarrabain, Moe Assaf, the Haymours and the Hamdons...They kept track of things and kept the construction moving forward." Everyone around the city was pleased that such a beautiful piece of architecture was added to Edmonton's skyline—during a downturn in the economy! The exterior of Al Rashid was so impressive that on the day of the dedication, Alberta Premier Peter Lougheed spent the whole morning with the people visiting the entire complex. The official opening took place in September 1982, with all the fanfare that the original had had with attendance by dignitaries, including Premier Lougheed, Mayor Hawrelak, Dr. Sherif, and large numbers of Edmonton community members. It was a red-letter day for the community.

Yet there were clouds in the sky. Mahmoud Tarrabain was treasurer from 1982 to 1984, during years of great austerity in Edmonton. By 1984, it was obvious to him that Al Rashid could not continue to thrive on the fragile financial foundation of community gifts. Mansour (2015) explained, "Bill (Mahmoud) Tarrabain was great…in a class by himself! He would drive the contractors. He carried a short stick like a field marshal…but he avoided me! Indeed, we never had an argument. I found him careful; [he] made serious decisions carefully." It was Mahmoud who could see that the costs of the mosque were unsustainable, especially given the city's economic woes. He had a plan, as Khalid Tarrabain (2014) explained: "We needed some kind of financing that will provide stability…We needed to make this mosque financially stable. After we completed the mosque, and we still had a strip of two acres beside it, I suggested that we use half of the acreage to construct an apartment building of thirty-two suites. I figured the suites would bring in circa $100,000 a year. This would put the mosque on a solid financial footing. It would also build equity on the land."

Mahmoud went to an architect and asked him to design a four-storey apartment building. The architect went to a contractor, who estimated the cost at around $1.2 million. Since it was 1984 and the economy was not flourishing, it was a time of cheap construction. The problem was that Mahmoud Tarrabain did not have one penny of that money. All he had was the land. So he called Tripoli to talk to Dr. Sherif. As recounted by Khalid Tarrabain (2014), his conversation went like this:

> "Dr. Sherif, I only have three days, because I'm a businessman. I need to meet with you. I will leave Friday and come back Sunday night."
> Dr. Sherif replied, "Come anytime!"
> So he went to Tripoli with his apartment plans.
> He reminded Dr. Sherif, "You helped us build this mosque, but we might die tomorrow and we want to plan for more financial stability for this mosque."

Mahmoud told him that he wanted to build an apartment building and asked Dr. Sherif to set up a business partnership with him. He explained that although the $1.5 million that had Dr. Sherif had provided was a gift and that ownership of the mosque as equally shared between them, under Canada's foreign investment laws, business partnerships could not be done the same way. The Canadian partner had to have majority ownership.

According to Chebli (2015), Mahmoud proposed that they enter into partnership of 49 per cent ownership for the donor and 51 per cent for the mosque. Dr. Sherif asked, "So we pay $600,000 and you will pay $600,000?" Mahmoud said, "We have a problem...We don't have $600,000! But we want you to pay the full $1.2 million. In exchange, you hold the piece of land (current estimated land value is $300,000); as for the remaining $900,000, you cover it, and then we pay you back from the dividend we receive from the $300,000 land value increase. So every year, there is a dividend from the land and apartment and we take 51 per cent, and it pays you 49 per cent. From our 51 per cent, we will pay you back the $300,000. So over the years you will get your money back." Dr. Sherif laughed, but he agreed and he signed the cheque.

The apartment building was finished in 1986. Since then, the dividend has been produced annually, and Al Rashid "continued to pay the dividend until it was completely paid off. It finished a few years ago," explained Khalid Tarrabain in a 2014 conversation. "We continue to stay in touch with them," he added. "They come and have meetings with us once a year; they look at our financial statements. This [arrangement] really helped to stabilize the finances of the mosque in the 1980s."

ORGANIZATIONAL SHIFTS AND CHALLENGES IN THE NEW AL RASHID

Changes were afoot in Alberta and Edmonton. The often-elected Conservative Party, with several powerful representatives from the Islamic community either in the legislature or in significant positions in the party, saw the growing Muslim population as a fertile area for development, and gave a nod to the Arab founders of the Edmonton community with an official recognition of one hundred years in Alberta. At the same time, Edmonton was booming and welcomed the flourishing Muslim as indicated by its new splendid mosque.

Still, the new Al Rashid faced a number of organizational challenges as it grew into its new space and alongside a changing culture. This section highlights several of the most pressing issues: the role of the imam, governance under the Arabian Muslim Association, the complex legal implications of the mosque's funding structure, and—intertwined with each of these issues— the strong personalities who shaped the community. The ad hoc organizational structures of earlier years were obviously not working as the size of the congregation grew. When the new Al Rashid rose into the sky, the board was aware that some things had to change. While the physical building was lovely, and a matter of pride, it was the people that needed care. The emphasis on construction that had obsessed the community from the late 1960s through the 1980s had exhausted the people. They now wanted services and provisions instead of worrying about physical plants.

With growth came the loosening of the ethnic factor; as we have seen, people from all over the world, with various shades of Islamic commitment came to Al Rashid. Al Rashid had established an identity like none other in Canada, and its stability drew both converts and immigrants. Yet Al Rashid had never been exclusively a Lebanese or even an Arab mosque. According to Judge Edward Saddy's (2015) recollection, his parents had explained that the lawyer who drew up the Arabian Muslim Association papers suggested the name based on the fact that they were all Arabic-speaking; it was not that the founding principals held ethnic identity to be a key factor in determining the character of the mosque or its emphasis. Like pioneer Mahmoud Tarrabain, Saddy himself had a long association with the AMA—from 1960 to 1990— so he had a unique perspective on the situation.

Identity issues were to bedevil the organization, including tensions between an implicit Lebanese character and a more widely encompassing Islam as a religious community. Islamic law teaches that believers belonged to the *ummah*, not to a congregation with any ethnic identity. Very early, then, even insiders referred to the AMA as the *Canadian* Muslim Association, the designation somehow better fitting their view of who they were. The term also resonated with the position the mosque was assuming in Canada. Even though people in the mosque community referred to themselves by *Canadian Islamic Centre, Al Rashid Mosque,* this specific name was never registered; nor were the official signatories with responsibility for the mosque ever moved to change the registration. Many of the issues discussed in this section may not have arisen had it not been for the continuing problem of financing the skills needed to address a sophisticated and diverse community.

In the early days, all roles in the mosque—from imam to president of the board to caretaker—were unpaid, a norm that Al Rashid's first imam, James Ailley, had established. Mosque-related work was considered a commitment to the community. This didn't sit well with imams, who, in the Middle East, were hired by mosques to take on a well-established set of duties after scholarly and religious training. Al Rashid addressed this issue, in part, by providing a home for the imam and his family, but early imams still had to find income somehow, especially if they had a family to feed. Members sometimes gave the imam money as gifts, but the ad hoc arrangement hindered the ability of the mosque to attract a highly trained imam. Given his responsibilities with the mosque, the imam often didn't have time or energy to work outside the mosque. Some imams found part-time work. Imam Chebli (2015), for example, drove a cab for a year when he first came from Lebanon.

Obtaining an imam who was sufficiently fluent in Arabic to deal with the continuing Arabic influence among the older members of the community *and* able to converse easily in English for the next generation was an ongoing problem. Indeed, the first study done on the group in the late 1970s had identified language as an issue (Waugh et al. 1983). It was expensive to search out proper candidates. There was also the pressure of finding someone capable of handling the many converts coming into the community. Most of these were spousal conversions, but there was no doubt that Islam was attracting a goodly number of inquisitive people who were dissatisfied with their current religious commitments. Special skills were needed to make these people feel welcome, and Arab imams did not often have the cultural sophistication to deal with seekers.

Enter Saleem Ganam again. As we have seen, Ganam had been a schoolteacher in Saskatchewan and Alberta, and he and his sister, Dr. Lila Fahlman, formed a vigorous team to promote Islam. The younger, English-speaking members of the community increasingly looked to Saleem, long an advocate of interfaith dialogue, for Islamic support and explanations. He also had a special sensitivity around Islamic marriage. He knew, for example, that some Canadian women converts were dissatisfied with the formal betrothal ceremony in which the woman said nothing; only a designated male spoke on their behalf. This did not sit well with Canadian women, who felt they played no part in stating their desire to marry their husband-to-be. Some remarked that the ceremony left them feeling that they were simply not married. Saleem responded to their feelings by setting up a mini-ceremony in which they could express their willingness to marry. He was also able to mediate at mixed funerals. His familiarity with Canadian ways made him a natural in handling these cultural issues. He increasingly called himself a leader of the community, and he was accorded an equivalent position as a result. As critical as these matters were, there were social and family counselling needs that required advanced skills; the community did not have the resources to support these kinds of needs.

The two individuals who were most involved in day-to-day care of the congregation were Yousef Chebli and Saleem Ganam. As we recall, since the early 1970s Imam Chebli had been funded by the Muslim World League, with headquarters in Saudi Arabia, in his work in Edmonton, through an organization identified as the Canadian Islamic Centre. Some members of the board and some members of the community were concerned that the model of Imam Najjib James Ailley—that is, of serving as imam without remuneration—was not being continued. Those who felt this way

Famous boxer Muhammad Ali visited Al Rashid Mosque
in 1984. With him is Al Rashid official Saleem Ganam.

rejected Chebli's assertion that Saleem Ganam should received
some stipend for his work in the Al Rashid community. The
difficulty was that Saleem had many expenses relating to meetings
and travel, which were unsupported, and he could not carry on
what he saw as necessary work for Islam. He proposed an organization that could issue receipts for tax purposes in order to fund
these activities.

In the 1990s, Saleem Ganam registered the name *Canadian Muslim Association*, with Mohammad al-Sassi, Imam Chebli, and himself as signatories, apparently hoping to disconnect the title from the Arabian Muslim Association that had initiated the mosque years earlier. A sub-name *Canadian Islamic Centre, Al Rashid Mosque* was indicated as part of the new association. The justification was that Ganam served in a leadership role through the 1980s into the 1990s without direct remuneration and was funded via an unknown allocation arrangement through WICS of Libya. The allocation was not approved or allocated through the regular mosque structure. In fact, the funds had a different accounting system altogether than Al Rashid, which continued to be funded under the regular gifts and alms of the people. These apparently legal actions were taken without the consent or awareness of the officials in the AMA, including Edward Saddy or Mahmoud Tarrabain. The board was naturally unhappy about this arrangement. The AMA board, responsible for the overall financial structures of the Al Rashid complex, was concerned with accountability of this dual situation.

One issue brought the divided situation to a head: whether Al Rashid, the religious complex (along with its imam and counsellors) had a different ownership structure than the other parts of the buildings in the complex, such as the gymnasium and the social hall attached to the mosque. A court case was launched by the AMA board to determine this question of ownership. Mohammad al-Sassi, a lawyer from Libya, requested clarification on who owned Al Rashid and the Canadian Islamic Society—was it was the Arabian Muslim Association or Islamic Call Society? Previous negotiations proposed that an organization would be formed as a holding unit titled the Call to Islam Society; all the physical plant associated with both the mosque and apartments would rest under this organization. Title to Al Rashid would be held by the Arabian Muslim Association, while the rest—the Canadian Islamic Centre and the Al Rashid Apartments—would be collectively held by the Arabian Muslim Association and the Call to Islam Society. This complicated relationship derived in part from the funds donated by Libya and the concern that the complex could be sold by an AMA board at some point.

The problem was, Ganam really had no legal authority to register the *Canadian Muslim Association*. He had never been an elected official on the AMA board, nor had he held a position on the holding association of the apartments, and from the point of view of the AMA board, to refer to himself as Al Rashid community leader was to distort the legal facts. The bank, under the impression that Ganam and al-Sassi were now in control of funds, had complied with changing them to being signatories. As is the case in most corporations, at least two signatories are required on cheques, and both Tarrabain's and Saddy's names had been removed and replaced with the new names. When Tarrabain and Saddy learned of this change, they called a lawyer. The lawyer approached Ganam and Chebli and suggested that they return the banking protocols to their original configuration or face legal action. They changed the names back to the original signatories, and the term *Canadian Islamic Centre, Al Rashid Mosque* was to return to its former role as purely an offhand way of speaking of the more formal and official AMA.

The conflict was not put to rest, however. The complicating factor was the protracted and serious difficulties the board had with Imam Chebli. Despite Chebli's charisma and his friendship with important families, the board was concerned with his ability to handle the diversity that was now Al Rashid. They worried about his public stance, which was activist and sometimes peculiar. They feared that he might stir up trouble in a city they had grown up in and loved. They also were concerned with his tendency to reshape the finances in ways amenable to his plans. They were uncomfortable with the fact that they gave him a free home, but he did not work at any other role to pay for his upkeep, and his initial funding had come from Saudi Arabia, and then later through an arrangement with the Islamic Call Society of Canada. In effect, his sources of funding were foreign governments—either Saudi Arabia or Libya—not the mosque community or employment. This ultimately meant that he could decide what he would do with his time and that he was not subject to board control. The impasse continued as the board met several times to dismiss him as imam. Each time they failed because he warned them he would not leave the house without a fight, and the people had no stomach for a court case to relieve the imam of his duties and legally remove him from their house. This state of affairs continued for many years, and all the while Chebli insisted that he was the imam of "the Canadian Islamic Centre, Al Rashid Mosque." The board finally relieved him of his imam duties in 1992.

Both Chebli and Ganam had accompanied Mahmoud Tarrabain to Libya as described earlier. Ganam's signature appeared on the agreement signed with the Libyans for the mosque funds, and at some point the issue of personal funding for Ganam and Chebli must have been raised. Apparently, both these men thought the mosque board had deliberately set aside funds from Libya that had been earmarked for them as leaders in the community. The board, on the other hand, insisted that only the president and the board were the leaders of the community and had the authority to direct funds. There was, in other words, serious disagreement over who constituted the genuine leadership of Al Rashid Mosque.

The issue boiled over in 2004. Ganam, Chebli, and al-Sassi again applied to register the *Canadian Islamic Centre, Al Rashid Mosque* as a separate entity, with provisions for them to gain financial control over funds from the mosque. They successfully registered the name and represented themselves as the leaders of the mosque community. They also approached the bank and had the signatories of bank accounts of the mosque transferred to their names. According to the documents filed in court, they did this because they deemed the board to be moving Al Rashid more vigorously towards Saudi control, especially towards its conservative Wahhabi roots, and focusing its finances in ways that were not particularly aiding the congregation. When the board learned of the new registration, they also registered the name so that the whole complex was connected to the Arabian Muslim Association, implying that the name of Al Rashid belonged to their jurisdiction. The question was, who then owned the name?

Another complicating factor was the funding arrangement (or corporation) that had been set up between the AMA and WICS in Libya to provide funds for paying mosque expenses through joint enterprises, one of which was the apartment complex. The agreement involved willingness to share revenues on the apartments that had been built by the Libyan organization in conjunction with the mosque leaders—that is, the board. As is the case in corporations, at least two signatories are required on cheques, and both Tarrabain's and Saddy's names had been removed and replaced with new names. Why were these funds not used to pay mosque personnel? When Tarrabain learned that a second attempt to change the names of signatories had been made to the bank by Ganam and al-Sassi, suggesting that they were now the community's true leaders, and hence should have signing authority over corporation funds, he immediately contacted Edward Saddy. On behalf of the AMA board, Saddy instituted a legal case, arguing that the financial stability of the organization was threatened by two sets of parties claiming ownership over the same entity.

Consequently, a court case was launched by AMA board against "the Canadian Islamic Centre, Al Rashid Mosque, Mohamed Sassi, Yousef Chebli, Omar Tarchichi, Ibrahim Majeed and Saleem A. Ganam." (See Court of Queen's Bench of Alberta: *Arabian Muslim Association v. Canadian Islamic Centre*, 2004 ABQB 784). In a judgement that ran over twenty pages, Madame Justice Veit ruled against the defendants (Chebli et al.) on the issue of who owned the name of the mosque and who had signing authority over the accounts with the Islamic Call Society. The judge noted that Chebli had represented himself as imam of Al Rashid when, in fact, he had been dismissed from that role. She also ruled that all along Al Rashid had been the mosque led by the officials of the board of AMA, that neither Chebli nor Ganam had ever been elected as board members so they could not claim to be leaders of the Canadian Islamic Centre, Al Rashid Mosque. During the trial, Chebli had also argued for an $80,000 payment from the AMA to cover their costs and the indebtednesses for services that the defendants conceived they had provided to the mosque, a demand the judge regarded as spurious. The judge also castigated Chebli for representing himself as the imam of the mosque to appeal to people to give money to invest in Nigeria, which they subsequently lost. She ruled that this was false representation, very costly for the people, and unacceptable for an individual in his claimed position. Judge Edward Saddy (2015) noted later that he felt the individuals had pursued a personal agenda incongruous with the role of community builder.

Since Chebli was no longer imam, his official role in the mosque was no longer in question, and, since the funding he claimed for his work was not granted by the court, he retreated into semi-retirement. Ganam continued his work in the university and in the larger community, funded by his contacts with Libya. Neither had any continuing responsibility in Al Rashid. But there were lessons learned. The AMA board saw clearly that it was increasingly difficult to operate a professional organization on a volunteer basis; the days of a tiny mosque in a prairie town were over.

THE ORGANIZATIONAL SHIFT

With Saleem Ganam working elsewhere, the focus on property and physical development in the mosque organization changed. The shift was signalled when Khalid Tarrabain became president of the AMA board in the early 1990s. The Al Rashid community was financially exhausted from the construction projects, and there was very little money for programs. Khalid believed that the people, not real estate investment, were the real financial bedrock of the mosque; lasting financial commitment was rooted in constructive and rewarding programs and services. Khalid (2014) explained in conversation, "When I came in 1992 I had a different vision. Funds for real estate were not available anymore. To make Al Rashid financially stable, we needed to create programs and services that people wanted. Wherever I looked, I saw a community in need. So we started lots of programs; the first step was to create programs for the youth, for the ladies, for seniors, and for funeral services."

The Board of Directors of AMA, Al Rashid Mosque, 2012.
LEFT TO RIGHT: Bassim Kadry, Imad Kaddoura, Khalid Mouallem, Tayssir Younes, Walid Zein, Khalid Tarrabain (front).
ABSENT: Jim Aboughouche, Tariq Deeb, Ameen Aboughouche and Nazir Umarji.

A few years before Khalid started his tenure as board president, the mosque made a conscious effort to prioritize the education of Muslim children and offer education as a key service. In earlier days, Al Rashid had programs like Sunday school, but in 1987, it established an Islamic school for children. (See Chapter 5 for a discussion of Al Rashid's education initiatives.) The fees for attending the school covered the salary of the teacher. As with most Canadian religious groups, the AMA board saw the pressures on young people and wanted to help. In addition to the more formal school, Al Rashid formed its own Scouts Canada troop. At the same time, it drew the male youth in by funding an Al Rashid Youth Club, started by the youth, run by the youth, for the youth. Similarly, it began an organization for young women called Generation of Change.

The Al Rashid Beaver Scouts, 1994.

Scout leaders, 1994.

Khalid (2014) noted that "some people wanted the youth activities separate [by gender], so we created two organizations." Generally, he explained, "There are six types of activities for all these youth: education, Scouts, sleepover once a month, camps twice a year, a kids' conference, trips. These youngsters go all over Canada to meet other Muslim kids. Now we even have groups of them who go on Umra (religious visit to the *hajj* territory). You name it, we concentrate heavily on our kids!"

Given that women historically played a key role in Al Rashid, it is not surprising that considerable resources were invested in programs by and for them. Since they had always had their own committee, with a president and vice president, they were understood to be a central part of Al Rashid. Khalid (2014) remarked,

> People ask us all the time about the role of women in the mosque. From day one, women were involved in our board meetings and it's in our constitution that they do so. They also have their own organization, the Al Rashid Ladies Association. It is surprising, but 80 per cent of my work is with the ladies and their activities. It is only about 20 per cent with men. The reason is simple: the ladies always deliver the vision…If we want something done, it will be the women that deliver it. The ladies run their own program for health and wellness; they visit people in the hospital and they actually have their own private organization. The work they can't do with men, they do on their own, especially the visits of care, funeral support, et cetera.

Al Rashid lives in a city of constant social need, and part of the organizational shift was to help address some of these issues in Edmonton by partnering with existing social service resources. Members recognized that Edmonton's proximity to the north, the constant stream of new immigrants, and the poverty and pain of urban living place a huge burden on social services across the

Members of the Al Rashid Ladies Association during the 1980s receive recognition at the Edmonton Islamic Academy Gala, 2012. FRONT, LEFT TO RIGHT: Maryam Hamdan, Zarifee Aboughouche, Gail Mouallem, and Amnee Nashman. BACK, LEFT TO RIGHT: Rangeena Saif, Jawdah Jorf, Khazma Assaf, Hanna Tarrabain and Fatin Almaouie. ABSENT: Halimi Abufarris, Fatima Assaf, Salma Chebli, Josephine Hamdon, Alice Jomha, and Bahijah Tarrabain.

city. In the mid-1990s, in particular, it became obvious that some institutions beyond the borders of Al Rashid were in dire need of community assistance. At the same time, the board recognized that some Muslims were using these Edmonton resources. Hence, Al Rashid responded with support to the Edmonton Food Bank. They also raised funds for the children's hospital through the Stollery Foundation. Given the trauma faced by families with serious illnesses, Al Rashid now moved to support the Cancer Society and the Kidney Foundation.

Additionally, Al Rashid initiated six funds, each with a specific social group or program as recipient. Each year, *zakat* (members' alms) goes to the Islamic Family and Social Services Assocation; food hampers for Muslim people who need assistance; food coupons at select stores; the Islamic Social Services Association; Boyle Street dinners; and Friday prayer at Alberta prisons. A collaborative initiative of all mosques in Alberta, the

Islamic Family and Social Services Association (IFSSA) was established in 1992. Al Rashid is a strong supporter of the association, and refers people to IFSSA because it has access to resources from a wide range of non-profit organizations. IFSSA is also useful for new immigrants who need support while they get settled. Four times a year, Al Rashid provides dinners to the local people of Boyle Street, a low-income neighbourhood in Edmonton's downtown. Finally, mindful that some of their people are in Alberta prisons, including maximum-security facilities, Al Rashid's Prison Committee meets with Muslim inmates every Friday for prayer.

Al Rashid also developed new services related to death during the 1990s. In our 2014 conversation, Khalid described the origins of these services, which included a unique funding initiative:

> We needed a cemetery. In 1993 we started work on the cemetery...We continue to do this even today and are developing 5,000 new graves. We have purchased 80 more acres and we are developing additional plots. Also, by 1995, we opened our own funeral home; we bought a cooler—it only cost us $10,000—and we applied for and received a licence. This opened a significant initiative for us...Once again we did not have the funding to do this...We were only 5,000 people. In order to buy the [original] 80 acres, which cost us $100,000 (an acre was around $12 at that time), we said, everyone will pay $500 for a membership and if you have a membership, you'll get a free plot along with [a plot for] your wife. People supported that. So we sold all the memberships. We got the land and we started the funeral home from the membership fees.

Establishing the cemetery provided a complete cycle of services for Sunni Muslims in the Edmonton area. Unlike some other Muslim communities in Canada, the mosque community was able to present a full range of religiously inspired services without any conflict with

the larger community. Al Rashid now could now be entirely
self-reliant for religious activities, but its connections with the
larger community made it a full partner with social agencies as
they linked with them for the population at large.

THE ROLE OF WOMEN IN MOSQUE PROGRAMMING

As we saw in Chapter 2, the first Al Rashid was built through
the energy of a group of women activists who worked diligently
to provide funding for its programs. The mosque has had an
active women's group throughout its history. That group also
sends a delegate to the board. Over the years, some women have
urged a more formal place in the senior administrative structure.
However, the majority of Al Rashid women have not been too
concerned with this, arguing that there is no doubt that women
have made and continue to make extraordinary contributions
to Al Rashid in so many ways beyond the formal. They remain
quite comfortable in the organizational structure as it has
evolved in Edmonton.

This is not to say, however, that the Muslim women of
Al Rashid were unaffected by the women's liberation movement
in Canada during the 1970s and 1980s. Middle Eastern women
had long had feminist advocates (at least from the late 1800s—
far earlier than the West), and careful scholars pointed out that
the Prophet himself argued for and legislated women's rights
(e.g., Mernissi 1991). But when Gloria Steinem and her American
and Canadian colleagues popularized the movement in the early
1970s by decrying the limited roles available to women, it didn't
resonate with the Muslim women in the mosque. As is sometimes
the case, however, the social movement embraced by the majority
would turn back to criticize those they thought outliers. The movement that initially attacked male dominance and argued against the
negative legacies of patriarchy found Islamic society an easy mark
for criticism. Once again Islam was placed on the defensive, and
once again Al Rashid women were forced to respond.

My colleague Jenny Wannas and I conducted an in-depth sociological study of Al Rashid women and their response to the women's movement in the 1980s (Waugh and Wannas 2003). We found that Al Rashid women developed what Leon Festinger calls cognitive dissonance, an uncomfortable state of tension resulting from the contradiction between one's belief system and one's actual lived experiences. Cognitive dissonance was a kind of strategy of accommodation to the women's liberation movement when it became part of Muslim women's lives. To reduce cognitive dissonance, individuals may avoid experiences that cause dissonance or increase experiences that cause consonance. Mustapha (1989) has used the term "doctrinal dissonance" to refer to the specific religious experience of dissonance of Muslim Canadians, and our study found this an apt description of how many women from Al Rashid viewed the feminist movement in the 1980s. In effect, they felt out of sync with it.

Our findings indicated that cognitive dissonance was part of the cultural adaptation process of Al Rashid women. They regularly weighed how actions would be interpreted and the kinds of criticisms that outsiders might make. We found that tensions varied according to three main factors—socioeconomic status, generational differences, and ethnicity/nation of origin. We further found that Al Rashid women reacted at least two ways in Canada. First, those women who were of higher economic status were more likely to have the capability to educate themselves and to learn how to master the "Canadian system." Many of them were used to upper-class living in the homeland and they occupied a privileged place among their associates in Canada. Some of them were older, had raised their families, and had witnessed the transition from one generation to the next.

They also had a strong will to preserve Islamic values. They appreciated their increased stature as they proceeded through the age ranks, a position that they attribute to Islamic culture. We found these women experienced cognitive dissonance with Canadian society less than those of lower socioeconomic status.

We speculated that it was because as they aged, they had built extended families and friendship networks in Canada.

Indeed, for some of these Al Rashid women, there was an increased dissonance with more recent immigrants who had been influenced by Islamist ideas in the Middle East. Some of the "established" women had little in common with those women who wanted to blame Western society for everything; they were at a loss to comprehend this blanket blame because they had a measure of success within the society that was being castigated.

They also knew very well the problems that women had back in the homeland and they were not about to trade what they had achieved in Canada for what they believed was an inferior situation back home. One way they handled this dissonance was to form social groups of women in Al Rashid from their socioeconomic class, where they met to discuss issues that were relevant to them. Some, but not all, of these women joined outside groups such as the Canadian Council of Muslim Women, and addressed broad liberal policy issues within the Canadian context, about which recent immigrant women would have had little comprehension.

The mosque environment provided opportunity to provide guidance for recent women immigrants. Because of their financial privilege and awareness of the system, Muslim women in the mosque who belonged to the older, first generation of immigrants were able to overcome most economic difficulties, which now were encountered by their more recent, less-informed immigrant sisters. Nevertheless, this was not always the case, for some recent immigrants with financial means also reflected some of this trend, but without the same convincing depth. Rather, the results indicated that there was a correlation among wealthy immigrant women and first-generation women who were deemed financially successful, and their families prospered for the very real reason that they both did not have to work outside the home to sustain their families. At the same time, both developed strategies to handle their respective situations.

This nimbleness in adapting is significant. Indeed, as Kevin Dwyer (1991) points out in the Moroccan case, Muslim women have a high degree of adaptability, developing networks and bilateral connections that best suit their needs. They are not bound by formal ideologies. In fact, what seems to hold in the Alberta case is that even recent immigrant women from lower socioeconomic classes or those who have a lower educational background reduce dissonance considerably because the local community continues to have an identity related to an Arab Muslim environment.

We asked participants if they felt any discord between the formal requirements of Islamic law and their experience in Canada. One woman, Sister Sayyida (not her real name), responded quite openly, "We are freer here because we can go to the four books of law (the four Sunni legal schools) and decide which one appeals to us, then ask the imam to apply that law. It gives us greater flexibility than back home where we are bound by the local law" (Waugh and Wannas 2003, 3). Salwa Kadri (2015), on the other hand, points out that most women in the community had little training in the four schools of law and there was little attention to differences in law among community people. In her experience within the community, she found little attempt to practice one kind of law over another.

Thus, while there may have been areas of dissonance, Muslim women negotiate the difficulties they face with confidence and resilience. In fact, the Al Rashid community is of such a size now that the women need not interact much with broader Canadian society. At least initially, this gives recent immigrant women a sense of security until they feel confident enough to branch out. It also allows Al Rashid to lower tensions between them and Canadian society as a whole.

We also found that women working outside the home, or working in the presence of male Canadians, which might traditionally have been regarded as problematic, was better handled by older, first-generation women, probably because they and their families adapted to Canadian culture in a less difficult period; they had less difficulty negotiating relationships in the office or in stores with Canadians. They knew very well the social lines in the sand that govern relationships of working men and women in

Canadian society, and they quickly learned how to deal with them. As Fatima, one first-generation woman who worked outside the home, put it, "Office relationships today are very much shaped by the feminist and women's rights movements, and most people have a level of banter that is acceptable, but we all know when the line has been crossed; what I like is that women office workers play an important role in defining that line. Knowing that I am Muslim also is a controlling factor" (Waugh and Wannas 2003, 5).

Furthermore, second- and third-generation Muslim women were more likely to be more adaptable than first-generation Muslim Canadians. Adaptation in this context refers to the ability to reach a "happy medium" between two often-opposing cultural value systems by the fusion of the cultural and religious values into one belief system. The process of adaptation for third, fourth, and consequent generations likely is eased by financial security established by earlier generations of Al Rashid Muslim Canadians. More recent generations were not as likely as first-generation Muslim Canadians to have had strong ties to the Middle East. Nor were they likely to know their native language well, whether it be Arabic, Indonesian, or Farsi.

In fact, third- and fourth-generation Muslim Canadian women experience some aspects of Middle Eastern life as completely alien. For example, as their eight- and ten-year-old daughters approached puberty, the parents of one family were concerned that the girls might have difficulty with acceptable marriage partners in Canada, and so they went back to Egypt after ten years in Calgary. The family returned within the year. They experienced significant dissonance with contemporary Egyptian culture—in business practices, educational possibilities, relationships between the family and their relatives, and even in attitudes towards their daughters by families in the homeland. As the girls put it, "Calgary is just a much cooler place to live, and we're not talking about the weather." This family's experience indicates that it would take considerable cultural adaptation to live comfortably there. As a parent who has immigrated to Canada stated, "although

I lived back home most of my life, going back is a real effort where even cab drivers and street vendors notice I've been away and I am treated like a foreigner" (Waugh and Wannas 2003, 7).

Many readers will wonder at Western feminism being an issue to take so much space; the truth is, feminist norms are a challenge in Canada, as we see in more recent issues such as responses to the wearing of the hijab and burqa. Almost none of the early founders of the community in Edmonton wore the hijab. The head shawl was only a sign of respect in the mosque when they went to pray. Indeed, even when they wore the hijab, they would remove it during household parties. Wearing the hijab was much more of a cultural than religious practice (Kadri 2015). Newcomers to Canada, however, opted to retain the hijab as a symbol of their connection to the homeland. The perception of the hijab as cultural element derived in part from the presence of French (Lebanon) and British (Palestine) occupying forces, with women donning the hijab as a differentiation symbol (Kadri 2015). According to Salwa Kadri, few Al Rashid women appear in public without some kind of hair covering. What is behind this shift?

Feminism and various interpretations of feminism made in the mainstream media have had a profound impact on Muslim women in Canada. What does it mean that women who resisted the Shah in Iran and wore the veil as a means of distancing themselves from his Westernizing tendencies suddenly had the veil imposed upon them as an official dress code of the revolution? Or, in Egypt, where removing the veil was a statement of independence in Nawal al-Sa'dawi's career, but is now almost universally espoused as proper Islamic dress for professional women in Cairo? From 1981 on, various studies have shown how complicated donning (or not donning) the veil is. Anthropologist Fedwa al-Guindi (1981) argues that the veil can be liberating, even emancipating, such as when a women is member of a conservative religious group in Egypt. Leila Ahmed (1982) suggests that conventional meanings attached to veiling and sex segregation could and often did have other significances: both were conducive to promoting sisterhood and women's empowerment. Salwa (personal communication 2015) argues that the hijab was once a cultural indicator of status and wealth, while the poor seldom wore it; she sees that as reversed in Canada.

Muslim women have a long history of being the flash point of debate. Recall that the British colonialists regarded veiling as a symbol of women's oppression in Muslim societies and opposed it as backward. Lord Cromer, the founding member and president of the Men's League for Opposing Women's Suffrage in England, immediately upon arrival in Egypt argued for Muslim women's liberation from the veil, for example (Kernaghan 1993). The debate has moved from issues of veiling to the way in which women and women's issues have been manipulated for the use of states and revolutionary movements. Even the veil itself has been used for political or cultural purposes that have little or nothing to do with Muslim women, as in its use by Western feminists for their own arguments. Chandra Mohanty (1984) has suggested that the discourses of Western feminist scholarship colonize "third-world" women by homogenizing them into a special category of "women"—when, in fact "Muslim women" are not a monolithic group. Yet they are inevitably depicted as a veiled person who is universally and wholly oppressed.

Canada has done much to sensitize Muslim women to the ways in which they are turned into something for political and ideological reasons. Discussion around the application of sharia in Canada, for example, involves gender-based discrimination. Muslim men marrying several women at one time, a feature of Islamic history and culture that often predominates Western perceptions of male–female relations in Islamic countries, surfaces in public discourse in Canada mainly in jokes and asides. Discussions of honour killing also turn Muslim women into problematic, stereotypical figures who are in turn used to uphold specific Western ideologies. Hence, Al Rashid women have ample experience of cognitive dissonance in accommodating Western feminist notions about their religious tradition long before the crises brought on after 2000.

THE EVOLUTION OF EDUCATION

Muslims almost universally extol education. Muslim families embrace education as a critical part of their religious outlook, and many Muslim parents will argue that providing a good education for children is as much Islamic as prayer. Once Al Rashid was well established, the potential for children to learn Arabic and to discover the great values inherent in the Qur'an both within the mosque and in advanced education at the University of Alberta were huge drawing cards for the city. Throughout the Middle East, opportunities for children to study in the West meant immense family outlays in terms of financing and support.

Fittingly, Zubayda, the wife of famous Abbasid ruler Harun Al Rashid, did not leave education to her husband to fund. She alone financed schools and accommodation for students quite apart from the government. She also made sure that proper roads to educational institutions were built, along with wells for the students as they travelled to school. Muslim women's involvement in education does not end there. The first official school in the Muslim world was established in Fes, Morocco, in 859. It was the University of Al-Karaouine, founded by a woman merchant named of Fatima al-Fihri. From that point on, major learning institutions graced the Muslim world. Al-Azhar University in Cairo, founded in 970, is to this day one of the great educational institutions in the Islamic world. Over a thousand years ago, learning was deemed to be one of the basic requirements of living a legitimate Muslim life.

As we've learned already, the earliest school was held in the basement of the original Al Rashid, where Ali Alex Ganam taught Arabic to a cluster of students, including some adults. Their curriculum was largely ad hoc: the rudiments of the language and some discussion of the Qur'an and religious law. What Canadians may not recognize is that the original mosque applied the model of historic Islamic cities: the mosque was a centre of learning as well as a place of prayer. Hence, Edmonton's Al Rashid was classical in the sense that the fundamentals of learning were established very early as part of the reason for the mosque. In short, Al Rashid had followed the

Summer day camp at Al Rashid, 2013.

Prophet's exhortation to "seek knowledge to the ends of the earth."
Al Rashid's educational contributions are foundational to its success.
It drew Muslims from all over for its emphasis on education.

In fact, as early as the 1970s, Dr. Lila Fahlman, Saleem
Ganam, and Yousef Chebli had actively lobbied for an Islamic
school, as an outgrowth of the classes held in the basement of the
old mosque before moving to Victoria Composite High School.
Fahlman, a public school teacher, championed Islamic education,
and her arguments made solid sense: Islamic history was deeply
intertwined with European movements, especially in areas of
philosophy, science, and medicine. She argued that students
should know the sources of these important fields of knowledge.
Eventually, the Edmonton Public School Board (EPSB) sat up and
listened; they set up a committee to identify how to address the
issues. It was to bear important fruit later.

Soraya Zaki Hafez, well-known leader in the Al Rashid
community and herself a teacher, was central to the next phase
of formal educational development. As in classical madrasa style,

The Arabic Bilingual Program started in the basement of Al Rashid Mosque
and then moved to Glengarry Elementary School in 1982.

professional instruction of Arabic in began in the basement of
Al Rashid in 1980 with Soraya teaching beginner's classes. During
this transitional phase, the EPSB financed Soraya's work to develop
a professional curriculum. She was also sent abroad to buy books
and find materials for the curriculum. The EPSB made a serious
investment in Arabic teaching.

Building a public bilingual English/Arabic program was
a dramatic move, but it has to be contextualized. It was the first
official acknowledgement that Edmonton's Muslim community was
now large enough to sustain such a program. Further, it was part
of EPSB's attempts to grapple with Canada's multicultural policy.
It was also a genuine attempt to address political pressures from
faith-based schools for provincial government funding. Language
was a start. Thus, Edmonton was the first in Canada to offer the
Arabic language from the first grade in a curriculum-developed
bilingual program. It was an auspicious moment, for it was the
herald of one of those things that Muslims wanted desperately
for their children to learn—the Arabic of the Qur'an.

Eventually, the Arabic class moved from Al Rashid's basement to Glengarry School in 1982 as a legitimate public offering. Soraya had experience teaching Arabic in Lac La Biche, and her ability in fundamental Arabic grammar made her a natural when the public school wanted to move into the field. Educational authorities recognize her today as a crucial part of this important phase of Arabic's acceptance in Edmonton's educational system. As of the 2017–18 school year, there are six schools in Edmonton with thriving bilingual Arabic programs: at the elementary level, Calder, Glengarry, Evansdale, and Malmo; junior high school, Killarney; and senior high school, Queen Elizabeth (Edmonton Public Schools 2017). Grace Martin School, a K–6 school also of the Edmonton Public School Board, offers the Sakinah Circle program (previously offered through the Sakinah Argyll Home Education Centre), which is the Alberta Learning curriculum through the lens of the Qur'anic worldview. During interviews, the existence of another educational facility in the city offering Islamic/Arabic education called Al-Mustafa was mentioned. Al-Mustafa, according to those I talked to, offers full-time home schooling programs, summer camps, and weekend classes.

With that ancient religious language available, Al Rashid's Muslims had basically established what their relatives in the Middle East took for granted—fluency in understanding the Book's sacred words. This model of education harked back to the earliest days of Islam, when madrasas or mosque schools sprang up all over the Muslim world, some funded by wealthy Muslims, some by governments. The madrasa concept is a simple one: bring students to a mosque, place a distinguished teacher at one of the pillars, and have the students gather around the teacher to learn Arabic, hear the Qur'an being recited, learn its truths, and understand how it shaped Islamic law and society. Later, subjects such as mathematics and science were added to the study. From this model grew the great centres of learning, such as Nizam al-Mulk schools and Al-Azhar. Eventually, Europeans picked up this model, which resulted in the establishment of the West's great universities in Paris and London. Al Rashid's model has a long and brilliant history.

This chapter has focused on a period of growth for Al Rashid—from the building of a new physical structure to new governance and programming initiatives. The thirty-some years covered in this chapter saw the development and evolution of many factors that contributed to the mosque's contemporary iconic position. We move now to one of the most fraught periods in the community's life, a new and potentially explosive chapter in Al Rashid's long story.

4

CONSERVING A CANADIAN ISLAMIC COMMUNITY DURING ADVERSITY

Al Rashid Post 9/11

2001–2010

THIS CHAPTER EXPLORES THE AL RASHID COMMUNITY'S PROGRAMMING immediately before the events of September 11, 2001, and considers how it responded to local, national, and international pressures arising from the 9/11 disaster. Words fail to convey the trauma that 2001 brought. For one, Canada became far more suspicious towards Muslims after 9/11. Distance from the event itself, however, shows us that the community found inner resources during this politically charged time. What role did Al Rashid play for the broader Canadian Muslim community in facing the difficulties of the post-9/11 period, 2001 to approximately 2010? What problems did Al Rashid experience during this unique time, and how did it respond to them?

As the flagship of Canadian Islam, Al Rashid's handling of various problems, including those of the post-9/11 environment, reflects the larger context of Islam's survival in a Western nation. Examining how Al Rashid set its agenda post-9/11 demonstrates the community's character and its shift to a wider vision. The Al Rashid community was faced with the media trend of critical

The Edmonton Islamic Academy, 2012.

interpretations of Islamic norms, especially those associated with Sunni Islam. Then there were public discussions of what stance a Canadian Muslim should take to the violent expression of a political Islam. Dealing with these issues leads to a significant examination of the Muslim notion of *belonging* to the *ummah*—that is, the universal community of Islam.

Having to confront such changes signals a major shift from the simple embrace of the Islam of Al Rashid's earlier experience and its embodiment in a building. Exploring key aspects of this shift is a primary task in this chapter. As a corollary, we need to look at the attitudinal orientations that guided the community through this traumatic period. Finally, we also need to gauge the reaction of Canadians to the Islamic tradition towards the end of this critical period.

While the mosque leadership was aware of buffeting cultural storm clouds post-9/11, we can see how they initially responded by what they did: they built. They turned again to a major building mission—this time, the establishment of the Edmonton Islamic Academy. The message was that this community was at home in

Edmonton, and Muslims wanted to build for the future of their children. This direction was not easy as the general population, the media, and even government was rife with suspicion towards Muslims after 9/11. Hence, the first section of this chapter will deal with the situation of the mosque as it headed into the fall of 2001, and in particular the background planning for a major educational thrust in the community. We then explore some responses to the catastrophe of 9/11, followed by a sketch the some of the broader, national legal issues that affected the community over the next decade. Finally, the chapter outlines the planning, design, and construction of the Edmonton Islamic Academy, and highlights some of the principal figures involved in this signature achievement for the community.

THE LIMITS OF MULTICULTURALISM

While it is a policy established by federal law, multiculturalism is also a central Canadian value with significant legal and emotional purchase. On the one hand, its emphasis on the acceptability of all types of difference, including religious difference, has allowed Muslims to engage positively with Canadian culture. We have seen how Muslims developed confidently in Canada because they were convinced of its welcome. But multiculturalism has implications for identity that Al Rashid also had to contend with. The federal model of belonging may not sync well with Muslim notions of being a member of the *ummah*.

Identity may well be the key issue. Multiculturalism has a deeper root in Canada than federal policy; it is possible, for example, that it goes back to Indigenous cultures, where identity is rooted in family, place, language, and group. Indigenous peoples argue that they do not have a "national" identity per se; there is nothing like the European notion of "race" among these cultures. In many Indigenous cultures, adoption was the way to obtain status. Establishing oneself in pre-Canada was based upon relating to and linking oneself with a local Indigenous community—in effect, a kind of cultural adoption into the group. This model is less monolithic, and more group-focused. Unfortunately, that is not the way that identity worked out in Canada for the Indigenous peoples and it may well not work out for Muslims.

For example, in their work carried out shortly after the Gulf War, Baha Abu-Laban and Sharon McIrvin Abu-Laban (1999) found that the Arab Canadian community was moving towards isolation within Canadian society. Moreover, Suleiman (1999), in his article "Islam, Muslims and Arabs in America: The Other of the Other of the Other," suggests that stereotyping had created several levels of "otherness" for Arab Muslims, and little headway had been made in changing that situation. Studies also showed that the second wave of immigrants that started in 1962 was far more educated than most, with the majority having managerial, professional, or technical skills and only a few taking up lower level, blue-collar occupations. In 1991, one of four Arab Canadians had a university degree, compared to 10 per cent of the Canadian population in general (Suleiman 1999). Soharwardy (2002) interprets the statistic that 75 per cent of these recent Muslim immigrants could not find jobs in their professions in Toronto as blatant racism and discrimination on the part of Canadian society. While that is clearly extreme (many other immigrants have the same experience), anecdotal evidence from members of the Muslim community in Alberta also confirms some discrimination. Certain members recall changing their names as a way to sidestep adaptation problems: Mahmoud Tarrabain used *Bill*, Ali Hamdon used *Alex Hamilton*, and so on. A recent student reported that he preferred to use his second name, Rushd, rather than his first, Muhammad, during a phone interview because he was afraid of being rejected based on his name (Emami 2012). Hence, one might think that the studies of Suleiman, Soharwardy, and the Abu-Labans seem to portend a dramatic downturn in Al Rashid's history of success.

However, not all Muslim migrants to Canada experienced discrimination; most of the early migrants faced little to none of the confrontations around race or culture that current migrants experience. Our study of Muslim women (Waugh and Wannas 2003) did not clearly reveal discrimination as a prominent experience in Canada, at least for our respondents, 80 per cent of whom were Arab Muslims. Rather, the responses of the Muslim women and our interviews with a variety of participants revealed that there was no general experience of isolationism. Rather, isolationism varied with socioeconomic class and between generations, and indicated decisive ethnicity/nation of origin.

Moreover, our analysis of the interviewees shows that they did not have the same revivalist/rebirth mentality present in the 2000s Islamic cultures, cultures that were struggling to modernize but at the same time remain true to Islamic values through reformist ideologies. So the facts are unclear. What can be accepted is that the attitude in Canada appears to have stiffened towards Muslim migrants, and especially after 9/11, even if we cannot accept Soharwardy's designation of this as "racism." Al Rashid has had to gauge and respond to this "stiffening."

In the case of Alberta, or more specifically in northern Alberta, immigrants from Muslims and Islamic countries represented potential; there was no overt racism involved in dealing with these groups. Rather, government officials and leading citizens wanted to engage the growing community through new businesses. Early in 2001, for example, I was contacted by two officials from Alberta Agricultural Food and Rural Development, along with a poultry corporation, to undertake a study of the market potential in developing halal products, specifically beef and chicken, with the view to providing for a flourishing local demand and ultimately to ship abroad to Saudi Arabia. The consortium behind this initiative included such well-known Edmontonians as Glen Sather, coach and general manager of the Oilers hockey franchise of the time, but it also had Muslim backers.

The initiative was supported by the Alberta government because of the growing market in Canada for halal products. The issues explored in the resulting report included discussions of maintaining halal practices on a modern slaughter line, the presence of female workers during slaughter, variation between Muslim jurisdictions in certification, and halal challenges for multiple-use slaughter lines in factories. The ultimate goal was to expand Alberta agriculture into a market that had become evident as Muslims found Alberta an attractive home and used their skills in expanding agricultural exports abroad. While this was deemed a business venture, and might not then be seen to have racial overtones, the fact is that seeing the Muslim community as a distinct one certainly could have had an impact from an investment point of view. "Race" was not even considered in discussions. It was only after the report was tendered in 2002, that is, immediately after 9/11, that the social situation had altered perceptions and singled out Muslims with a decidedly negative cast. Before that, at least in Edmonton at the time, the Muslim community represented a highly attractive business opportunity.

DEALING WITH THE METAPHOR OF REBIRTH

For over two centuries in the other parts of the world, countries with dominant Islamic populations weathered a variety of colonialist and repressive regimes; yet they have found resources within their religious consciousnesses to shape compatible institutions and new kinds of government. Despite its critics, Islam has been very inventive in its response to such crises. It has formulated a type of rebirth that is distinctively its own—various countries shaping reforms of education, social policy, cultural and political history, to name a few, in order to integrate into the contemporary world. This has been an international movement, but it does not rely on Western forms of renewal for its inspiration; in fact, the religious culture of Islam has been the catalyst for this "rebirth" ideology. This factor seems to be lost on many Western observers, who tend to look to the renaissance in Europe as the quintessential rebirth motif. The problem is partly verbal: no single English word captures the equivalence in its entirety of this rebirth—be it revival, renewal, renaissance, reform, rejuvenation, or revolution. However it is designated, it is real and vibrant. Immigrants have transported these ideals, hopes, and fears with them in coming to Canada, and these notions play a role in settlement and achievement. We should expect the leadership of Al Rashid to be sensitive to that reformist strain in contemporary Islam and to rejuvenate Islam within a similar rebirth spectrum. Indeed, the mosque has been very inventive in responding to change.

Canadian responses to Islamic rebirth are likewise not univocal. Indeed, as Nesbitt-Larking (2007) argues, Canada reflects both negative and positive responses to the phenomenon. In a 2011 study, my colleague Razavy classified these responses as "reactive" and "affective"; a third category—"transitional," potential response areas that are not yet clear in their ultimate significance, also exists (Waugh, Razavy, and Sheikh 2011). The point is that although Al Rashid stood alone in its early history as a trailblazer, history no longer allows it that leisure. Rather, the mosque community is part of what might be called a "response map" to the Islamic renaissance, some of which clash with Canadian values.

By the early 2000s, Al Rashid no longer had the maneuverability to ignore world events, or to distance itself from international Islamic cultural trends. As far as Canadians were concerned, its place in the pantheon of mosques immediately put it in the spotlight. On the other hand, Al Rashid Muslims were constantly required to justify actions by Muslims abroad. Why should an action committed by a Muslim in some other part of the world suddenly require local Muslims to automatically be guilty?

There are important reasons for this conundrum. First, Sunni doctrinal teaching about the unity of the *ummah* allows for no unique—that is, Canadian—creations of Islamic belief. The very universality of doctrine implies similarity of values. Second, Sunni Islam has traditionally deferred to Saudi Arabian definitions of "true" Islam, and there is a cultural attitude that other forms are somehow held to be derivative. The catastrophe of 9/11 shows how problematic Saudi connections can be. Third, the influence of Wahhabism—a conservative and even anti-historical Islamist movement—has come to play a key role in contemporary definitions of Sunni Islam abroad, even if it is difficult to determine precisely how this movement impacted Canadian and Al Rashid Sunnism. Some writers see Saudi political intent behind the exportation of Wahhabism. Fourth, to retain its leading position in Canada (and around the world), Al Rashid could not buck the prevailing interpretations of major issues, so regardless of its exalted place in Canadian Islam, it also had to be aware of the wider Muslim world's opinion. Fifth, financing of mosques in the West from Middle Eastern Arab funds has perhaps skewed doctrine and custom in the benefactor's direction; as the saying goes, he who pays the piper calls the tune. This feature has been both a blessing and a curse—a blessing in that a small community can receive assistance to develop a mosque program, and a curse in that critics see it as playing the role of a fifth column in Western circles. Al Rashid has had to deal with these critics. Sixth, Muslim leadership has had differences with those within who gravitated to the view that Islamic rebirth was entirely expressed in Muslim Brotherhood terms. During the period leading up to the turn of the millennium, this orientation was rapidly gaining adherents in the heartland areas, and it has spilled over into communities in the West.

In public discourses in Canada, Muslims may be reluctant to say much about the Muslim Brotherhood, or Islamism, or the more radical jihadist (this word is an invention of the West; no Muslim group invented the term) wing because they do not want to clash with viewpoints of their own community on the one hand, or they are fearful of antagonisms by larger North American society on the other. In engagements with the Canadian public, they are more apt to hew to a conservative line because of peer pressure within the community, where they may not wish to be known as anything less than a "true" Muslim. Canadians as a whole are confused by this apparent lack of transparency.

While there may be no overt sympathy for jihadist views among most Muslims, its presence has made Muslims aware that even sympathetic Westerners are likely to be suspicious of conservative Islamic views. Contrarily, one may even find the younger generation more conservative than elder parents, a feature that has been found by scholars in studies of the second-generation migrant population. While spokespeople from within Muslim communities stress the minority character of these new branches of Islam, and may even deny their existence as distinctive groups, Canadians scarcely believe that they are not present; they just don't know how much. The result is a continuing, undefined tension over just what constitutes Islam and Al Rashid's relation to it.

In Canada, we are seeing a jockeying for position within the Canadian public mind about just what constitutes "true" Islam and who is said to express it. Thus, like multiculturalism, there are several circulating discourses and none can be said to predominate. Al Rashid has had to live with this indefinite situation, but it has not turned inward or moved away from engagement with the larger community, which is itself is a significant achievement given the difficulties of the post-9/11 world.

LOOKING TOWARDS THE FUTURE IN THE YEARS BEFORE 9/11

While it is tempting to move directly from the construction of the new Al Rashid in the 1980s and the growth of the Canadian Islamic Centre to the tragedy of 9/11, that is to distort the facts. A wide range of activities was underway within the community, which indicates a community at peace with itself and planning for a vigorous future in Edmonton and Canada. Unbeknownst to Al Rashid at the time, these activities set the stage for the community's responses to the 9/11 crisis and a changed, post-9/11 world.

Increasing Provincial Government Awareness

As we have seen, the community had been brilliantly successful at connecting with other Canadians in a meaningful way throughout the early days. How to keep connected and how to make new

Legislative Assembly of Alberta

CONGRATULATIONS

to the

**Muslim Community
of Alberta**

on your

*100-th ANNIVERSARY
of Settlement in Canada!*

*"Thank you for your outstanding contribution
to the cultural, educational, social and
economic strengths of our province and
our country!"*

Presented May 1, 1999, by:

Gene Zwozdesky

Gene Zwozdesky, MLA Edmonton Mill Creek
On behalf of the Government of Alberta

Statement honouring the province's Muslim community
from the Legislative Assembly of Alberta, 1999.

connections became a central issue for the Muslim leadership.
We will have occasion below to explore more thoroughly their
strategies, but here it is sufficient to point out that one way was to
entrench an Islamic awareness in the highest form of provincial
consciousness through an official governmental celebration
of Eid within the legislative body. Thus, while most provincial
governments recognize Eid celebrations either by proclamations
or official congratulations, in Alberta where Larry Shaban served
as the first Muslim minister in the provincial cabinet during the
1970s and 1980s, it was introduced as a traditional breaking-of-
the-fast celebration at the Legislature Building itself, hosted by the
ruling Conservative government. It was an official expression of the

Al Rashid is committed to enhancing and strengthening cultural ties and interfaith dialogue. Cold Lake Catholic School visits Al Rashid Mosque, April 2016, with Outreach Imam Sadique Pathan. The tour taught students about world history and religion.

Government of Alberta. That tradition has been maintained, long after Larry Shaban left office. Indeed, the national government has followed suit, with special Muslim celebrations given the stamp of governmental approval. How significant and unique this official recognition is easily discernable: despite the formative role of Indigenous peoples in Canada, no official celebration marks their ritual presence in legislative bodies.

Meeting the Social Needs of a Growing Population

The immigration trends in Edmonton pre-9/11 indicate a self-confident community struggling not with other Canadians but with the overwhelming task of finding homes and jobs for the flood of Muslim brothers and sisters who swept into the city, hopeful that Al Rashid would help them settle. A few numbers help illustrate this scenario: Muslims made up the largest non-Christian community in ten out of twenty-five Canadian cities (Hamdani 1997).

In 1991, census data indicated the presence of 253,265 Muslims in Canada; 2001 Canadian census data estimated the number of Canadian Muslims to be around 800,000, and Statistics Canada predicted an increase of approximately 160 per cent in the number of Muslims in Canada by 2015 (Bélanger and Malenfant 2005). The 2011 National Household Survey counted over one million Muslims in Canada, largely concentrated in Canada's largest metropolitan cities (Statistics Canada 2017). One way Al Rashid responded to the flood of immigrants was to support initiatives in other parts of the city. Edmonton has significant suburban sprawl, and cheaper housing is almost always available in the outskirts. Not surprisingly, immigrant populations often settle in these more remote suburbs, and, in Edmonton's case, mosques soon follow. Al Rashid has been instrumental in developing several of the mosques in the Edmonton area. Providing this kind of assistance echoes the actions of the old Al Rashid Mosque, when the dome of the old mosque was donated to the mosque in Lac La Biche. Since then, several other mosques, including Markaz al-Islam in Edmonton's Mill Woods community, have sprung up with assistance from various members of Al Rashid.

While Al Rashid rejoiced in so many joining them, the larger Canadian community reacted with fear. Some Canadians feared this rapid growth as a "Muslim takeover." Yet in a country that brings in around 250,000 immigrants annually, this is not really a Muslim "flood"; much of this fear is driven by the visibility of Muslims, especially women, and not by Canadian communities being inundated with Muslims. This is Canada's expression of Islamophobia, that ambiguous experience of dread that has swept other parts of the Western world. Al Rashid had to face this. As Al Rashid settled into its new mosque quarters in 1982, Muslims were conscious that Islamophobia was spreading throughout the Western world (Hamdon 2010). Al Rashid continued to respond with initiatives that worked towards a thorough integration into the fabric of a Canadian city.

A case in point is social services. To address a growing population and the problems generated by Muslim immigrants from a wide range of backgrounds and cultures, Al Rashid had worked with the City of Edmonton to establish a social net to assist families. As we saw in Chapter 3, the founding of the Islamic Family and Social Services Association (IFSSA) in 1992 reflected an awareness that migration did not always provide the outcomes promised. This was specially the case for women who came to Canada assuming that their menfolk would naturally take on the same role they had in their home countries, which did not necessarily happen. The result was heartache for some families—fathers who sat at home without work, mothers who worked part-time at cleaning jobs and brought in what little they could. Long-established roles were disrupted. Relationships soured.

The IFSSA realized that families faced these kinds of difficulties and provided a sensitive arm of support. Towards the end of 2010, the IFSSA had an annual revenue of $212,000 (K. Tarrabain 2014) and was addressing the full spectrum of social problems; it provided a food bank for young people estranged from their families, counselling services for families, parenting programs, and an active outreach to the community through their Boyle Street dinner program.

Lobbying for Islamic Education

Another indication of Al Rashid's orientation, in the two years before the events of 9/11, is the honours accorded to Dr. Lila Fahlman. Fahlman was born in Manitoba, and early in her career played an active role in Girl Guides. She took great pride in the fact that she was the honour guard when King George VI and Queen Elizabeth I made an official visit to Canada in 1939 (Edmonton Public Schools 2017). Fahlman was a longtime teacher with the Edmonton Public School Board, and spent her entire public career in the public system. She played critical roles in several educational areas. She argued vigorously for both the public recognition of Arabic through teaching the language in public schools as well as the legitimacy of an Islamic school. There was an active debate around both of these issues.

Jewish schools, for example, had operated within the public system for many years, but there were mixed reports about restrictions on what could be taught and how much religious training could be added to the curriculum. Fahlman had expressed similar Muslim interests as she advocated for Islamic schools. Furthermore, in 1994, the province had approved public support of charter schools, the only province in Canada with such legislation. Shepherded through the system by Ralph Klein, colourful premier of Alberta, the goal of the legislation was to allow for various approaches to education that might include a distinctive religious perspective as long as the province's curriculum was followed. The Al Rashid community likewise focused on this option for Arab Muslim students.

Fahlman was opposed to this model of schooling. In the first place, she did not want Muslim students segregated from the other students. She thought there was immediate value in other students learning that Muslim students were first and foremost students just like them; they had a recognizably different religious background that needed to be learned about and encountered. She saw charter schools as a recipe for discrimination. Finally, she saw Islamic teachings as worthy of public support just as much as separate (Catholic) schools in the province.

The debate was resolved in May 2001 when the Arabic Language and Culture Three- and Six-Year Programs of Studies were approved by the Edmonton Public School Board under superintendent Ernie Dosdall. This program had been very near and dear to Lila's heart, and she rejoiced when it was announced.

This issue was not the only educational initiative on Lila's mind; as we shall explore below, she also had a hand in the development of the Islamic school. But Lila was known for her long service to the Muslim community through interfaith dialogue activism and her staunch opposition to violence against women. One example: the ambassador visited Edmonton to give a public lecture about Saudi Arabia. Lila had just returned from performing the *hajj* and she was incensed at the way she had been beaten by mosque police as she tried to enter the mosque in Mecca when the crowds were thronging the entranceway. In the melee that followed, the police used sticks to beat back those who did not obey their orders, including Lila. During his question period, Lila lambasted the Saudi ambassador for the uncouth behaviour of the mosque police and demanded why she should not have had equal freedom to the mosque entrance as the stronger men. After withering questioning, the ambassador looked about, as if to find a hiding place. She spoke up, "Women are equal in piety to men in Islam and men have no right to act so violently towards women in the holy places!" She was loudly applauded.

In 2001, Fahlman became the first Muslim to receive the Order of Canada for her service to the Muslim community, violence against women, and interfaith dialogue. After her death in 2006, the Canadian Council of Muslim Women, a group she co-founded, honoured her name by establishing the Lila Fahlman Scholarship for Muslim Women; it is offered annually from Winnipeg. The Dr. Lila Fahlman School in Edmonton opened in September 2017, to students from kindergarten to grade nine.

Validating Ethnic Identity with the Edmonton Heritage Festival

Edmonton's Heritage Festival, a local celebration of diversity held every year since 1976 in William Hawrelak Park during the August long weekend, has played a significantly positive role in affirming ethnic identities. With over sixty pavilions and eighty-five different groups, the festival has become a favourite gathering for visitors and immigrants alike. At the festival, food and entertainment assert that difference is not only good, it's essential to the fabric of Canada. Newcomers find its atmosphere welcoming and open. Muslims from all over the globe often found the reflection of their ethnicity a pleasing element of the festival and recognized the event as a public acknowledgement of diversity. Immigrant Muslims have intense pride in their countries of origin; they appreciate the cultural achievements of their homeland. Thus, part of Canadian Muslim identity is linked irrevocably to other places, even if, after the first generation, they were born in Canada.

The Heritage Festival, in a small way, assists in this validation of identity. For many immigrants, their homeland cultures are far older than those they encounter in Canada. Some immigrants experience a disconnect between the relative rich cultural wealth of their homeland and its financial poverty when compared to the West; for many newcomers, the West, or Canada specifically, despite its financial wealth, is culturally inferior. While there are no acceptable indicators of how resentments generated by these factors register with Muslims, or whether some have greater difficulty adapting than others, there is no doubt that ethnic difference plays a role in adaptability.

While not strictly religious in scope, belief systems played into the history of the Heritage Festival: during their first few years in Edmonton, the Ismailis had a pavilion that sketched some of their history. Later they withdrew when it was pointed out that they were hardly an ethnic group in the way others were; nevertheless, it made Edmontonians aware that the word *Muslim* does not apply exclusively to Arabs. In a fascinating way, this reduced the need for Al Rashid to be the only source in town of Islamic ideas. Arabs, of course, had had a pavilion for years, usually supported by the Canadian Arab Friendship Association or some other cross-religious community organization, such as the Canadian Arab Businessmen's Association. Many Muslims from Al Rashid participated in these organizations and assisted with the Heritage Festival. Hence, religion, while not dominant, did have a representation of sorts at the festival, giving recent immigrants insight into how Canada separated the ethnic from the religious.

Accommodating to a Distinctive Shia Relationship

In Canada, Shi'is from Iran do not necessarily feel at home with Shi'is from Pakistan. As we know, distinctions are also to be found between various types of Shia believers (e.g., Twelvers [Iran], Ismailis [India, Pakistan, Afghanistan, Africa], and Ibadis [Oman, Yemen]). Most importantly, immigrant believers from these groups have not moved uniformly into Western society, and they also have higher percentages in places like Edmonton than in the general population of Islam in the world. This has had significant ramifications for Al Rashid. For example, Ismailis have been extraordinarily successful in Canada and have developed strong connections to Canadian public life, but Iranian Muslims have not been so publicly engaged. In Edmonton, Ismaili influence is disproportionate to their numbers vis-à-vis Sunnis. In terms of aggregate numbers, though, Sunnis remain the largest Muslim group, comprising at least 75 per cent of all believers in Canada. It is important, then, to notice that numbers may not necessarily be the critical feature in discerning influence. Al Rashid, with an identity rooted in the superior numbers of Sunnis around the world, has had to accommodate itself to sharing a Muslim presence with a Shi'ism that is proportionately impressive and has very fine political skills.

RESPONDING TO 9/11

This section discusses the major responses of Al Rashid and its Edmonton neighbours to the events of 9/11. The mosque was thrust into an international catastrophe for which it had no previous understanding and for which its leadership had no training. Amin Malak (2008) describes one of the first gestures made by other religious leaders, who recognized the imminent difficulties 9/11 would bring to Al Rashid and Muslims in Canada. He writes,

> In the turbulent days immediately following the 9/11 horror, the leaders of the Jewish and Christian communities of Edmonton realized that the Muslims of Alberta's capital were in for a rough time. In an impressive gesture of solidarity, the leaders of the two Abrahamic faiths, accompanied by senator Doug Roche and religious studies professor Earle Waugh, went to Al-Rasheed mosque, the largest in the city, and

publicly attended the Friday prayer. Some joined the worshippers in the prayer hall—normally accessible only to Muslims. A minister from the United Church of Canada, Bruce Miller, even prayed with the Muslim worshippers, emulating their ritualistic gestures: bowing, kneeling, standing, and mouthing the Muslim article of faith.

Only a confident, caring culture can perform such an elegant proactive gesture. Only a genuinely generous community appreciates the generosity of other communities extending such a warm hand. (Malak 2008, 74)

Muslim groups responded to the 9/11 situation creatively, which generated considerable goodwill. Many mosques, including Al Rashid, opened their doors to the public, held information sessions, invited clergy to prayers, and generally abandoned a policy of "keeping their heads down." Al Rashid sent material to almost every Alberta Muslim establishment to use as public information. They also sent information packages on Islam to institutions, hospitals, mayors' offices, and so on to counter the negative impacts of 9/11. Inspired by Al Rashid leadership, many institutions around the world issued statements decrying the carnage created by the jihadists. They also made public statements of condemnation of the 9/11 attacks, and many mainstream organizations issued public repudiation of Osama bin Laden. While they were hampered by an incredulous population and a media bent on undermining their stance, Canadians as a whole came to understand that Islam too had its divisions, just like Christianity, and that some of them could be violent. Furthermore, the similar destructive nature of some Christian groups, such as the Irish Republican Army, was not lost on Canadians. In general, the average Canadian was willing to give the benefit of the doubt to Muslims when media and other hotheads railed against Islam.

Creating the Edmonton Council of Muslim Communities

Larry Shaban, former Alberta MLA and cabinet minister, and supported by former mayor of Edmonton Bill Smith, recognized the danger of individual mosques operating alone. Each mosque community, roughly defined, elected its own mosque council, whose role it was to oversee all matters dealing with the local mosque and its community. In the larger centres of Calgary and Edmonton, there were collective organizations, such as the Inter-Mosque Working Group, to address the larger concerns of the community as a whole. This working group had spent a good deal of time monitoring relations between the public and three Sunni mosques in the Edmonton area. But there was no organization that bridged all Muslims. Shaban thought this made them weaker when they had to confront a political event or tragedy such as 9/11. He chaired a meeting of the leadership of all Muslims—Sunni, Ismaili, Shia—at Al Rashid in the spring of 2002. His only stipulation was, "Leave you egos at the door. We are all equal in this."

The result was the Edmonton Council of Muslim Communities (ECMC). In its 2005 edition of *Towards Understanding Muslims in Canada*, the ECMC describes its rationale and lists its early achievements:

> From the outset of its formation in early 2002, the ECMC has recognized that in order to understand Islam, one needs to understand its rich heritage of multiplicity of ethnicities, languages and traditions which have been part of its history for over fourteen centuries. At the same time, one needs to deepen one's understanding of other faiths as well as various interpretations within Islam, to enrich the society that we live in. Based on this recognition, the Council has successfully helped establish the first community-endowed Chair in Islamic Studies in Canada, at the University of Alberta, to provide various courses in Islam and its history—an accomplishment

which all Albertans can be proud of. During this time, the Council has also partnered with Alberta Learning in shaping the Social Studies curriculum to include certain modules in Islamic Civilization. Further, driven by the spirit of discussion and dialogue, the Council has either initiated or otherwise participated in numerous interfaith dialogues and interactions among the various faith groups in the city. The ECMC has supported local institutions such as the Edmonton Police Service through its Hate-Bias Crime Unit and the Chief's Advisory Committee as a multilateral partner. The Council has also participated in and supported a dialogue with representatives of the Jewish community, which has since lead to the formation of the Phoenix Multi-Faith Society for Harmony within the city.

The ECMC has been a very activist outgrowth of Al Rashid's presence in the city. Its formation is regarded as one of Shaban's outstanding achievements in a career of firsts. In 2008, after a short bout with cancer, Larry Shaban passed on, leaving Al Rashid in its strongest position in the city and the province in its history.

Violent Responses from Edmontonians

In the first few months after 9/11, there were several incidents in and around Al Rashid. The mosque was egged one night, a stone was thrown through the window, and women wearing the hijab were accosted and ridiculed. School children were bullied and assaulted; there was at least one case of a child being kept home from school because he was so badly frightened. In other places, mosques were burned. Al Rashid asked for additional protection from the police and kept security people on scene during late nights. The concern was not just for the building. It was for the way that Islam was being portrayed in the media as well as in everyday conversations. There was also worry that hotheaded youth might take things into their own hands and act in ways that the Muslim community would not want. They especially did not want someone acting in their name or speaking for them in ways that they did not approve. Al Rashid members also worried about unprovoked reprisals—that is, unsuspecting Muslims might be attacked at any time because of who they were. Women were particularly afraid. In general, however, violence was minimal, reflecting, perhaps, the long-standing amicable relationship between Al Rashid and the people of Edmonton.

The Canadian Security Intelligence Service

Immediately after 9/11, the Canadian Security Intelligence Service (CSIS) developed a number of strategies to deal with the aftermath of the terrorist attacks and their related challenges. CSIS's surveillance strategy involved what scholars have called Canada's policy of "securitization of Arabs." Zainab Amery (2013) writes of the "securitization and racialization of Arabs" as distinctive products of Canada's immigration and citizenship policies as well. On the ground, the infiltration of Muslim communities by security intelligence officers and pointed delays at airports reinforced a "them and us" ideology. CSIS sent its agents to major cities to ascertain whether al Qaeda had infiltrated local communities. Sometimes they tried to procure inside information by contacting local Muslim leaders and asking them to provide details about the community, with the implication that a good Canadian citizen would spy on his neighbour if he had nothing to hide. That Muslim communities were under surveillance was disconcerting to Canadian Muslims, many of whom had, for a long time, led successful and exemplary lives in Canada. That CSIS knew whom to contact in the local community was also a source of dismay, for it meant that the whole community had been strategically surveilled and identified by security intelligence offices.

CSIS landed in Edmonton shortly after 9/11. Members of Al Rashid and the Arab community received phone calls from people who wanted to know as much as they could about certain individuals. When members did not give information, CSIS used other ruses—invitations to become an agent of CSIS, encouragement to sit down and talk about the community with people they never heard of before, requests for interviews out of the blue, and requests to "teach me Arabic." Richard Awid, whose roots reach to the founding members of the community, was contacted almost immediately. In a 2014 interview with me, he recounted, "They called me up and said things like, 'We have information about the community that you should have.' I responded with, 'Then why not come to the Canadian Arab Businessmen's Association and present it to all of us?' If they did come, they didn't have much to say, and it merely was an attempt to dig around and find out about us." Soraya Zaki Hafez, a well-respected Arabic teacher, received several requests to teach Arabic. On one occasion, she was invited downtown to a federal building and presented with an application to be a member of CSIS so she could be paid for teaching. She responded, "I am not interested in signing any contract with CSIS. Besides I do not know what this commits me to do for you. I do not wish to be an informant for you" (2014).

Both Awid and Hafez noted that there was a great deal of pressure to provide information to the agents and insights about the community. They believe that there was a significant push to find willing people within the community who would "monitor" members for CSIS. From the perspective of Al Rashid, this was an attempt to infiltrate the community, as if its members were suspected of being involved with terrorist activities or at least had some insider knowledge. These experiences made the community even more doubtful about the federal government's concern for them.

The Media, the Canadian Public, and Islamic Sensitivities

As a visible minority in Canada, many Muslims had experienced some form of prejudice before 9/11, but the events of 9/11 triggered a widespread public unease that made Muslims more vulnerable to discrimination. Rhetoric produced by the federal government and the mainstream media contributed to the problem. The Canadian government's anti-terrorist rhetoric was particularly problematic for the Muslim community. In concert with the media on both sides of the Canada–US border, Canada's government often referred to "terrorists" or the "threat of terrorism" when discussing security threats. After 9/11, the media increasingly made direct associations between Islam and violence, and, according to some Al Rashid community members, soon after 9/11 the Canadian government created a list of organizations that had business or charitable interests in "potentially problematic" areas of the world. This list immediately branded certain organizations as "pro-Taliban or pro-violence," and the government withdrew these organizations' charitable status, which effectively cut off their funding. Canadian Islamic Centre president Khalid Tarrabain was the director of one of these groups—the Islamic Society of North America-IDB Education Trust, which lost its charitable status based on claims that its funds were not providing charity but creating politicians. As media sources became even more conservative, taking strong anti-Islamist stances, and press coverage became decidedly less independent and discerning, Canada's traditional liberal democratic stance narrowed, and the Al Rashid community felt the implications of this shift. Their freedom to travel, for example, was affected, and support for Muslim and Arab enterprises dropped.

Zogby (2001) polled Arabs in America from various countries after 9/11 and found that more than 75 per cent of respondents condemned the attacks and over 80 per cent were sympathetic to the United States for its pain. The strange thing is that in 2004, the same Arab citizens expressed only 2 per cent sympathy for America. All post-9/11 goodwill had disappeared. Perhaps it had something to do with the disruption of the normally independent public opinion and the negative media representation of Muslims.

An editorial published in the *Edmonton Journal* on April 2, 2002 is a case in point. The editorial demonstrated a distinct lack of impartiality: "Wherever one looks along the perimeter of Islam, Muslims have problems living peaceably with their neighbours... The conflicts within Islam have also been more numerous than those in any other civilization, including tribal conflicts in Africa...

But even by the barbaric standards of the Arab Middle East, Yasser Arafat and the Palestinian terrorist organizations that operate freely under his writ have hit new lows." Naturally, the Arab Muslims of Al Rashid were offended by these remarks, and they took action. A team of young members, headed by Nizar Ali of the World Lebanese Cultural Union, brought together supporters to form the Coalition for Media Fairness, and they presented their case to the Alberta Human Rights Commission. Because the Alberta government was scrapping the section in the Alberta Human Rights Act that dealt with freedom of the press, the very section that was in question, eventually the coalition had to give up the case. The expense of taking the matter to a higher court would be prohibitive. While there seemed to be good grounds for bringing minority rights into the discussion, the bottom line was that public opinion saw the case as one of freedom of expression, with Muslims being against it. The case died, but the results were not lost on Muslims: Canadian law does not necessarily protect citizens from press bigotry. The result left Al Rashid members and other coalition members feeling unsettled.

Some members of Al Rashid remained concerned that no one was speaking out against what they saw as blatant aggression against their Arab brothers and sisters. As the Iraq War swept everything in front of it, Edmontonians reacted. In one of the largest anti-war marches in Canada in 2002, Shia convert Buff Perry, Saleem Ganam, and Al Rashid Imam Yousef Chebli carried a banner against the intervention as they led thousands of protesters through the streets of Edmonton. While Al Rashid had not many any public statements about the war, it was obvious that many Muslims were concerned that the invasion would have grave repercussions.

Issues of freedom of expression were also involved in another scenario that placed Al Rashid on the defensive. On February 13, 2006, the *Western Standard* published the widely distributed cartoon of the Prophet Muhammad that had earlier appeared in the *Free Jewish Press* in Calgary and originally on the front page of *Jyllands-Posten*, Denmark's largest daily newspaper, on September 30, 2005. *Jyllands-Posten* editor-in-chief Carsten Juste claimed that the publication of twelve cartoons, most of which represented the Prophet, was advertising for someone to draw pictures of the Prophet for a children's book. He had asked for cartoonists to respond because no one would draw Muhammad's face. It was a matter of freedom of expression, claimed the editor. The result reverberated all over the world. When the picture appeared in the Calgary newspaper, the Islamic Supreme Council of Canada in Calgary and the ECMC teamed up to have the Human Rights Commission ban the picture. In 2007, the Crown Prosecutor said the picture did not fall within the criminal hate category (Bonnell 2008), so the prosecution could go no further. Once again, Muslims saw how ineffectual Canadian law was in protecting their religious values.

Both the Canadian Council of Muslim Women (Edmonton Chapter) and Al Rashid were queried about a book by Irshad Manji called *The Trouble with Islam Today* (2004). Manji, a disaffected Ismaili who describes herself in the book as a "Muslim refusenik," argues that the apparently rigid Islamic doctrine cannot possibly handle contemporary issues. Manji's follow-up PBS documentary, *Faith without Fear* (2007), maintains that Islam is out of touch with contemporary culture and enthralled with old-fashioned ideas. She vigorously claims that Islam is out of touch because it has abandoned the principle of *ijtihad* (independent reasoning in application of law). Since she had received death threats, these reactions were taken as proof of what she was saying. Once again, freedom of expression became the touchstone of difference.

Finally, when Al Rashid had pieces of pork scattered around its door, mosque officials regarded this as a hate message. Khalid Tarrabain responded to the media, "Muslims don't eat pork, it's forbidden. It's a religious thing," he said. "It's not a vandalism or anything, but it has a meaning" (2006). The incident received very little press and rather desultory opinion of it as a hate message.

NAVIGATING ISSUES POST 9/11

This section sketches the welter of cases and legal problems that Al Rashid leadership faced as the mosque had to respond to nation-wide issues. The leadership's responses were both reactive and proactive. This section focuses on the reactive because this category stresses activities that are perceptively negative for Islam in Canada and for Al Rashid. This analysis focuses on four significant areas: restrictions on immigration through containment; restrictions of rights; rejection of sharia-based mediations; and legal curbs on hijab use. Obviously, Al Rashid is not directly involved in these issues, but their responses to these issues were carefully watched by Muslims across the country.

Following 9/11, many Muslims who previously had had little interaction with Al Rashid made contact and supported the mosque's programs, even if they did not worship there. The extra support helped Al Rashid as it tried to stay a steady course in a world that had suddenly grown antagonistic. On the other hand, some disapproved of how Al Rashid's leadership, whose response to outside criticism had been to reflect a very conservative party line (almost Wahhabi, as one member stated), restricted the meaning of Islam for the media to one closer to the Saudi Arabian model. In fact, many disliked modelling mosque ideology around any particular Islamic country's ideology.

Muslim Immigration Containment Strategies

Canada has contained Muslim immigration by setting fairly high educational expectations for full-citizen immigrant applications; Immigration, Refugees and Citizenship Canada requires a completed university degree or certified program for a trade. Al Rashid's first founders would not have made it here under these rules. While the norms were not constructed specifically to target Muslims, they did affect Muslims, given the significant number of applicants from Muslim-dominated areas like Pakistan and Bangladesh, and, as we have seen, Al Rashid was now home to a wide variety of Muslims from diverse countries, including these two. According to Statistics Canada

(2016b), of those who immigrated between 2001 and 2006, 51 per cent had a university degree—more than twice the proportion of degree holders among the Canadian-born population. In fact, as of 2016, Canada had the highest proportion of post-secondary immigrants in both the OECD and G7 (Statistics Canada 2016a). Canada's privileging of immigrants with university degrees can, perhaps generously, be interpreted as a strategy to encourage and support smoother integration (although there are less generous interpretations, as well).

The second containment strategy involved restrictions on marriages abroad. Everyone in Edmonton has heard of a marriage that dissolved after the parties landed in Canada. In the fall of 2010, Jason Kenney, then minister of citizenship and immigration, did a series of town halls across Canada to discuss the topic of fraudulent marriages. As part of the government's attempt to address the problem, an online survey was posted, asking respondents for their thoughts on "marriages of convenience" and how they should be dealt with. Such marriages were deemed fraudulent following that Canada-wide survey (Meurrens 2011). Canadians were apparently scandalized by these marriages. Rumour had it that money passed under the table from bogus spouses to accelerate access to Canada. Muslim groups were often cited as using these kinds of arrangements to bring cousins and other acquaintances to Canada, and then to use *talaq* (divorce) immediately after arriving to free the person to make his or her own way in the country. The government's response was to institute a year's wait time before the spouse would be allowed into the country as well as a provision that allowed the alleged miscreant to be sent back to his or her country of origin if the marriage was deemed illegitimate. Following that initial response, the federal government instituted a wait period of two years before permanent residence would be granted (that limitation has since been stayed as of April 2017) (Government of Canada 2017).

In short, containment became a constant theme in Canadian governments after 9/11. An even more alarming trend was the restriction of the rights of Muslims in Canada, a process that ran counter to Canada's longstanding embrace of multiculturalism.

Restriction of Rights:
The Cases of Maher Arar and Omar Khadr

The restriction of Canadian Muslims' rights remains a sensitive topic for those within and outside the Al Rashid community. Not long after 9/11, Dr. Baha Abu-Laban (2002), well-known Edmonton academic and sociologist, said that he would not travel to the United States again because he feared the profiling to which so many of his Arab friends had been subjected. From general murmurings of differential treatment in airports to the ongoing developments of two high-profile cases involving Canadian Muslims, the restriction of rights debate in Canada continues to unfold against the backdrop of one of the most celebrated charters of rights in the world. The cases of Maher Arar and Omar Khadr reveal the problematic line that separates the protection of fundamental rights and freedoms of Canadian citizens and the promulgation of a national security program shaped largely by an atmosphere of Islamophobia.

On September 26, 2002, while returning from a family vacation in Tunisia, a routine stopover in New York became the beginning of a human rights violation case that would cost the Canadian government millions of dollars in financial compensation. US officials detained Maher Arar, a well-educated Canadian citizen, married with two children, on charges of links with al-Qaeda. Notwithstanding the fact that Arar was travelling on a Canadian passport, US officials deported him to his native Syria where, as a Canadian government investigation revealed, Arar was "interrogated, tortured, and held in degrading and inhumane conditions" for almost a year, despite the fact that he "ha[d] never been charged with any offence in Canada, the United States or Syria" (Commission of Inquiry 2006, 9). The final report published by Commission of Inquiry into the Actions of Canadian Officials in Relation to Maher Arar also reveals that RCMP reports described Arar and his wife, Dr. Monia Mazigh, as "Islamic Extremist individuals suspected of being linked to the Al-Qaeda terrorist movement," although there was no indication that "Mr. Arar committed an offense or that his activities constitute[d] a threat to the security of Canada" (Commission of Inquiry 2006, 9).

In addition to citing a lack of credible evidence that resulted in the deportation, inhumane treatment, and torture of Arar, critics raised some significant concerns regarding Canadian officials' actions upon Arar's return to Canada in October 2003. Shortly following Canadian investigations into the Arar affair, evidence turned up indicating that Canadian officials had disseminated "confidential and sometimes inaccurate information about the case to the media for the purpose of damaging Mr. Arar's reputation or protecting their self-interests or government interests" (Commission of Inquiry 2006, 16). In January 2007, the Canadian government issued a formal apology to Arar and his family and announced that Arar would receive a $10.5 million settlement. As of 2011, Arar and his family were still on the United States' No Fly List. In a 2016 article in the *Washington Post*, Arar remarked that "he believes he remains on the United States' No Fly List—something he would only know for sure if he tried to fly into America, which he has no interest in doing" (Itkowitz 2016). What happened to Arar was precisely why Edmontonian Abu-Laban and his friends refuse to fly into the United States.

The Arar affair is a clear case of a Canadian citizen's rights—severely, and without adequate explanation—curtailed. While the Maher Arar case has come to some sort of a conclusion, another Canadian-related case continues to grip the attention of many worldwide, including those working within human rights fields—the litigious case of Omar Khadr.

The Khadr saga began with the capture of fifteen-year-old Omar Khadr by American soldiers on July 27, 2002, following a firefight in Eastern Afghanistan. US officials alleged that Khadr threw a grenade that had killed an American soldier. Khadr himself was injured as a result of the firefight, having been shot twice in the back, and wounded in the eye. Subsequent to his capture, Khadr was airlifted to Bagram Airbase before he was taken to Guantanamo Bay.

While many agree that American authorities transgressed certain basic human rights in their treatment of Khadr, what makes this particular case so controversial is the questionable role that Canadian authorities played and continue to play in securing and protecting Khadr's rights as a Canadian citizen. Khadr is one of the youngest prisoners to ever be held in Guantanamo, and has often been referred to as a "child soldier" (Gorham 2008). Despite his age, however, US officials and, more importantly, Canadian officials have failed to recognize this status and by extension all the protections pertaining to the treatment of child combatants under international laws and conventions that are afforded globally to such children (these include the International Covenant on Civil and Political Rights and the Convention on the Rights of the Child). Such laws and agreements are meant to ensure that child soldiers have access to "special safeguards and care, including legal protections appropriate to their age" and "that they be treated in a manner that takes into account their particular vulnerability and relative culpability as children, and focuses primarily on rehabilitation and reintegration" (Human Rights Watch 2007, 1). While the US government clearly chose not to comply with many of the juvenile justice standards that would typically apply to a case such as that of Khadr's, the lackluster role played by the Canadian government in pressing for these and similar rights for Khadr has been more troubling.

Khadr's detainment and treatment while in Guantanamo, and the Canadian response to it, have not fared much better. Reports indicate that while in Guantanamo, Khadr was mostly kept in solitary confinement or in interrogation. During his stay, interrogators "subjected him to stress positions, used attack dogs to scare him...and used him as a human mop to clean up his own urine" (Rangaviz 2011, 256). A briefing to the Committee Against Torture presented by Lawyers' Rights Watch Canada and the International Civil Liberties Monitoring Group implicated Canada in the matter, stating that the nation was "both a direct participant and/or directly complicit" in violating Convention standards by failing to prevent and punish the torture of Omar Khadr, "to take effective measures...to ensure that Khadr was granted rights to 'independent legal assistance, independent medical assistance'" and "to take jurisdiction over, investigate, and prosecute offenders in Canada" (Lawyers' Rights Watch 2012, 4).

After counsel of various organizations, including UNICEF, the Canadian Bar Association, and Amnesty International, Khadr was extradited to Canada in 2012 and placed in a maximum-security prison in Edmonton in 2013. Notably, Canada was the last Western nation to repatriate one of its citizens from Guantanamo. In 2010, after years of detainment at Guantanamo, and increasing pressure by various human rights groups, the Supreme Court of Canada finally ruled that Khadr's Charter rights to life, liberty, and security of the person had indeed been breached, but the court stopped short of forcing his return. On October 25, 2010, Khadr pleaded guilty to various charges of murder, conspiracy, and terrorism. In return for his guilty plea, Khadr was to serve one more year, in solitary confinement, in Guantanamo preceding his return to Canada. In 2013, he was installed in federal prison in Edmonton. Khadr has also had strong support from both the students and professors at King's University, a Christian school in Edmonton, where he took courses. Khadr was freed on bail on strict conditions, including living with his lawyer, Dennis Edney, on May 7, 2015. Khadr's story and the question of Canada's violation of Khadr's rights have been in the spotlight again with the Liberal government's July 2017 announcement that they will compensate Khadr with a $10.5 million settlement (Fife 2017).

Clearly, the cases of Omar Khadr and Maher Arar reveal shortcomings of the Canadian government when it comes to their own stated-protection of citizen rights. These cases have taken place, however, in large part against the backdrop of a rather apprehensive Canadian public that expects that certain rights will be curtailed in the name of national security. To what degree the curtailment of these rights, where Canadian Muslims are concerned, will become a standard and expected practice remains to be seen. Al Rashid Mosque leadership has kept a low profile on these cases, but there is no doubt that many members are concerned with the way Muslims seem to be singled out for negative treatment. The issue remains below the surface, and usually officials will speak off the record about it.

Rejection of Sharia-Based Options

Another issue that came to the forefront of Canadian debates on restriction of rights after 9/11 is the role that sharia courts can play alongside formalized Canadian legal systems. For years, various faiths have used formal religious dispute resolution systems, opting out of the secular court system and allowing clerical courts to settle matters related to uncomplicated cases of divorce, child custody, and inheritance rights according to the tenets of respective belief systems (a practice that was made possible through provincial arbitration acts). In October 2003, the Islamic Institute of Civil Justice announced its intent to open an arbitration business that would offer Muslim Canadians in Ontario arbitration services in certain areas of family law, guided by Islamic principles and legal frameworks. The announcement quickly drew a firestorm of controversy from both within the Muslim community and outside, as issues of women's rights, freedom of religious practice, and equality rights quickly took centre stage in Canadian public debates.

The issue of sharia arbitration had its opponents and supporters, but the matter seemed to consistently gravitate around the rights of women and Canada's commitment to guaranteed equality rights versus guaranteed freedom of religion rights. Opponents of Islamic-based arbitration courts argued that faith-based arbitration, as an alternative legal system, had the potential to contradict equality protections accorded to women in section 15 of Canadian Charter of Rights and Freedoms, which guarantees "every individual...[the] right to equal protection and benefit of the law...without discrimination based on race, national or ethnic origin, colour, religion, sex, age, or mental or physical disability."

In fact, the issue of gender equality, especially as contested through Islamic law, was the main thrust of virtually all of the opponents' arguments against faith-based arbitration. Contending that Islamic law, for the most part, is an archaic and male-oriented system of jurisprudence, opponents argued that the implementation of such a dated system of law would be detrimental to women. Those against the implementation of sharia law in Canada often pointed to certain aspects of Islamic law, such as a man's unilateral right to divorce, unequal inheritance rights between men and women, and child custody laws that give preferential treatment to fathers as examples of the inherent gender equality that could result from sharia rulings. Pointing to these specific legal interpretations, opponents argued that Islamic law stood in direct conflict with Canadian laws, which demand equal rights between genders.

Opponents also argued that religious arbitration courts would disadvantage Muslim women because the courts would ignore power hierarchies that they believed defined many Muslim households. They suggested that, for many Muslim women, who were often characterized as recent immigrants with minimal English language skills and little to no knowledge of their rights as Canadian citizens, the notion of free choice underestimated not only their position in society but also the intrinsic power dynamics of many Muslim families, where, critics insisted, men hold an authoritative position over women. For opponents, the establishment of Islamic-based arbitration courts was not a realization of true multiculturalism but an exercise in discrimination that would work against women's rights (Razavy 2010).

Alternately, advocates of Islamic-based arbitration courts based many of their arguments on well-established Canadian laws and policies on religious freedom, multiculturalism, and diversity. For the most part, proponents' arguments centred on section 2 of Canada's Charter of Rights and Freedoms, which guarantees the right to "freedom of conscience and religion." Individuals must be able to practice their faith without constraints and coercion, and no citizen should be forced to act in a way that is contrary to his or her belief or conscience. As proponents of the system argued, the inability to worship as dictated by the tenets of one's faith (in this case living by the codes of sharia) presented a restriction on one's capacity to exercise religious freedom. In the minds of many proponents of faith-based arbitration, these constraints proved inconsistent with essential freedoms guaranteed by the government and as interpreted through the courts.

Supporters of Islamic-based arbitration courts also argued that Muslims were entitled, under section 15 of the Charter, to be given equal treatment "before and under the law." They felt that the government had failed to administer equal protection through the application of neutral "secular" laws on religious adherents and through a display of preference for one belief system over another, as evidenced by the fact that for so many years other faiths had established arbitration courts.

In response to the public outcry over the Islamic Institute of Civil Justice's proposal, the Government of Ontario requested Ontario's attorney general, and former minister responsible for women's issues, Marion Boyd, to review how the province's Arbitration Act, which established family faith-based tribunals in 1991, was working and whether it adversely affected vulnerable people, including women, the elderly, and people with disabilities (Sturcke 2008). Boyd's full report, submitted in December 2004, generally found the faith-based tribunals effective and supported the establishment of an Islamic arbitration court in Ontario. The report's findings, unfortunately, never came to fruition. Against Boyd's advice, on September 11, 2005, Ontario Premier Dalton McGuinty turned down the Islamic Institute of Civil Justice's proposal to establish Islamic-based arbitration courts, and by extension all faith-based arbitration tribunals (Freeze and Howlett 2005).

Unfortunately, missing from these debates was discourse about how banning faith-based arbitration would contribute to gender inequality. As many critics of McGuinty's decision pointed out, leaving arbitration out of formal channels would do little to help protect women as the practice would continue to operate underground, away from external scrutiny. In fact, as critics of the decision contended, the argument to ban faith-based arbitration on grounds of human rights abuses stemming from gender discrimination only holds ground on the assumption that removing faith-based arbitration from the Ontario Arbitration Act would discourage people from using it. So far, this does not appear to have been the case as Islamic arbitration courts continue

Dr. Lila Fahlman, educator, social justice advocate, and one of the founders of the Canadian Council of Muslim Women, was the first woman in Canada to obtain her PhD in educational psychology and the first Muslim woman to be awarded the Order of Canada.

to operate, particularly in Canada's larger urban centres. Rather, Ontario's decision to ban faith-based arbitration was viewed not only as a disservice to religious groups but also as a failed occasion to create an environment of support and protection for Muslim women in Canada, and the development of a uniquely Canadian system of sharia (Emon 2005).

In the midst of these debates, which were ostensibly about all faith-based arbitration, the Islamic faith became the centre of controversy over communal pressures and inequality towards women. Debates that should have focused on the role of arbitration in all matters of personal law quickly spun into Islamophobic discourse. Muslim men were characterized as controlling, women as incompetent and powerless, and the whole community as backward, incapable of self-governing, critical thinking, and modernity—a community in need of protection by Western laws and norms. Al Rashid opted to give quiet support to the local branch of the Canadian Council of Muslim Women, originally founded by Lila Fahlman, through its local president Soraya Zaki Hafez. There seems little overt support for such a tribunal in Edmonton, perhaps because of a long awareness of divisions within Islamic law itself.

Legislation Concerning the Hijab: The Case of Quebec

A certain notoriety surrounds the soccer official who, in spring 2011, banned a girl from playing soccer in Laval, Quebec, because she was wearing a hijab. He argued that the headgear was not official clothing for soccer and therefore the girl should not play. When challenged, he suggested that the child's safety was at risk in the event that the scarf became entangled. News of this incident spread across the country and was widely discussed in Edmonton where many Muslim girls play soccer—some while wearing the hijab. The case was debated because the official was from a national sports league, suggesting that any official game would require a similar ban. *Ottawa Citizen* journalist Kelly Egan (2007) wrote, "In miniature, this is the Laval situation. Should the child be asked to remove the hijab—and 'integrate' with the other players—or should the rules be flexible to meet her halfway? Put another way, what did we think would happen to immigrant Muslims who became Canadians? They'd become Anglicans and put on ball caps? Citizenship does not come with an asterisk. You get all the rights, not just the half your neighbour wants to put up with." Hijab discussions have catalyzed much of the public discourse around Muslim women, and in no place has this discussion been more pronounced than in Quebec. It is important to state this in a book about Al Rashid because immigrants come to Canada assuming that the laws will apply equally throughout all jurisdictions when, in fact, they do not.

Singular among Canadian provinces for its French-speaking majority and unique heritage, Quebec takes a significantly different approach to religion from the rest of Canada. Not only is Quebec guided by French civil law, as opposed to the rest of Canada where English common law is the norm, but its adherence to its Charte des droits et libertés de la personne and the influence of French principles of secularism (*laïcité*) have translated into a different approach on accommodation that focuses more on integration through secularist practices. While Quebec follows the Canadian Charter of Rights and Freedoms, it nevertheless remains Canada's only official secular jurisdiction, separating all religious and civil affairs since the 1960s.

Quebec indicated there would be no discussion of sharia courts as there had been in Ontario; the application of religious laws would never be allowed. The fact is that Quebec's embrace of secularism, however, has had implications beyond the use of sharia courts. The ways in which the province approaches social issues, and how it deals with minority groups, have translated into a great debate over religious symbols in the public sphere, including the Islamic hijab and niqab, of course.

Debates regarding the public place of religion in Quebec society have pitted the interests of the majority of Quebecers who wish to assert their local identity through practices of secularism and integration against those of the minority segment of the population who wish to live their lives according to the tenets of their faith. Those who oppose legislation, such as Bill 94, which prohibits "government employees and those accessing government services from wearing veils where issues of security, identification or communication are involved" (Barnett 2011, 5), feel that the subtext of such legal frameworks are Islamophobic and marginalize certain segments of the population rather than better integrate them into larger Québécois society. What remains to be seen is how Quebec will deal with the issue of religious accommodation in an effort to assert its unique identity as increased migratory influx into the province continues.

Attitudes towards women and the hijab have changed considerably at Al Rashid over the years. Women now pray upstairs in a balcony overlooking the mithrab, so they are officially segregated from the men; women uniformly wear the hijab when praying, and most even when they are in the mosque precincts; most women now wear the hijab or an equivalent when they are out and about in the community, in contrast to the founders, who did not wear the hijab in public; the Edmonton Islamic Academy mandates a hijab for all girls as part of their uniform when they reach a certain age. By 2010, the debates had pretty well subsided on these issues in the mosque, even though they continue in Quebec. A kind of conservative norm set in, which makes some uncomfortable. For others, this is the price of difference.

By the end of the first decade of the new millennium, public opinion in Canada concerning Muslims in general had moved decidedly from neutral to negative. Al Rashid, on the other hand, moved away from confronting this kind of cultural antagonism by returning to its roots: it stated its affirmation that it was here to stay. And it began to build again.

THE TRIUMPH OF MUSLIM EDUCATION

In the face of much depressing news, it is truly extraordinary that the community had the will and drive to undertake two exhilarating and groundbreaking projects: the establishment of the ECMC Chair in Islamic Studies at the University of Alberta in January 2006, and the construction of the Edmonton Islamic Academy (Cairney 2006). Both initiatives required significant financial commitments from Al Rashid members, and were carried out with class, perhaps even with brilliance. Furthermore, both projects built on the vision set many years earlier by Al Rashid's founders: to establish the highest standards of an integrated mosque in a contemporary Canadian city.

The ECMC Chair is unique in North America. It is the only university chair that is a joint project across Islamic sectarian divides for purposes of furthering the study of Islam as an academic field. The idea arose during a time of cutbacks to the university and the subsequent awareness that Islamic studies may be left without a professor. ECMC stepped in to say that they would raise $1 million, which would then be matched by the University of Alberta and the Government of Alberta, to institutionalize Islamic studies. Given the strain between Islamic groups in Canada and official institutions at the time, the establishment of the chair was a dramatic commitment. It reflects the quality of various Muslim groups that were part of the ECMC team.

This was not the first time that the community had contributed to high-level academic study. During the 1990s, the community had donated a sum of money to the Faculty of Arts to foster the teaching of subjects related to Arabic society. Furthermore, Qatar had fostered graduate studies in Islamic studies by providing funding of $30,000 for graduate stipends. But these amounts paled against the need of $1 million. The ECMC community took several years to procure the funding. As of this writing, the government has completed its part of the commitment, but the university has not yet been able to supply the funds necessary for full funding.

Despite funding issues, in 2008 Dr. Ibrahim Abu-Rabi, a Palestinian Sunni scholar of Islamic studies at Hartford Theological Seminary, was hired as the inaugural ECMC Chair of Islamic Studies. Joining the university in fall 2008, he taught courses in Islamic studies, political science, and related areas. He also brought in over a dozen graduate students in various areas of Islamic scholarship, providing the university with an enviable program. He spent much of his time in Edmonton in creating and promoting interfaith dialogue, and was dearly loved by students, colleagues, and the community. His early death in July 2, 2011 was a shock to everyone associated with ECMC and set the whole project into eclipse. (The university, with no funds to provide its matching funding, has laboured to find an acceptable internationally recognized scholar to fulfill the chair position, and in 2015 opted to elevate a current University of Alberta professor to the chair. As of 2017, Professor Mojtaba Mahdavi from the Department of Political Science holds the chair.)

The second initiative has been much a more durable achievement, perhaps because it was entirely an Al Rashid project. The goal was to plan, design, and construct a state-of-the-art school (first for kindergarten to grade nine, but eventually for kindergarten to grade twelve). Arising out of a need to provide students with and awareness of their cultural and religious roots, the Edmonton Islamic Academy (EIA) began as an initiative of Al Rashid in 1987, with the establishment of a school in the mosque's basement. The school opened with twenty-one students, but it grew quickly. Within ten years, 186 students were registered. It was clear that the school needed proper infrastructure.

As with earlier building projects, an Edmonton Islamic Academy committee was formed. The goal was not just to build a school but to craft an Islamic school that was visibly Canadian. Once again, size and cost were factors, and once again the community decided to build for the future. Khalil Mohamed Rahime, who had immigrated to Canada in 1972, was a founding member of that committee, as was the legendary Larry Shaban. Conceptually, the building had to represent the community and its aspirations. It also had to address the importance of Islamic education as an expression of Muslim piety, and it had to be built for community purposes. As Issam Saleh (2008), teacher and board of trustees member, remarked, "We wanted the Academy to be the nucleus of our community—a place where everyone feels a tie of some kind. Whether you or your child is a member of the school community, people should still feel that ownership and connection. Community members may come to the Academy for prayers, sports activities, or other events; the hope is that the Academy serves as a bridge that will enable the community to come together regularly in some way." In short, the school was envisioned as a place of genuine community building. In that sense, the EIA carried on the idea of the mosque as a social centre, a concept long ago instituted by Hilwie Hamdon and her colleagues. This was a huge project that required enormous efforts and sacrifices and involved the whole Edmonton Muslim community.

Early in the process, the community toyed with turning the Alberta Registry building, which they had purchased from the provincial government for $1 million, into a school, but the community response was overwhelmingly negative. They objected to its location in the city's northwest, an industrial area, and questioned the site's general fit for a school. Consequently, the decision was made to sell the building and look for a more compatible site closer to the majority of Muslims in the northeast of the city. Having given up on the easy alternative, the community was aware that a purpose-built school would be costly. In 2005, they found a property on 127 Street in the Barenow district that housed a greenhouse and garden complex, sitting on eight acres of land. An adjacent parcel of four acres was also purchased with the funds partially recovered from the northwest site. Then the business of bringing concept to reality began.

Mahmoud Tarrabain and Saleem Ganam had an extensive network of contacts, which included Dr. Gulzhar Haider, the dean of engineering at Carlton University in Ottawa. Haider responded warmly to Al Rashid's overture to design an Islamic school, and he was joined by Steve Barr of Scheffer Andrew Ltd. Haider had many ideas for a distinctive Canadian Islamic building and began putting concept to paper. Conceptually, what emerged was a blend of Canadian and traditional ideas: Canadian in that the central visual feature of the building, a square needle standing against the sky, is a reflection on Canada's coastal seascape, with icebergs sailing majestically through the icy waters. Group of Seven founder Lawren Harris's famous painting *The Old Stump, Lake Superior,* in which a stump stands resolutely against a brilliant sky, also provided design inspiration. Yet, now, from a distance, the school is reminiscent of the Phoenician/Lebanese sea-going galleys with the high prow cleaving the waters of the Mediterranean. Haider brought a rich patina to the design of the building, and wove around that the central courtyard of classical Muslim home architecture. The result is a delightful blend of several cultures.

Sine Chadi, well-known entrepreneur, was pressed into helping with negotiations on the building since his company had a record of industrial structures. He also had a long history of bringing his skills to the community. Chadi's grandfather, Sine, was a pioneer in Lac La Biche, arriving in 1895 with his ten-year-old nephew, Ali, from the Levant in search of Klondike gold. Thwarted by the failure of that venture, he settled in the hamlet of Lac La Biche and began the life of a trader and peddler. Soon he set up a grocery and dry goods store. The elder Sine treated Ali like a son and showed him the ropes in business; he learned quickly and followed Sine into the trading and importing business. The Chadi name was firmly established by the time young Sine was born into the Lac La Biche establishment. He went on to be a successful businessman and realtor in the town. Investment became his forte. By the 1980s, he had moved to Edmonton and had set up his company, Imperial Equities Inc. With these credentials, it is easy to see the wisdom of handing him the oversight of the financial and building dimensions of the new school.

Haider came back to the community with his initial conceptual drawings and a price tag. The concept was to build a structure that reminded people of Mecca but that looked and felt like a genuine Canadian building. It was large enough to house major community gatherings but structured enough to serve the interests of schooling and students. The immediate visual plane is the front of the building with its dramatic arabesque design and, in Kufic Arabic, the inscription, "There is no God but God; In the Name of God, the Merciful, the Beneficent; Muhammad is his Prophet." Attached to it is a square brick structure reflective of many schools in the province. Further out, pale yellow buildings array around the central doorway. Behind the inscription is the central courtyard where prayers can be held. The hiddenness of this section creates curiosity: Is that spire a minaret? But this is not a mosque! Perhaps it is a lookout or a stylized pointer to the heavens.

Inside, the spacious environment is evocative of a Middle Eastern souk or a pillared mosque with classic caps reminiscent of medieval architecture. The space is open and calming, resembling classical Muslim homes with a quiet inner courtyard. The classrooms open onto this pleasant space where prayers can be said and children can mingle. Proceeding right, we enter a major hall for activities such as dinners, conferences, and community gatherings. At 135,000 square feet, the hall combines community and utilitarian educational purposes. The price tag was $14.7 million for the whole building. The community once again realized they were building for the future. They all agreed. Chadi organized his team into committees to raise the necessary funds.

View of the geometric design of the interior of the Prayer Hall
and the foyer at the Edmonton Islamic Academy.

Chadi looked about for a construction company that had
a sense of what an Islamic building was, and found it in Ismaili
contractor Sheraz Jiwani and his Aman Construction Company.
The company had a good track record of building schools. Because
the community did not have the cash in hand, the fundraising
committee had to track funding with the pace of construction.
Chadi established several working committees to handle fundraising in each major sector of the community, among professions
(physicians, accountants, engineers, businessmen, builders, etc.),
ordinary folks, and outside businesses and corporations.

Chadi had some confidence in what they were doing. He
is well known among investors in northern Alberta. He also is
on a first-name basis with some of the region's most successful
businessmen. By his own calculation, there are in excess of five
thousand successful businesses in northern Alberta, with assets
in the several billions of dollars. At the first fundraising dinner

in 2003 among the eighty-five physicians in the Edmonton area, the committee raised over $1 million in half an hour. The process was repeated for each professional group. He also put together a program for a more general Al Rashid membership; the School Nurturing Project asked each Muslim family to contribute a set amount per month and arrange to have it automatically debited from their bank account. Whether $50 or $500, each family contributed regularly for two years. The result was that the building committee had a predictable amount to promise the contractor at each period of construction.

Construction began on the new Edmonton Islamic Academy in the spring of 2004. Like most communities, there were differences of opinion on a number of things—colours, the speed of construction, the drain on resources. A couple issues were more serious—namely, how to deal with the Islamic doctrine about interest. Some Al Rashid members were reluctant to fund an Islamic building by borrowing because of the Qur'anic injunction against usury.

Al Rashid had contacted the Islamic World League about borrowing from the Saudi-controlled Islamic Development Bank. Under that bank's jurisdiction, no interest is paid for the loan. An official from the bank came to Edmonton, looked over the plans, and said that this was as good or better than any of the 150 or so projects they had sponsored around the world. They would need a letter of commitment from the community since as a foreign entity they could not own the building outright. And, incidentally there would be fees.

Sine Chadi was dismayed. Fees but no interest? In fact, the fees came to about the cost of borrowing money at the bank. Chadi balked. With appreciation, he bade goodbye to the official and decided the community would fund the building in another way. At the same time, Chadi had gone to the Royal Bank of Canada and had invested money that was sitting in a bank account at the going rate of interest—something like 4 per cent, a very good rate. When he relayed this to the committee, they rebelled. They did not want Muslim money receiving interest. So Chadi went back to the bank and negotiated away the interest they would pay on the money

Breaking ground at the Edmonton Islamic Academy, April 24, 2004.
The Academy was open and fully functioning on September 1, 2006.

they held from the mosque, but arranged for the bank to make an
$80,000 gift to the school as a gesture for the use of their money for
free. Indeed, Chadi (2015) confessed, at times, he had to cover costs
with his own money if construction outpaced giving.

This genuinely gold standard of a building was ready to host
the school in September 2006. As of 2017, over seven hundred
students attend the Edmonton Islamic Academy from kindergarten
through grade nine. (It now includes all grade levels). There is no
uniform ethnic identity in EIA; about sixty-five different ethnicities
are represented in the student body.

The inclusion of a community hall within the school has
resulted in a new industry: Academy banquets. The spacious
Academy banquet hall, complete with state-of-the art appliances,
functions as the EIA's cafeteria during class time and is available
at other times for conferences, weddings, funerals, congregational
meetings, and community forums.

The structure was funded through the initial fundraising that provided $1 million, and the city had loaned the community some money on the basis of the community centre concept. That money was to be paid back over twenty-five years. By 2006, the Royal Bank of Canada had loaned the Al Rashid community $9.75 million, but in two short years, over $2 million had been raised to reduce the debt. With the goal of paying off $100,000 a month, the community was debt-free by 2012.

A structure of this type sets the norms for Muslim construction across the continent. It is not just a building. It is first and foremost an educational institution that aims to provide the best in Muslim education in the West. But its overall goal is excellence in education, on par with or better than the sterling reports of Edmonton's school systems. A key ingredient of its success is the policies that guide its processes. The community has placed that oversight in the hands of a board of trustees drawn initially from seasoned members of the community: Mickey Jomha, Mahmoud Tarrabain, Mohamed "Rony" Jomha, Abdu Ghafour Rana, and Dr. Mohammad Shoush. Shoush, a retired professor of religious studies at the University of Alberta, provided an academic perspective and a guiding hand on the building of the Islamic content of EIA's program. Soon after the Academy's inception, Khalid Tarrabain joined the group. Board membership rotates between business and professional individuals in the community.

Give a world of sectarian violence, and the rise of jihadist trends in Africa, the Middle East, Afghanistan, and Pakistan, steering a major educational enterprise around the shoals cannot be an easy job. Jawdah Jorf (2015), superintendent of EIA, described how they have been able to shape the school's impressive program:

> We stay solidly in the middle on Islamic issues. We do
> not veer to the right or to the left in how we run the
> school. We do not tolerate breaking our rules. This is
> a traditional Sunni school with the goal to present
> the best education within the guidelines provided

by Alberta. We aim for excellence. Our student achievements show we are successful. Indeed, we are so successful that professional families move to Edmonton to place their children here. At the same time, students are vetted before they are accepted, and those who show signs of little commitment to our goals are rejected, even if they are from recognized families in the community. Our dedication is clear: we want to be the best school in Alberta!

Such a firm hand on the helm is reflected, too, in the school's organizational pattern: a general superintendent with responsibility for the overall running of the school is supported by three principals who run the day-to-day programs at the elementary, junior high, and high school levels. (A pre-school program is also housed at the Al Rashid Mosque.) The direction and responsibility for of all these programs rests with the board of trustees and the school administration.

The EIA operates under Alberta's private school legislation and meets the guidelines provided by the Accredited Funded Private School Act. The school is granted funding according to its ability to meet teaching and programmatic requirements as drafted by the Department of Education. The EIA teaches the Alberta Learning curriculum, but adds intensive Arabic instead of French and conducts additional studies in Islamic studies during an extra forty-minute block per day.

In the 2013–14 academic year, the school received $4 million from the provincial government. As Jorf pointed out, education is expensive, and none of the programming is built on foreign funds. Each student pays graduated fees: elementary, $3,000 first child, $2,700 second child, $2,500 all other children in family; high school, $3,500 first child, $3,000 second, $2,700 third, etc. Obviously, some families cannot afford these costs, but children are not turned away. When the fees are an issue, the superintendent arranges a meeting between parents and Khalid Tarrabain of

Al Rashid where finances are discussed and evidence of the family's finances is explained. Children may be subsidized out of regular mosque offerings that are placed in a fund for that purpose.

The Academy's Department of Islamic Studies has a vice principal who closely monitors the curriculum, and all Islamic teachers are monitored by instructors with at least a BA in the area. The result of this arrangement is that graduates can now move directly into programs at the University of Alberta without doing remedial courses. According to Jorf, graduating students relate directly to the Department of Modern Languages and Cultural Studies at the university so the move from EIA to the university is seamless.

Care is also taken to integrate Islamic studies into the regular offerings in classes. For example, an English class writing assignment can use Muslim writers who write in English as the basis of a project. Since the school is Sunni, it also pays attention to the four traditional *madhdhabs* (schools of thought) of law; in turn, any one or all can be cited as resources on legal matters. The result is that students do not find a disconnect between the topics they study and their Islamic heritage. Islam is integrated into the whole knowledge base. Nor is stress laid upon doctrinal differences with the Shia population, since they are a significant minority in the school. In conversation, Jorf pointed out that the school is non-sectarian in other senses: there are both Muslim and non-Muslim teachers in the school, and classes are not segregated by gender. She remarked, "These students live in Canada, they are going to relate directly with both non-Muslims and work in non-Muslim environments. They will always be in non-segregated situations. What sense is it to impose a different cultural standard on them as they learn? That is unrealistic."

EIA philosophy promotes active curricular and extracurricular leadership roles among students. Volunteering is highly regarded, so students have set records in collecting for the poor, cleaning highways, and helping at shelters. They readily gather hampers for families at Ramadan and other times of the year. During the 2007 Ramadan food drive, the children of EIA collected a huge donation of food. The campaign, which ran from September 14 to October 14, donated 5,449 food items to the Edmonton Food Bank. Jorf insists that instilling the values of responsible citizenship is fundamental to school policy. It is no surprise, then, that students also fundraise annually for the Stollery Children's Hospital and for autism and cerebral palsy research. (Parenthetically, at our interview, Jorf proudly noted that in 2014 a student-organized drive raised $10,000 in a few short weeks for the families of the military killed by deranged militants in Ottawa and near Montreal.)

The school's policies seem to be working. From its beginning with twenty-one students in 1987, expansion has been dramatic: as of the time of our interview, there were a thousand students. Some students go to M.E. LaZerte High School for the international baccalaureate program; LaZerte's co-ordinator would welcome more EIA students because they display strong leadership roles there as well. The EIA also has a program where alumni return to talk to current classes and inspire students by their example. This kind of reciprocity extends to teaching staff as well; five of the current teachers were themselves students in the school. With local support at such incredible levels, and the community firmly behind their efforts, the school is fully engaged with other Canadian students. The EIA sends sports teams to local meets, for example, and fosters twelve local teams across many different fields, including a girls' team that recently won bronze at a meet.

Jorf notes there are always those who disagree with the school's middle-of-the-road philosophy. Some might be unhappy with girls wearing the hijab so early, or they might object to the mandatory uniform, for instance. Yet it is much easier handling disciplinary issues with a uniform than imposing a dress code where public taste sets the standard. By requiring both girls and boys to adhere to a uniform, EIA has side-stepped many of the issues that other schools find difficult, such as dealing with the latest styles. Besides it does not have to deal with cultural differences in dress styles, since, for example, 30 per cent of the student population is Somali, with very colourful options in their ethnic background. At EIA, distinction between grades is maintained through colour-coding: elementary, red and black; junior high, green and black; senior girls wear an abaya with a head scarf. Non-Muslim teachers are not required to wear hijab. Sports outfits are respectful and yet allow for ease of movement.

In this period, Edmonton Islamic Academy took its place as one of the city's premier schools, backed by a sympathetic Alberta culture and supported by an equally important business and professional Muslim community. The Academy, along with North America's first cross-sectarian-sponsored chair in Islamic studies, places the Al Rashid community at the forefront of a genuine Canadian Islam that confidently builds for the future. The history affirms that this is an extraordinary community firmly rooted in Alberta and Edmonton and fully committed to the next phase of growth.

Consensus is that Al Rashid could have been crippled by post-9/11 backlash had it not had strong leadership during this time, one of the most stressful of periods in the community's history. At the same time, had the community not been successfully integrated into the larger community, both that community and Al Rashid people could have retreated into standoff positions. None of that happened. Even during the darkest days of the 9/11 crisis, the school remained open and fully functioning. Al Rashid stood its ground as one of the great achievements of Muslims in the West, and the city honoured the Muslim community by supporting it during this difficult period. It responded by making Al Rashid part of its colour and its spiritual legacy. We have discussed what rancour there was, but it is clear: the Muslim community of Al Rashid is now part of Edmonton's fabric, like Ukrainians, Indigenous peoples, and Scandinavians. As we move now to the most contemporary, we see some of the elements that make up that fabric in a different light.

5

TRANSITIONING
INTO THE
FUTURE
2010s and Beyond

THIS CHAPTER SKETCHES AL RASHID'S TRANSITIONS to a happier time—beyond the decade of the 2000s and the post-9/11 troubles—to a progressive and more fruitful period of the 2010s. We explore some new directions the community took as it overcame the obstacles inherent in the earlier social disruptions and the issues it faced as it looked towards a more prosperous time. We follow Al Rashid as it revised its governance structures to address the growth and diversity of the Muslim community in Edmonton, celebrated its seventy-fifth anniversary, planned new social services, and envisioned its future to 2030. These new directions lead naturally to a reflection on the community's sense of place and confidence, and provide insights into the continuing character of the Al Rashid community.

NEW GOVERNANCE STRUCTURES

As we saw in the last chapter, Al Rashid's response to 9/11 was to take a business-as-usual approach and to martial the community into a new building program—the groundbreaking Edmonton Islamic Academy. At the same time, the administration realized that the various groups and programs required a much more dedicated supervision from the community at large than had been the case in earlier days. For one thing, it was now obvious that the many dimensions of Al Rashid's outreach could scarcely be handled by one small board. Consequently, Al Rashid streamlined its governance structure to bring into the decision-making apparatus a broader coalition of viewpoints. As the board realized, not all of the views within Al Rashid's congregation were represented by the board and administration.

A number of factors influenced the change in governance. First, the community was growing so rapidly that no single individual could keep track of the newcomers' circumstances or the community's needs. Second, the mosque community now embraced a dynamic educational program, along with major demands for accommodation to children and youth programming. These were areas that needed attention from an organization attuned to their growth. Third, the new phenomenon of Islamophobia, especially in eastern Canada, required attention; the board realized they needed help to deal with external communication concerns. Fourth, the administrative structures had not been revisited since the first mosque was built in the late 1930s with $5,000; with a contemporary annual budget in excess of $5 million, the administration was labouring under the load. Finally, the early community had been the only Muslims in town; now there were over sixty-two ethnicities represented at Friday prayers, and somehow Al Rashid had to deal with such diversity.

The Al Rashid community was diversifying rapidly and the AMA board realized it had to develop internally to cope with the demands being made on its administration. Over the years, various suggestions for streamlining activities had been made, but now a serious effort was made to update the inner workings of the organization and make it more responsive to community needs. Finally, after several board and committee meetings, a revised organizational structure was brought to the Al Rashid community. Discussions ensued through 2010 and 2011, and a new governance structure was proposed.

First, there are several principal organizational units: Al Rashid Mosque/Canadian Islamic Centre, Edmonton Islamic Academy, Helping Hands Society, Islamic Funeral Society, Islamic Investment Corporation, Al Rashid Cultural Society. Each unit is led by a community-elected director who answers to Al Rashid's board and, through the board, the community. Second, while the board had existed since Al Rashid's early days, its role was further formalized during this conscious effort to assure effective governance. The board includes a president, vice president, secretary, treasurer, and five directors at large, all of whom are elected by mosque members at an electoral general meeting. The board also includes, as voting members, the two immediate past presidents. If these members are elected to another position at the electoral general meeting, then they step down from the board to serve in their new capacity. In previous versions, the president served for a two-year term only; there had been continuity as a member of the previous board replaced the incumbent. For example, Khalid Tarrabain has been re-elected regularly since 1990, and he continues to be re-elected under a new version of the constitution. The new version extends the length of the term for each elected director to four years; the term begins on the thirty-first day after the election and ends thirty days from the following election.

Finally, under the terms of the new constitution (January 19, 2011), elections are to be held every two years so that positions do not all rotate at the same time. Regularizing this framework has been an important part of the transitioning to the future for the organizational structure. Further, in the event that one or both of the past presidents hold an elected position on the board or are unable or decide against sitting on the board, then the previous past presidents of the AMA board shall be invited to sit on the board of directors. The invitation shall be extended to the next previous past president until both positions are filled. The current holders of all positions are found on the mosque website. Notably, the cohort represents a diligent attempt to move towards the inclusion of younger members.

THE EDUCATIONAL THRUST

In the previous chapters, we noted the strategy for maintaining community cohesion was to enlarge the vision of the people with construction projects; buildings moved the community vision ahead. Now the thrust was on education. The decade's number one priority is the creation of an educational future that is second to none in North America—a large order given the size of communities elsewhere. (Toronto, for example, has the largest Muslim population of any city in North America.) The community is undaunted by the challenge, given their historic accomplishments, the quality of the current mosque and school they have built, the generosity of the people, and the support of the larger community. They look now to a larger educational vision.

Mindful that Islamic education was one of the great achievements in classical Islamic society, Al Rashid has looked for ways to provide a depth of understanding for its own people and for the citizens of Edmonton. It is, for the majority of the community, a kind of trust delivered to them from the past that they are compelled to maintain and extend. Briefly, Al Rashid has been instrumental in working with the province and the Edmonton Public School Board to introduce significant dimensions of Islamic history and cultural achievements into the public sphere. Apart from the existing programs of bilingual Arabic and various public schools, and effort has been undertaken to develop a wider range of Islamic topics in home schooling and summer programs (see Sakinah Circle program integrated in the Alberta Learning curricula).

Education beyond the classes at the Edmonton Islamic Academy is also a matter of discussion and development. Goals, curriculum, Qur'anic studies, and other Muslim topics are part of ongoing conversations about the school as it expands high school offerings and even contemplates college-level courses. This means that intellectual resources will have to be developed at a much higher level than now exist within the mosque environment.

Complaints are often made by writers about Muslim countries on how little education is valued and how few women are on an education pathway. Many Muslims are weary of these criticisms, which usually revolve around different notions of education and educational structures. As we have seen, the Al Rashid community has moved decisively to address the educational needs of youngsters from within Canada. Mindful of the necessity of providing the means for youngsters to advance into higher education, Sameeh Salama, a local businessman in technology development, brought like-minded individuals together to form the Al Rashid Education Foundation (AREF).

The goal of this organization is to ensure that young people have the resources to achieve the best there is in education. Aware that it is a competitive environment for scholarships and grants, the foundation's aim is "to give Muslim youth the tools and support they need to succeed in today's competitive education system" (Salama 2015). Salama and Majeda Fyith promote their program through fundraisers and building bridges to those who are concerned that Muslim youth have access to higher education. Their mechanism derives from an old Muslim source of funding— an *awqaf* (endowment), a favourite way in the Muslim world to direct funding towards a project. Indeed, *awqafs* have a long and rich tradition, dating back to the early days of Islam. Salama notes, "*Awqafs* are the responsible stewardship of community donations for sustainable development, and we determined that Muslim youth are a critical area of growth for the community." The result has been the Light the Legacy Endowment, which provides scholarships and grants to young men and women to pursue advanced education. With 40 per cent to 50 per cent of Edmonton's Muslim community under the age of thirty-five, the endowment is a lifeline for families without the means to send bright children on to higher education.

Following 9/11, Al Rashid leadership recognized that keeping its head down and not participating in public education was having a detrimental effect on the public's perception of Islam. The community appeared secretive with a belief system few understood. More recently, in response to this perception, the Al Rashid community decided to open up. They've held educational forums, offered information sessions at the mosque, and published brochures and programs on social media, in press releases, and in public venues. In earlier days, under Saleem Ganam and Ibrahim Abu-Rabi, interfaith discussions had occurred, but they were largely hosted by the Interfaith Centre, and Al Rashid was not an explicit participant.

In an unprecedented move in 2012, the mosque formed an annual interfaith Christian-Muslim Dialogue with many Christian churches in Edmonton. Certainly, people from the mosque had participated in such discussions before, but this was the first collaborative effort with important Christian groups. In 2016 the event was held at Al Rashid Mosque, in which Muslim and Christian representatives of Indigenous, settler, and refugee groups partici-pated. The format allowed for both Muslim and Christian speakers to explain their distinctive religious viewpoints. It was a genuine sharing without any attempt to confront the other on doctrine or stance. While some complained that it was "mild," and did not change any minds, the leaders stated that that is exactly what they wanted. Personal testimony, music, and the Qur'an were generously shared. The event garnered considerable praise from the three hundred or so in attendance.

FACING UNPRECEDENTED GROWTH

One might assume that the negativity and Islamophobia post 9/11 would dent the growth of the Muslim population in Edmonton. In fact, this has not been the case. Mid-way through this decade, the Edmonton Council of Muslim Communities commissioned a major study through Mitacs, a national, not-for-profit organization that designs and conducts research and training programs in Canada, on the direction of the entire Muslim community as it moves towards 2030. The resulting report, of which I am a co-author, is called *Embracing 2030* (Waugh, Razavy, and Sheikh 2011).

One of the issues we struggled with was the degree and scope of growth. Available statistics showed that Edmonton's population in 2010 sat anywhere between 722,000 and 812,000. Published estimates indicated that this population would increase to between 890,800 (City of Edmonton 2010a) and 1,062,997 (Government of Alberta 2007) by 2030.

Calculating Muslim growth, however, is as problematic as calculating the city's growth. If we examine national figures, Muslim presence will grow dramatically. Earlier, we noted that those identifying themselves as Muslim in Canada had the largest increase from 1991 to 579,600 in 2001, representing 2 per cent of the Canadian population (Statistics Canada 2003). What the impact of new immigrants (such as those from Syria) will have is unknown.

In our study, we calculated the Muslim population for Canada using our previous data and found that the Muslim population in Canada in 2030 would be roughly 2.64 million. Using this data, we then interpolated for the Muslim population in the city of Edmonton for 2030 using varied sets of data (refer to Appendix 1 in *Embracing 2030*). We came up with three possible populations: 80,341; 59,260; 58,792. Regardless of which scenario turns out to be most accurate, these numbers suggest that Al Rashid will need to plan for a variety of issues that arise from population growth.

Hence the educational thrust will entail more construction. Such planning will involve another major building project, since the school is already nearing capacity, and additional programming will require further physical construction. It will not be sufficient to just provide classrooms. Students also require social stimulation, such as that offered by health and fitness facilities. Any building project would also require some way of integrating a growing population and meeting community needs. Several projects—already in the planning stages or currently underway—will carry the community well into the end of the 2030s.

DEALING WITH PUBLIC PERCEPTIONS

As we have seen, Al Rashid charted a solid course through one of the most tragic periods of Islamic history, but it also encountered several, more local, festering issues in the post-9/11 context, including the perpetual question of Islam's treatment of women, fears of radicalization among youth, homophobia in the community, and links between the mosque and terrorism. This section looks briefly at these issues and how Al Rashid has addressed them in recent years.

Despite its own history of dominant women, Al Rashid constantly has faced a skeptical public in any issue involving Muslim women. Several issues since 9/11 have attempted to paint Islam as a backward religion when it comes to women's rights: hijabs, burqas, clitoridectomies, girls' education, human rights abuses, arranged marriages, honour killings all have been used in the media to portray Islam as out of step with Western society. From the broader Muslim community's viewpoint, there has been little interest on the part of Western and Canadian media to present a balanced point of view or to understand the doctrinal or cultural nuances of these issues.

Leadership on these issues came not directly from the mosque itself but from an Al Rashid stalwart, Soraya Zaki Hafez. Through the Canadian Council of Muslim Women (Edmonton Chapter), a number of initiatives were undertaken to present a more nuanced view of women's issues. In 2009, Hafez and Dr. Zohra Husaini, with the council, teamed up to receive a grant addressing universal human rights, Islamic tradition, and Canadian Muslim women. The funding was a joint initiative of the Alberta Human Rights, Citizenship and Multiculturalism Education Fund, and the Federal Human Rights Program of the Department of Canadian Heritage. The critical section of the resulting study attempted to bring about reconciliation between the international conventions and rights of women as reflected in sharia traditions. Interestingly, the report uses the Qur'an and the Constitution of Medina as justification for speaking of universal human rights

Members of the Canadian Council of Muslim Women (Edmonton Chapter) celebrating the seventy-fifth anniversary of the Al Rashid Mosque at the Legislative Assembly of Alberta, 2013.

in Islam (Husaini 2011). It argues that the Islamic sources provide a foundation for justice and the equality of women in Islam, that the spiritual values of the religion indicate the basis for human rights, and that there are commonalities between Islamic values and Canadian Charter values. The report insists that violations of universal human rights are as much against Islam as they are against the Canadian Charter and international human rights conventions. As part of the project, the researchers held meetings with Muslim women to make them aware of their rights and the legacy of Islam for themselves so they can speak knowledgeably about their tradition in the face of criticism.

A high-profile case of family violence and murder incited the federal government to institute awareness campaigns concerning honour killing. The issue of families murdering young women who wished to marry someone not approved by the family had a direct impact on Edmonton-area Muslim women. In March 2014,

Rona Ambrose, minister for the status of women, funded a workshop on violence against women, which addressed issues such as violence against women and girls in the family, forced marriages, femicide, and genital mutilation. The event was co-sponsored by the Canadian Council of Muslim Women (Edmonton Chapter) and the Multicultural Women and Seniors Services Association. In October 2013, a group known as American Freedom Defense Initiative sponsored poster advertisements that ran briefly on Edmonton city buses. The ads were purportedly meant to increase awareness of honour killing, and portrayed girls dressed in hijabs. A number of people from all faiths were incensed that the ads implied that Canadian Muslim girls are at risk for honour killing, and objected. Subsequently, the City removed the bus posters and was sued by the American Freedom Defense Initiative, arguing that the City buckled from Muslim pressure. They argued that some Muslim governments had reduced penalties for so-called honour murderers and that Canadian girls were subject to these cultural issues. The case concluded in October 2016, with the judgement that the City was justified in removing the posters.

Education was not only necessary for the general public, however. The mosque leadership recognized that some in-house education was also necessary; community members had to understand their traditions and what their presence meant in Edmonton. So while a great deal of emphasis was placed on the school, the board also advocated for extracurricular activities to teach values and heritage. For boys and young men, for example, a Scouts group that was originally established in the 1990s was rejuvenated. Al Rashid's emphasis on educating children has significant dividends. As Khalid Tarrabain (2014) remarked, "We want our kids to know who they are, to know what Islam is and to feel connected to it and the community. We can't guarantee that kids won't get involved in these things—after all we believe in freedom of religion in Canada—but we do make sure that we have programs in place for them to learn exactly what is going on in the world and to provide a way for they to move up in the world. That's how we deal with that problem. But really, there is little evidence of radicalism among Al Rashid's youth populations."

The mosque also recognizes a responsibility to adults who know little about their religion, and with such a diversity of cultures and varieties of ethnicities making up Islamic society in Edmonton now, many women have had little exposure to the teaching of sharia or their rights under Canadian law. Within the mosque itself, Hanna Tarrabain and Khazma Assaf have brought women together to address contemporary problems in chats with the imam after Friday prayers. This kind of educational initiative allows members to address issues as they arise in the Al Rashid community.

Another issue that caused a local stir was the accusation that the Imam Mustafa Khattab had voiced an opinion on homosexuality to a class at the Edmonton Islamic Academy, early in 2013. The offending remark was an offhand comment, made during a break in class, and recorded on an iPhone. Subsequently, Alberta Liberal education critic Kent Hehr released a statement condemning the comments. During a CBC Edmonton radio program, he remarked, "No educational institution in Alberta should be allowed to discriminate or promote hate, much less receive public tax dollars to do so" (June 2013). The issue has been contentious in Alberta in particular because of the well-known *Vriend v. Alberta* (1998) case, in which Delwin Vriend sued King's College, a private Christian post-secondary school in Edmonton, for dismissing him because he was gay. The Alberta government sided with the college, but Alberta Court of Queen's Bench sided with Vriend; however, the Alberta Court of Appeal overturned the ruling. Vriend took the case to the Supreme Court, which ruled on April 2, 1998 that sexual orientation was a protected status, overthrowing both the Appeal's ruling and Alberta's Individual Rights Protection Act. This situation with Khattab attracted attention in part because the EIA was receiving over $4 million in funding from the Alberta government. The government, however, responded by noting that these were personal views—not the school's. Khattab, a very popular imam, had already moved to another position out of town and the issue died down.

A further issue, generated from the statements of Al Rashid's former teacher and developer, Issam Saleh, related to the Muslim Brotherhood. He had moved to the Muslim Association of Canada (MAC) mosque in the west end of the city, shortly after leaving the EIA. Both he and a director of the MAC mosque in Toronto had expressed approval of the Muslim Brotherhood in public statements: MAC's national website originally connected itself to "the Islamic revival of the early 20th century, culminating in the movement of the Muslim Brotherhood" (although this statement has been removed), and Dr. El-Tantawy Attia, a retired engineer originally from Alexandria, Egypt, says he preaches "middle of the road Islam." "Here, we follow the teachings of the Muslim Brotherhood," he said (Hume 2011). The Muslim Brotherhood has been associated for many years with the Islamic revivalist movement that culminated in Islamism, a modern political Islam. The group has subsequently been banned in Egypt's military coup. A group opposed to MAC's plans at the suburban Edmonton mosque argued that the mosque might be funding terrorism, which occasioned Saleh to threaten legal action. That conflict has subsided.

Relatedly, more worrisome accusations have been made against Al Rashid—namely, that it funds groups like Hamas in Palestine. Several Western governments have repealed Hamas's charitable status after questions about its funding political activities in Israel. Al Rashid's treasurer has thoroughly and publicly denied any connection to Hamas. At the same time, a group calling themselves the Terrorism and Security Experts of Canada Network has suggested that groups that support terrorism are widespread in Canada, and that these groups "constitute a greater threat to Canada than al-Qaeda" (Quiggin 2014).

Author of the Terrorism and Security Experts of Canada Network report, Tom Quiggin, cites former Prime Minister Stephen Harper's sources as saying that the National Council of Canadian Muslims is "an organization with documented ties to a terrorist organization such as Hamas." The National Council of Canadian Muslims instituted legal action against the Prime Minster's Office,

which, of course has died now that Harper is no longer
prime minister.

Writing in *Maclean's* magazine, Adnan Khan (2014) discounts
the whole Quiggan report; he says this is fear mongering, and that
there is little to no evidence of widespread support in Canada for
either the Muslim Brotherhood or al-Qaeda. He sees Quiggan and
his organization as a blatant attempt to import Islamophobia into
Canada and to paint Muslim charities in a bad light. Judging by the
meek response in the media to the allegations against Al Rashid,
most Edmontonians have given little credence to the idea that the
mosque has connections to terrorist organizations. The allegations
have gone nowhere.

Instead of harming the reputation of the Al Rashid Mosque
and wearing the community members down, these situations
appears to have done the opposite: they have solidified Al Rashid's
commitment to building a strong and healthy Canadian community
based on a faith commitment. The goal set years ago is bearing fruit
today in a robust community that can take these kinds of suspicions
in stride and continue to build a viable Canadian Islam here.
Edmontonians continue to support Al Rashid's community despite
the tendency of the media to distort events.

Nonetheless, for many in the community, after more than
five years of negative press about Islam, it was a relief to see
Edmonton City Council and Edmonton Police Service approve a
hijab for on-duty police officers in 2013. After concurrent conflicts
in Quebec about women wearing the veil and the proposed Quebec
charter of values, the announcement came like a breath of fresh air
to Muslims in Edmonton. City councillor Scott McKeen indicated
that this was a "gesture of inclusion" towards the Muslim community and a counterbalance to the widespread belief that Alberta was
antagonistic to diversity. "One of the perceptions about Edmonton
and Alberta is that we're kind of redneck," he told reporters. "The
decision," he said, "is sort of saying that we want to have a diverse
police service that reflects the diversity and multicultural aspects
of Edmonton" (Brean 2013).

Al Rashid Mosque celebrating its seventy-fifth anniversary
at Fort Edmonton Park, 2013.

SEVENTY-FIFTH ANNIVERSARY CELEBRATIONS

On September 17, 2013, the Al Rashid community turned from the
negativity of the past decade to rejoicing in their achievements: the
mosque and its community had a birthday party! At seventy-five
years old, the community of Al Rashid gloried in its past and
enthused about its future. The crowds that gathered in Fort
Edmonton Park that day felt a sense of relief that, while they

were not unscathed, they were not defeated. Al Rashid stood firmly in place. They had survived some major problems and were stronger than ever. The celebration's opening remarks by Soraya Zaki Hafez (2013) indicate the depth of public celebration, and the guest list reflects the respect and appreciation that the larger public has for the mosque and its place in Edmonton and Canada:

> Minister Lukaszuk, Mayor Mandel, MLAs, Party Leaders, Councillors, Community Leaders, Ladies and Gentlemen,
>
> *Assalamu Alikum.* Peace be upon you all.
>
> It's my greatest honour to welcome you all here to the seventy-fifth anniversary of Canada's first mosque.
>
> In 1988 as the Canadian Council of Muslim Women, Edmonton Chapter, was having a meeting to organize a fiftieth anniversary for Canada's first mosque, we realized that the mosque was supposed to be demolished. It didn't sound right to celebrate one day and the next day the mosque could be demolished. We all were in agreement that it should be saved. It was saved because of its importance to the Edmonton community at large and to the Muslim community. It's part of Edmonton's history, built by the Muslim pioneers during the Depression to preserve their religion and their culture. What a struggle for it to be built and a struggle to move it.
>
> Please welcome, too, Councillor Heather MacKenzie on behalf of Mayor Stephen Mandel, though he has another commitment, he still wanted to come to celebrate and say a few words; Ms. Janice Sarich, MLA Decore North (Since Premier Alison Redford couldn't be with us tonight, Ms. Sarich will speak on behalf of the premier. She is accompanied by Barbara North, constituency office assistant, and Lisa Wildman, constituency office manager); Dr. Raj Sherman, the

leader of Alberta Liberal Party; Mr. Brian Mason, the leader of Alberta New Democrat Party; Mr. Moe Amery, MLA Calgary East.

Later, I would like to read a letter sent from the Speaker of the House, Gene Zwozdesky.

I would like also to introduce some very special guests: Ms. Linda Duncan, MP Strathcona; Edmonton city councillors, Ed Gibbons, Heather MacKenzie, and Dave Loken.

I appreciate the presence of the member of the Interfaith Board, and I am proud to introduce leaders from the Muslim community: Mr. Masood Peracha, chair, Edmonton Council of Muslim Communities; Mr. Khalid Tarrabain, president, Canadian Islamic Centre; Mr. Ayaz Bhanji President, Ismaili Council.

Please join me in greeting the sons and daughters of the Muslim pioneers who built this mosque and brought us together today to celebrate: Mr. Richard Awid, retired teacher, community historian, and a son of Ahmed Ali Awid Amerey, who was one of the pioneers who built the mosque; and Dr. Zohra Husaini, project director with CCMW.

I'd like to thank all of you for coming and sharing this happy celebration with everyone. Special thanks to the speakers who made it here despite their heavy commitments. Special thanks to my board members who spent time and long hours to make sure everything is done right. And finally, thanks to Fort Edmonton staff for helping to make the arrangements for the event to go so smoothly.

For the Al Rashid community, this was a banner day, for the celebration not only recognized the importance of the mosque building, but the presence of so many dignitaries from the city and province signalled Islam as a founding religion history within the city and province itself.

CHARTING THE FUTURE WITH THE
EMBRACING 2030 STUDY

Leadership and Intellectual Issues

Mindful of the increased attention to Islamic activities on the
part of media and government organizations, the ECMC board
wished to engage academic sources to help sort out priorities. For
example, the Sunni community faced important intellectual issues
around the training of its imams and leadership. The *Embracing
2030* study suggested that, apart from special training facilities
for imams, it may be difficult in the future to provide the spiritual,
psychological, and counselling dimensions demanded of today's
imams. Interviews conducted during the study reveal that there is
a disconnect between many youths and the clerical leadership in
some mosques in the Edmonton region. More often than not, youth
go to their peers for advice and information, as they find their peers
more in touch with pressures and issues facing youth today than
the leadership. This finding is not surprising or unique to mosques;
the same complaint circulates in churches and synagogues. One of
the individuals with whom we spoke felt that a younger, Canadian,
moderate imam would be a wonderful idea, but that it would not be
feasible because mosque leadership often equates religiosity with
conservatism, and a more forward-thinking imam would not mesh
well with mosque leadership.

One solution might be to develop a Canadian training
institute for clergy, drawing from Canada's Muslim youth. Many
of the issues at the heart of conflicts with Canadian society have to
do with assumptions of Mediterranean cultural values implicit in
much of Islam's doctrine and structure, and planning a college for
imams could be a catalyst for a new direction in Islamic studies. Yet
it is clear from the makeup of the mosque community today that
born-in-Canada Muslims outnumber the immigrant cohort. This is
a tension within the community that may have an important impact
in the years that lie ahead.

A corollary of this in the future may be the fashioning of a
distinctively Canadian fatwas system, whereby carefully crafted

understandings of Canadian issues could express a genuine Canadian Islamic value system. Whether such a system would be just the replica of what Middle Eastern authorities say is a matter of debate. When I expressed the view in Damascus in 2012 that we were growing a Canadian Islam, the local scholars objected, arguing that Islam was the same all over the world. Whatever the outcome of this debate, one thing is clear: the Canadian community feels quite resolute in its perception of its Islamic competence, and needs no authority to dictate to it. At the very least, an advisory commission of learned people might mediate these issues and might add an additional dimension to the intellectual life of the community. But the issue remains: Do Canadian-born Muslims represent a distinctive community within the Islamic family?

Another issue in Islam's intellectual life is likely in the near future; it relates to the very category of identity: How relevant is the issue of hybrid identities (Canadian Muslim) in Al Rashid's future? How important is the portrayal of Muslims in Canadian society post 9/11 and what role does the intellectual establishment and the media have in shaping that image? When the study raised the question of hybrid identities, we found that several of the mosques around the city offered workshops addressing this issue—what it means to be a Canadian Muslims, how one's Muslim identity plays into one's civil obligations, and how Muslims should operate within Canadian society. The youth, in particular, felt that addressing these needs through the mosque was both necessary and beneficial. On the point of Muslims post 9/11, many of the mosque groups that we spoke with felt that Muslims in Edmonton had to do more in terms of civic engagement to raise a more positive profile of Islam. The argument was that many Muslim communities might volunteer at soup kitchens, Habitat for Humanity, or the Red Cross, and they might make the effort to participate significantly in many interfaith programs, trying to increase others' knowledge of Islam that way. Furthermore, they would like to see some positive media treatment of this community work.

Migrants to Europe and North America have been subjected to several types of social pressures that have ultimately shunted them into being outsiders, or "others." The very social and political structures of nation-states make outsiders into others, those who do not belong. Groups that do not belong are structurally marginalized and reduced to minority status. The result, in the Muslim case, is the permanent non-belonging implied in Western culture. This otherness is addressed in *Making Muslim Space in North America and Europe*, a collection of essays that centres on the way in which a word-centred tradition (i.e., the Qur'an and sharia) translates itself into a tradition with claims on the physical and emotional space of America and Europe (Metcalf 1996). It is precisely this right to space and place that is part of the ongoing dialogue throughout the world concerning the sharia. The sharia becomes not just a law but a code word for Muslim space; it is a way of turning the otherness of veiling and religious law concerning divorce into a way of shaping a distinctive Muslim presence. By espousing otherness, a technique of becoming has been found within the West. If the West will insist on sharia as otherness, it is likely to find Islam moving increasingly towards a personal and community ethnicity in which sharia will have a continuing cultural impact. If this occurs, some form of sharia-orientedness within a Muslim Canadian life will be inescapable, and it will play a role as Islam develops in the West. A host of questions arise from that issue: Will it result in a rejection by Muslim intellectuals of the Western definition of the human? Will Canadian Muslim intellectual offer an alternative? Can some détente come about between a modernized sharia and Canadian law?

The Mosque and Personnel

If the Muslim population and mosque attendance continue to grow at their current rates, new mosques will be needed in the Edmonton area. Moreover, with the average age of the population approaching the twenty-five to thirty-five range, the most productive age for family development, we will likely see significant growth in required services. Al Rashid, as the mother mosque of the city, will be called upon to assist in covering this growth.

All mosque personnel admit that the situation cannot be sustained at its current level; the demands on imams and mosque personnel is increasing beyond capability (Kadri 2015). Immigrants, for example, rely increasingly on mosque personnel, including the imam, for guidance in a whole range of issues from financing a home to obtaining a passport. With the size of population, the diversity and vigour of growth, a single imam looking after spiritual affairs may no longer be viable. Congregations of Christian churches have found it impossible to keep up with counselling demands, and it may be that Al Rashid will find the same. In addition, the mosque may have to give imams special training to handle the complexity of cases that are now coming to them for help. Legal, financial, psychological, spiritual are all bundled together. Most imams with young families may be stretched too thin, and the community itself is so large and complex that a division of labour, even with professionally trained personnel (psychologists, social workers) may be necessary. The *Embracing 2030* study considered that Al Rashid's service sector would take on increasing importance, as outlined below.

Seniors

Factors such as the aging baby-boomer generation and increasing life expectancy means that Edmonton's population is aging rapidly. According to the 2009 City of Edmonton Population census (the most recent available statistics for the *Embracing 2030* study), 55 per cent of Edmonton's population is between the ages of 20 and 54 (City of Edmonton 2010b). These statistics suggest that the average age of Edmontonians will increase from 36 years (average age in 2005) to over 42 years by 2030. Furthermore, the number of people between the ages of 65 and 84 is projected to increase by a staggering 129 per cent, while the number of people ages 85 and above can increase by up to 158 per cent by the year 2030 (City of Edmonton 2010b). A 2010 Government of Alberta (2010) report also suggested that by 2031, approximately 1 in every 5 Albertans will be a senior. The shifting age profile of the city has implications for the provision and delivery of services, particularly with respect to infrastructure, care, and social services.

In our *Embracing 2030* study, we interpolated the projected number of Edmonton Muslim seniors through to the year 2030 and propose three possible populations: 18,077; 13,333; 13,228. These findings suggest that the Edmonton Muslim senior population would grow anywhere between 516 to 741 per cent, a percentage higher than the average rate of growth suggested by the city of 287 per cent. In other words, while the Edmonton Muslim population is projected to grow rapidly, the Muslim senior population will assume a large portion of this growth.

In effect, by 2018, the number of seniors in the city will move beyond the number of young children. The emphasis, then, on building for children may face an issue of priorities. While it may be attractive to provide funding for youngsters, it is also clear that families likely will not be able to provide for seniors. Nor are there available homes for Muslim seniors. Since this population is likely to have multiple health conditions, many of them chronic, the future does not look pleasing. Al Rashid is aging, although it may not appear so at the moment. It shows few signs of being invaded by white hair, but, like all religious organizations in Canada, it is growing older. This is a cross-religion issue that requires important consideration.

Traditionally, Muslim populations have felt a strong commitment caring for aging family members; the strategy has been for aging parents to move into the home of the senior son, where they are cared for daily by the senior son's wife and their grandchildren. There are a number of problems in applying this model in Canada and Alberta. First, the model works best in a village or small town, where commuting—to doctors, stores, and relatives—is not an issue. In major centres, transportation becomes a critical problem, for the aged often can no longer drive and significant distances must be travelled to reach hospitals and physicians (Alberta Caregivers Association 2008). Second, families are not as homogenous in Canada as in traditional cultures; wives may work outside the home, be incapacitated, or be culturally resistant to homecare, and thus cannot care for senior members of the family. Third, seniors are known to have health issues that require specialized treatment that is often best addressed in residents for seniors with nursing care. Fourth, families in Canada move about far more for work, rendering it impossible for the traditional pattern to be adopted.

It is also now probable that aging family members are reluctant to leave the homes they have loved and valued for many years, and family members are reluctant to bring dislocation because of that concern. Society is now aware that seniors living in homes, often in subdivisions far from children and relatives, are in danger of loneliness and feelings of abandonment. When they were younger they had no problem with this isolation, but with poor public transportation and no one able to drive, isolation is a real problem. Indeed, many may become what geriatric specialists call "elder orphans" (Carney 2015). Al Rashid may want to plan sooner rather than later for a branch of administration to deal specifically with seniors.

New Canadians

There is evidence that only about 25 per cent of immigrants to Edmonton make contact with settlement agencies in the community (K. Tarrabain 2014). Most seek out information about the city through family, friends, libraries, schools, post-secondary institutions, and the City of Edmonton's recreation, leisure, and community centres. This means that 75 per cent of new arrivals do not make contact with, or take advantage of, established settlement agencies that provide important services. On the face of it, it seems that family and friends are still the best way for newcomers to relate to the city.

On the other hand, as the sophistication of the mosque and its personnel increases, and their connections to the larger social service industry in the city and the province develops, it is quite possible that governments will be calling on Al Rashid to help integrate refugees. The mosque does maintain housing in its apartments, but it might make sense for the mosque to convert some of these units into reception housing for those who were displaced from their homes in Iraq, Syria, Somalia, and Ethiopia, for example. This will mean an expansion of its relationship with organizations such as the Edmonton Mennonite Centre for Newcomers. The centre has long carried a sizable caseload of those moving into the province and the city. Given the ongoing dislocation in the largely Muslim Middle East and the continual fighting reported there, many families have been broken. They will need essential trauma support. Theoretically, Al Rashid could become a place of solace for those from war-torn regions, with an expanded social team to assist in integration. With its important legacy of service, Al Rashid might find itself called upon to provide a Canadian answer to some of the dislocation in the Middle East. It certainly has the intellectual resources to be a welcoming face for Canada.

As of December 2015, there were 63.5 million displaced people in the world (UNHCR 2015). Over 70 per cent of those displaced or living as refugees in the world are Muslim (Maloof and Ross-Sheriff 2003). Arab refugees from major conflict zones in the Middle East continue to be a critical world problem. While many settle in Europe, some eventually arrive in Canada. With little else, they rely on their religious commitments to sustain them, and this means turning to Islamic organizations. The Middle East has been in turmoil now for over one hundred years, with the establishment of the State of Israel a major flashpoint for Palestinian refugees, some of whom ended up in Canada. The traumas brought on by this tidal wave of misery cannot be quantified in numbers, but it must be significant. Mental health issues become an ongoing reality, even when safely ensconced in Canada. Given the importance of religion for many of these Muslims, local mosques are challenged by the psychological damage.

Al Rashid is not immune to this misery and must maintain a staff to handle requests. About ten serious social calls are fielded a month, with workers assigned to counsel people on everything from passport applications to divorce. Within the contemporary mosque structure, then, it is not sufficient just to provide place for prayer, but the whole range of life services, including funerary services. In fact, Al Rashid deals with over eighty funerals a year, which means that the community also arranges a wide variety of services for the bereaved. Some of these people are seldom seen at prayers, yet when death comes, they seek out the mosque. It is a role that few in the larger community would associate with the building, but it highlights the fact that the mosque is more than a building: it is the centre of an ever-expanding community of support.

Funeral and Cemetery

If planning is in place for the living, it is also in place for those who have passed on. As discussed earlier, the community has purchased ground for the expansion of the Muslim cemetery, but it is still it fairly rough condition; the community continues to upgrade it. Examining what needs to be done in this area suggests that the community has to look ahead. With Al Rashid's community growing, and with the Islamic Funeral Society a key part of current offerings, there is already talk of expanding the ground, not for the next year or so, but well into the future.

As we have seen, the mosque very early developed its own funeral structure to handle the deaths of its community members, and we have documented the initiatives in expanding the base for Muslim burials. The statistics, however, suggest that with the increasing age of Muslims, this area will need increasing support and development. It might well be an issue that will require a cross-mosque agreement, since growth will likely put strains on the current facilities.

The trajectory going forward as mapped out by the leadership of the mosque indicates a full engagement with demands of a rapidly growing, technology-savvy, youth-oriented religious complex. This is clearly a multidimensional task, involving governmental and civic organizations in Edmonton and Alberta, while remaining steadfast to a moderately conservative Sunni doctrine. At the same time, Al Rashid is evolving. It is stepping forward to shoulder many demands and requirements imposed on it from its social and religious milieu. Clearly, it wishes to retain its place at the head of Islamic development in the city, the province, and indeed Canada. Whether it can martial the resources to meet all future expectations has yet to be determined. But there can be no doubt that it relies heavily on the solid foundation on which the early leaders of the Arabian Muslim Association built.

EPILOGUE

The Iconic Al Rashid, Its Community, and Rihla

THIS BOOK HAS DESCRIBED SOME OF THE VALUES that have built and sustained Al Rashid. The community has considerable reason to be proud. The pioneers were partners with all others in building Canada, and they always saw themselves as part of Canada's development in Edmonton. Difference was not a characteristic that isolated them. Rather, it was as strength that contributed to the whole. In effect, Al Rashid constructed itself as a Canadian enterprise from the beginning. This is one reason for its unflappability and resilience in the face of the many challenges.

A significant aspect of Hamdani's 2015 study of Canadian Muslims is the economic clarity with which he sketches diversity within the Muslim community in Canada and the nature of its professional profile. Of singular importance is the shift towards a Canadian Islam—that is, a community whose identity is firmly Islamic but that also sees itself and reacts as Canadian. This perception holds for the Al Rashid community, too. This community, however, will work out what this identity is not through some ideological articulation of a reified Islam but through an application of the knowledge and values its has developed in carving out a singular place in Canadian history. The story this book tells seems to indicate that Al Rashid has worked out a sophisticated and solid sense of belonging to Canada and Islam that is of singular importance. Al Rashid has articulated a distinctive Canadian Islam. Its new identity might best be described as Al Rashid-as-Islamic-Canadian.

The history of this mosque says something about Canada. It points to the role of religion as a medium through which some people become Canadian. First, by affirming the mosque as a community enterprise and not an exclusive religious club, Al Rashid has taken its place as an expression of Canadian religiosity—not as a foreign implant. This point highlights that Al Rashid is not a matter of a building funded by a foreign country and placed here by wealth from abroad. Rather, it was money from Jews, Christians, Muslims, Druze, and so on, all in agreement that this tradition has its place among the family of religions in Canada and should be supported by the body politic. Being Muslim is not the antithesis of being Canadian, the way some media would like to portray it. It is part of the Canadian fabric. It is part of the community's *rihla* in this part of the world.

Al Rashid's existence does challenge Canada's intellectual perception of itself, in somewhat the same way that accepting Indigenous cultures as the basis of Canadian society will have dramatic effects on Canada's identity. It is easier to see the intellectual problem by referring to Canada's constitution. One way this can be illustrated is to return to the sharia debate. A fundamental principle of religious law and the state's control of it are at the heart of the debate. There would seem to be a contradiction within the Canadian constitution between the claims that the state has "control" over all religion, when Canada insists that Canadians accord belief in God as absolutely primary in their constitution. What that means goes back to notions of law as articulated by former Chief Justice Antonio Lamer (Quig 2004), who suggested that some basis for law rests in public acceptance of religious belief—that is, religious belief has some area of primacy quite apart from that which the state grants as law. Canada already acknowledges laws from other jurisdictions as foundational, such as British common law, or French secular law in the case of Quebec. What role will ancient religious laws, such as those of Indigenous peoples, or Jewish or Muslim law have in Canada of the future? Canada has yet to grapple with this issue.

To this issue can be added the ticklish subject of the role of Muslim family law in Canada. As is well known, Muslim family law is a composite one. On the one hand, regulations and injunctions from the Qur'an are united with practices of the Prophet, *ijma* (widely accepted opinions) of the scholars, and various legal emphases and interpretations of the *madhhabs* (schools). Muslim family norms are mediated by values arising out of the central heartland's dominance of Islamic traditions, usually seen as the Mediterranean family structure mixed with Islamic religious hegemony. Does that embeddedness in Mediterranean symbol systems commit sharia to that framework in all contexts? This is an issue that calls for the Canadian Muslim community to intellectually engage in a larger task of articulating what Muslim family law could mean within Canada. So far, no Muslim body, and certainly not the intellectuals within Al Rashid, has taken this up.

On the other hand, these issues could arise directly if taken up by Jewish and Islamic groups in the Supreme Court, but it will also surely have some purchase in discussions about respecting Indigenous truth claims that are grounded in different value systems. The intellectual discourses that will follow from this would benefit from an examination of the way in which Al Rashid has worked out its position within Canadian society, and that too has potential to engage a new generation of Al Rashid community members in articulating a Muslim Canadian perspective.

The history of Al Rashid indicates that long before the doctrine of multiculturalism, the principles of that ideology were already in play in the experience of the early pioneers. The rihla of this community is still unfolding. It is a story of individuals relying on friends, family, relatives, cultural connections, and common interests to find work, to contribute to the whole. This gives Al Rashid an intangible sense of connectedness. Some would call it family, but it is larger than that, and is deeper in its reach. Nor is the mosque's identity just ethic or ideology writ large. While those who are religiously inclined will argue Al Rashid is distinctively religious—that is, the notion of global *ummah*—it is probably closer to the old notion of an accepted sense of common cultural values that formed the foundation of a now past Islamic commonality. That commonality embraced all religions and all points of view of the time. There seems no doubt that the community summoned this ancient perception of its background as it was formulating itself in Edmonton. By doing so, it has pointed to a richness in the Canadian identity that has not hitherto been explored.

Finally, for the naysayers within Canadian culture, there is a message here. It is not ideology, nor the doctrinaire, nor the letter of the law, nor the affirmation of difference that has placed this community where it is today—as a vanguard within Canadian culture. It is co-operation, collaboration, the seeking of community, and resisting influences that would undermine those values that are central to its history. It is problematic to chart that sense of worth and it is unlikely this book has been successful. Judging by its past, Al Rashid will be around for others to try. There is one current consolation: we can see Al Rashid in action in the lives and initiatives of its community, and celebrate its success with it. After all, Al Rashid will mark one hundred years in Edmonton in 2028.

CREATIVITY IN THE AL RASHID COMMUNITY

Selected Profiles

AS CRUCIAL AS THE AL RASHID BUILDING IS, the creative community behind the mosque gives the building its depth and significance. This appendix explores the more innovative and artistic dimensions of the Al Rashid community, which reveal some of the strengths and diversity of this talented community. Unfortunately, we cannot profile everyone involved in the community, but those described here stand for the many. Cumulatively, these profiles show something very real and special about this Edmonton community.

THE CREATIVE SECTOR OF BUSINESS

One of the more successful family business profiles is that associated with the name of Elsafadi. A family- and community-embracing business, the Elsafadi enterprise is a singular achievement within the community.

Mohammed Elsafadi was born in the village of Lala, Lebanon, and came to Canada in 1954. Like many others, he was lured to this country by those who were already here and who appreciated the freedom and opportunity—the Amereys, the Gutnys, the Tarrabains, and Abougouches. He arrived with five dollars in his pocket and immediately set to work for the Canadian National Railway. Meanwhile, his brother had established a peddler's delivery route among farmers north of Edmonton, Legal, Morinville, Smoky Lake, and so on—bringing them fresh vegetables and foodstuff by horse and carriage and later truck. When his brother moved into the grocery business, Mohammed took over his territory, drawing upon established customers to develop a thriving route.

Mohammed returned home to Lala to marry Khadijah and brought her to Edmonton to begin one of the most successful small businesses in the region. For some time, he not only sold groceries on his route but he kept a garage full of supplies. More and more local people and friends were coming to purchase supplies at his garage stockpile. The garage sales grew rapidly and the street became very busy. When the city objected that he had no licence to do this and recommended that he find a retail outlet, he chose to rent a store near the mosque and sell from that location. In September 1987, Mohammed rented the former M&M Food Market on the corner of 113 Street and 134 Avenue. After successive rental contracts proved increasingly costly, the company bought the whole building. Mohammed continued to maintain his connections to the north for over thirty years.

Meanwhile, he and his wife had three sons, Waleed, Anwar, and Ali, all of whom grew up helping in the business. The Elsafadi Market initially purchased supplies, especially foreign canned goods, through both Western Grocers and Dominion Wholesalers out of Montreal. The store became a staple for the burgeoning Muslim community in the northern part of the city, supplying a wide range of groceries, halal meats, festive supplies, and memorabilia. Eventually, the store could not keep up with demand. When space became available, they added the Mediterranean Bakery around the corner, and specialized in Middle Eastern bread and sweets.

To take pressure off the 134 Avenue store, and to better serve
the growing populations in the north part of the city, Mohammed
Elsafadi bought a plaza store in the Castle Downs neighbourhood.
The new plaza store had ample parking and access to a community
that was now centred on the mosque and the Islamic school. With a
niche market growing all across the northern parts of city, the older
store gravitated towards a convenience format, while the Castle
Downs location combined all dimensions of the larger market more
effectively. All three Elsafadi sons worked in different aspects of the
business: Anwar focused on the Castle Downs store; Waleed worked
in the 134 Avenue outlet, and Ali planned on expanding to the city's
south side. Tragically, Ali died from cancer in 2013, and the expansion has been put on hold. Anwar and Waleed look to their children
and their nephews and nieces to join the family business. With
twelve children among their families, some are bound to continue
the Elsafadi story.

As the Elsafadi brand became well known in the wider
community, the store switched to a Mediterranean focus to cash in
on the public interest in Mediterranean diets and wholesome foods.
At the same time, the company shifted from local store sheets and
community newspapers to radio advertising, and the company
placed more resources into promoting the Elsafadi brand. The
move was very successful, bringing new customers from among
non-traditional buyers, especially young Edmontonians and
other Canadians. In tandem, the store moved to import specialty
foods from across Canada, including foods from Newfoundland.
Meanwhile, facing declining health, Mohammed retired in 1983,
bequeathing the northern business to the Elsafadi chain. That chain
had expanded to include a wholesale component that supplies stores
and businesses not only in Alberta's north but east into Manitoba
and Saskatchewan. As the store became more broadly based financially, and the demands for its services expanded, the contacts in
the Middle East became more reliable, and Elsafadi moved to direct
purchasing, eliminating the middleman in Montreal and Toronto.
With a capitalization in excess of $25 million, the Elsafadi brand is

looking towards the future. The firm is now known widely across northern Alberta among devoted customers, and is a staple for people in the Arab, Muslim, and Canadian communities who are looking for Mediterranean specialties.

Asked about the family's success story, Waleed (2015) had this to say:

> We copied Mom and Dad's legacy—"Your name is everything," they said. We have therefore maintained a direct contact with our customers…We are in the store and on the ground where people can see us, talk to us, and feel that we will help them personally. Our secret for over thirty years has been the same: customers are part of our family. We go to their weddings, rejoice when their children are born, support widely their community charities. This is our great community. We want to keep that personal meaning, that feeling, that touch, with it. That name is everything. That's the secret of our success.

Another star in the Al Rashid firmament of extraordinary businessmen is Sine Chadi. Sine's ancestral roots also lie in Lala, Lebanon, but his business acumen has been honed by Alberta's boom and bust cycles. He began his rise as the grandson of an immigrant and as a teenager in Lac La Biche, Alberta, that northern town with the highest percentage of Muslims in Canada. He worked for his father in the fur industry until it dried up. In 1975, he switched to real estate—a move that shaped backbone of his enterprise ever since. For nearly a decade, he rode the elevator of boom development—buying and selling farms, houses, and raw land, and adding subdivisions, residential acreages, and land development projects to his quiver. He even owned truck stops throughout the province. As he remarked in conversation, "I set my sights on being a millionaire by twenty-five, and I was" (2015).

Then down went the economy in Alberta. By 1985, real estate had crashed. Sine moved to Edmonton, cobbling together funds to buy real estate at fire-sale prices and working on his next dream: serving the community through government. He won a seat as a Liberal in a notoriously Conservative province, and served from 1993 to 1997. When he saw that elected representatives had little clout unless they were part of the party in power in Alberta, he turned back to private business and rode the rise of the economy.

In 1999, he put together a plan to build a billion-dollar company called Imperial Equities Inc. He began simply. He shaped a company of three million shares at twenty cents each and peddled them to over three hundred partners and friends, satisfying the requirement to become a publicly traded corporation. With that, he bought and sold real estate, mortgages, businesses, and distributions firms, and once again rode the elevator to the top: he has at least a dozen companies and subsidiaries under his jurisdiction, including Imperial Equities Inc., Imperial Distributors Canada, a wholly owned subsidiary that handles drug delivery for all major pharmaceutical companies in Canada; Sable Inc., which manages the extensive portfolio of rental properties the firms owns; Transport Division, which owns and operates the shipping components for the distribution system; Venture Capital Division of Imperial Distributors, with 70 per cent invested in the Edmonton area and the rest across the country; the Real Estate Investment Division, which buys, sells, and leases industrial holdings, such as the Imperial West Industrial Park and other holdings in Fort McMurray, Red Deer, and Edmonton; and three Top-Flight Truck Stops. As of March 2015, the Imperial stable of assets stood at over $167 million with annual revenues of over $75 million—not bad for a forty-year run. Despite Alberta's recent downturn and the addition of millions of shares, Imperial's shares still hold strong at more than twenty-five times their original value.

Being recognized as a meaningful player on the landscape of Canadian business speaks volumes about Sine's achievements. The July 2014 issue of the *Globe and Mail's Report on Business* magazine ranked Imperial Equities 425 in its list of Canada's top 1,000 most profitable publicly traded companies. "Being included in the ranks of some of Canada's most successful corporations is not only flattering but inspirational," said Sine (2015).

Sine's dedication to Muslim charities is as impressive as his business sense. As we have seen, he chaired the fundraising committee for the $20 million Islamic Academy Project (and at times had to dip into his own pocket to keep the project on track and on time), and he was a major donor to the ECMC's Chair in Islamic Studies at the University of Alberta. Sine continues to be a liberal supporter of the charities associated with Al Rashid Mosque. He is also a major supporter and board member of many charitable organizations throughout Canada related to health care, children, seniors, sports, and the arts.

Sine's charitable work has not gone unnoticed. In 2002, on the occasion of the fiftieth anniversary of the accession of Her Majesty Queen Elizabeth II to the throne, Sine was awarded the Golden Jubilee Medal in recognition of his contributions to Canada. In 2005, he was awarded the Alberta Centennial Medal for outstanding service to the people and province of Alberta. In 2008, Sine was a finalist for the Ernst & Young Entrepreneur of the Year Award, and in 2012, he was awarded the Queen Elizabeth II Diamond Jubilee Medal in commemoration of the sixtieth anniversary of Her Majesty's accession to the throne. In 2013, Sine was inducted into the City of Edmonton's Hall of Fame.

Sine's career is reflective of the way the Al Rashid community has expanded and grown, with a major component of its success deriving from dedicated businessmen dating right back to the beginning of the Muslim community in Alberta. Asked about those with similar profiles, Sine responded, "I don't think I'm exceptional. There must be thousands of individuals throughout Alberta with a connection to this community who have millions in their portfolios. It is just a great community with a strong sense of commitment and a desire to build a better world. It's part of a Muslim legacy that I'm proud of. And yes, I'd like to see my children take it over after I'm done" (2015).

REACHING OUT TO OTHERS IN FUNDRAISING
AND PHILANTHROPY

Several years ago, in part inspired by the impact of 9/11, the board decided to welcome outsiders to the mosque during Ramadan. In a way, this gesture was not new. The old Al Rashid had been the scene of great festivity dating back to its beginning when all kinds of folks showed up for the wonderful food that the community women had prepared. About 2011, however, the board realized that food at the new Al Rashid was only feeding those who already had plenty at home. Thus began the Taste of Ramadan. Every year since, the organizers of this charitable event have reached out to feed the whole community, including the homeless and other visitors who might simply enjoy Middle Eastern cuisine. In 2015, because of local celebrations and festivities in Churchill Square, the event was held on Centennial Plaza, behind the Stanley A. Milner Library in down-town Edmonton. Scores of purple-shirted volunteers served those who had waited excitedly in long lineups. Games, face painting, and Middle Eastern music made it a true celebration. Everyone agreed: the spirit Hilwie Hamdon, known among the community for bringing the women of the mosque together in its earliest days, lives on right in the centre of the city!

In another act of reaching out to others, Summayah Arid was an undergrad student in science at the University of Alberta in the early 2010s when she noted that young Muslims on campus had no unique cause to support. A member of the university's Students' Union, she met with Ranya Haydar and a few others in a café and hatched a plan. They would sell tickets for a gala evening of dinner and art sales, and make it a young people's adventure. They decided that an auction format was best. They began with the notion of auctioning off parents to students, and it developed rapidly into companies and groups combining forces to raise funds for orphans.

Their inspiration was the tremendous need to help children who were left without parents because of war, disruption, and illness. With thousands of children in this situation around the world, she elected to work with the Red Cross and Red Crescent. She discovered the non-profit organizations Serving Orphans Worldwide and Worldwide Orphans Foundation Canada, and she and her group reached out beyond the student body to host a gala dinner to raise funds for orphans. The group learned that it costs around $600 a year to feed one child in a refugee camp or in an orphanage, and that figure became the basis for how many orphans would be fed every year by the student group. She set the goal at $200,000 the first year and raised $172,000 with sufficient funding to support some 258 orphans. Every year since, she and her group have topped this figure. She teamed up with a group of students in Calgary, and began a friendly competition between the Calgary and Edmonton groups for incentive.

In 2015, the goal was to top the $360,000 raised in Calgary for over 350 orphans. With a guest list of 500 people, the fundraiser was aiming for $400,000. The speaker was Dr. Munir al-Kassem, scholar and imam from London, Ontario, who had spoken at Worldwide Orphans Foundation Canada before and was well known to Edmontonians. Suffice it to say, they beat Calgary!

WRITERS, POETS, MUSICIANS, AND VISUAL ARTISTS

How one's identity can drive an articulation in prose is one of those eternal mysteries often probed by sociologists and political theorists but never quite clear to the rest of us. Likewise, how the Al Rashid community in its larger and less tethered sense could inspire excellence in writing is not easily described; yet it is true. This section begins by profiling a couple of writers, one a dyed-in-the-wool professional and one who has written out of a heart plea.

One could not have predicted that a child of Slave Lake–area Arabs would have ended up being feted by Edmonton's *Avenue* magazine as one of the city's Top 40 under 40! When Omar Mouallem's mother, Tamam, married his father, Ahmed, in 1980, they had known each other from the time they were kids in Kab Elias. This is a town in the famed Beqaa Valley of Lebanon, a valley that spawned so many other migrants to northern Alberta. It is a town where Muslims and Christians lived and worked together side by side for hundreds of years. The family grew up in High Prairie and then in Edmonton after Ahmed and Tamam left the restaurant industry and semi-retired to be near other Muslims. By then, their three kids were adults. That's where Omar cut his writing teeth.

Omar was and is challenged by the huge disconnect between the average Canadian's knowledge of the Middle East, Arabs, and Muslims in Canada and the diversity of origins of Muslims in Canada. While somewhat distanced from the idea of belonging to a Muslim community and the issues facing the community, he nevertheless feels a moral pull to try and set the record straight. So, he writes about identity issues, but they do not overwhelm his creativity. He writes from the variety of experiences he sees as interesting and vibrant. In spring 2015 alone, he explained, "I've immersed myself with gun nuts, orthodox Jews and a porn producer—so really, great stories will always be paramount to me, and they come from a variety of places."

He first broke into the literary scene through film (even directed some films for this author) because his dream was to be a screenwriter, and by eighteen he had written four screenplays and hung around Vancouver's "Hollywood North." Disillusioned with that, he moved to Edmonton, where his siblings and parents lived, and took an internship with city magazine *Avenue*, which grew into a full-time editorial job and had him exploring the unknown soft underside of the city's vibrant culture. He remarked, "It was during this tenure—writing, editing, fact-checking and managing the magazine's digital presence, everything centred around Edmonton—that I fell in love with the Alberta capital and its changing identity" (2015). In 2013, he was honoured with the city's Northlands Award for an Emerging Artist at the Mayor's Celebration of the Arts. That same year, at just twenty-seven, he served as the Edmonton Public Library's Writer in Residence.

Between 2008 and 2015, his work garnered at least sixteen awards. He has written on a wide range of topics (including a book about cats called *Amazing Cats*), but it's the stories about the Arab Canadian and Muslim Canadian experience that he's most proud of. These stories include an extensive profile of a colourful and dissident Arab businessman ("The Kingdom of Haymour") and an essay about growing up Muslim at Christmas time ("Children of a Lesser Santa"). His writings can be found in the local newspaper *Metro News*, and in literary outlets such as *Wired*, *Eighteen Bridges*, and *The Walrus*.

Not easily pigeonholed, Omar has many other interests: for instance, he raps. He performs under the moniker A.O.K. Both older folks and youngsters enjoy his creative workshops on everything from hip hop to how to use social media. Lest his local emphasis be seen to detract from his excellence, it is important to note he won top prizes from the Professional Writers Association of Canada and the National Magazine Awards in 2014—splendid achievements.

Carmen Taha Jarrah published her first book, *Smuggled Stories from the Holy Land*, in 2015. A *cri de coeur*, the book is a lament of the situation in Israel/Palestine. Its theme is her people's struggle to live ordinary lives among the repression and conflict of everyday life in that part of the world. It was inspired by her attempt to reconnect with her Palestinian roots through joining tours of the Holy Land. During her first tour, in 2009, she was as part of a team of eight members of the Arab Jewish Women's Peace Coalition from Edmonton. Following that experience, she decided to volunteer to help Palestinians pick their olives in the Bethlehem District in 2010. The following year, a Canadian interfaith group that comprised Jews, Christians, and Muslims went on the Path of Abraham tour. This tour was designed to be a kind of pilgrimage to various respective holy sites, and the goal was to share each other's religious rituals and traditions: praying at the Western Wall on the Sabbath, attending a Christian service in the Garden of Gethsemane, and performing communal prayers at the Al-Aqsa Mosque. What she experienced was not just religious connections, but life under occupation. In her book, she writes, "I walked along 'sterilized' streets, ancient streets and Jewish-only streets, explored olden medinas and the ramparts of the Old City of Jerusalem. I experienced military checkpoints and the Wall up close, the ghettoes and virtual open-air prisons left in their wake. I saw confiscated Palestinian hilltops, demolished homes and uprooted olive groves. I witnessed the lack of freedoms and daily humiliations. Hopefulness and hopelessness round every corner. I saw ancient ruins and ruined lives and antiquity and modernity existing side-by-side" (2015, vii). When she returned home, her diaries of her time abroad helped her to bring into discussion the other side of the occupation, as both Jews and Palestinians, living side by side for generations, suffer under a regime foreign to their friendships with each other. *Smuggled Stories from the Holy Land* is her attempt to tell stories that never get into the press— stories of ordinary people living under unbelievable conditions.

Islamic poetry has always been the queen of expression in Islam, with many at the time of the Prophet accusing him of being inspired by the *jinn*, just as they often held poets of the period to be similarly inspired. After all, the great poetic Olympics were held in pre-Islamic Mecca and the winner received wealth and adulation for the year. Poets held a higher place than warriors in the society. It is no surprise, then, that the Al Rashid community values spoken word poetry. Probably the community's best-known poet, Ahmed Knowmadic, won the 2011 Canadian Festival of Spoken Word, and from there he has not turned back. In 2012, he was given the RISE Award for community involvement in the arts and culture and, in 2013, he was Artist in Residence at the Langston Hughes Performing Arts Institute in Seattle, Washington.

Ahmed is a Somali-born Canadian described by the *Edmonton Journal* in 2012 as a "difference maker" in poetry, and indeed he has won awards and accolades every year since then. He is one of the founders and organizers of the Breath In Poetry collective, a young poets' group that features spoken word literacy. Ahmed's work has been published in *alt.theatre*, *The Great Black North*, and various online publications, and through Rubicon Publishing.

Adam Zaimul also has a following within the community for his spoken word poetry. He has performed for Calgary Mayor Naheed Nenshi as part of the Navroz celebration at Calgary City Hall.

Spoken word poets are part of the broader environment created in North America by rap artists, an art form that developed out of the black ghetto experience in the United States. What began as an alternative and minority-spoken form rapidly became the language of the rebel and the oppressed. Muslim rappers picked up the form and turned it into an alternative religious chant expression that addresses contemporary Muslim life in America. It has now found a compatible form in women artists, such as those represented locally by Sara Al Souqi. Sara's spoken word performances and videos are available on YouTube (search for her Breath In Poetry, Edmonton, performance at the 2012 Canadian Festival of Spoken Word, for example).

Musicians have been in Al Rashid's family beginning with King Ganam and his cowboy tours and popular music. A number of current expressions are known, not the least of which is Michael Frishkopf's Middle Eastern and North African Music Ensemble at the University of Alberta. Following along the same line is the Tarabish Collective, a collaborative project made up of five talented performers living in the Edmonton area. The group—Jenny Boutros (vocals), Etelka Nyilasi (violin), Andrew Asraelsen (bass), Mazi Jvd (tar and wind instruments), and Kevin Johnson (darbuka)— interprets music from various Middle Eastern traditions as well as contemporary pop culture. These musicians fuse their diverse musical skills and backgrounds to offer audiences unique sounds and expressions. In addition, local musicians such as Nizar Ali and Yasmeen Najmeddine often use YouTube or other social media outlets to reflect a creative strand within the community that finds a ready audience in Canada.

Canadians naturally see painting as one of the core fine arts, but painting is linked to European and medieval cultural expressions. Islamic societies did not initially invest in this form of art. Nonetheless, Islam has an incredible artistic legacy, and the expression of Islamic art provides us with a different window through which to examine the growth of the community. Indeed, painting continues to attract Muslim artistic expression. For example, traditional paintings that feature Middle Eastern cultural idioms, such as mosques, Arabic writing, traditional dress, and village scenes, can be found in oil paintings by local artist Khalid al-Mudallal; they are popular in Muslim homes and find a ready market.

Khalid is an engineer of Iraqi origin who worked for over seventeen years in architecture. Born in Baghdad, he was recognized for his artistic abilities early as he progressed from pencil to watercolours and then to acrylics. He won his first medal for art at eight. He then moved on to join the Iraqi Children Cultural House, a centre for training and developing talent. After two years there, he joined the International Animation Centre in Baghdad where he learned to paint backgrounds for cartoons. All these influences can be seen in his current oeuvre. Khalid currently works out of Fort McMurray and lives in Edmonton. His work has been displayed in places as widely disparate as Abu Dhabi, Iraq, and Alberta.

The settings he uses are Middle Eastern, perhaps even Iraqi. The artist takes great care to portray architectural detail, demonstrating an almost devotional sympathy for the style. The colours reflect a benevolent, rosy-hued feel for both people and buildings, almost as if they live in a dream environment. Traditional dress places the figures in relationship to village or local scenes. Still, the influence of Europe and Canada is evident— for the paintings' themes emphasize what might be called the classical artistic expression. Furthermore, Middle Eastern painters were universally part of personal and private collections, as is the case here.

Another painter who finds traditional imagery an attractive area of exploration is Ranya Aldayeh. Ranya came to Alberta via Kuwait, where her Palestinian parents ended up after being disposed. She studied fine arts at the University of Alberta. Passionate about painting, she explores various mediums, techniques, and styles. Often the themes she produces derive from traditional imagery, but she applies contemporary techniques in expression.

Madhi Hasan Neamah takes a different approach in his painting. Madhi finds the abstract form to be far more amenable for expression than traditional scenes. A product of Canada, he received his master's degree in fine arts in 1982, and since then has been creating very abstract oil paintings. His work has a space-time focus, often with an atomic fusion sensitivity and a disembodied world of fantasy and play. His colours tend to be surreal, with a Dali-like quality. Madhi's paintings root him solidly in the contemporary world and appeal to a generation that has grown up with space travel and cosmic proportions as a legitimate part of the current scene.

Many other talented artists exist in this community, indicating that a lively and flourishing artistic community exists below the radar of public awareness. Certainly, this dimension of Al Rashid's expression demonstrates similarities to the wider creative talent in the Edmonton region and justifies greater public attention to the creative side of the religious community sustaining it.

The classical artistic form most emphasized in the community is calligraphy, a long-respected talent within Muslim circles. Young people, such as Issam Kaddoura, a twenty-two-year-old Palestinian Canadian Muslim, are following in ancient footsteps. Issam, formerly a student of forest technology at NAIT, began practicing amateur calligraphy at the age of thirteen after hearing a presentation about the Ottoman Empire.

One of the most promising community artists is Dalia Saafan. Dalia hails from Egypt. She began her career in Canada as an arts and craft instructor, exploring various art forms with students. Creatively, she designed classroom doors for each of her colleagues at Earl Buxton School in Edmonton and her fame began to spread. So did her skills. She expanded into painting and then interior design, experimenting with applying the ancient Islamic technique of geometric patterning in the Canadian context. But 2005 was a watershed year for Dalia: she began working in glass. The rest, as they say, is history. Her works have been widely acclaimed for their incorporation of everything from Islamic calligraphy to Bedouin forms and textures to rural colours and expressions. Her work is displayed in many homes, and is available at the Alberta Arts Council.

A self-taught artist, Adnan Elladen works in industrial materials. He has a distinctive style, and his work demonstrates a synergy of several mediums such as digital, carbon fibre, and 3D installations in plexiglass. Adnan incorporates architecture, industrial design, and automotive design into his eclectic work. His series of works, *Arthiteckt*, combines the architectural workflow and process with IC3 designs artwork configuration. This involves using the conventional principles used by architects to create and design and then reinterpreting them according to artistic form. The results are fascinating. Shaw TV Edmonton profiled Adnan in January 2017. Search for "Adnan Elladen Artwork" on YouTube to see the video and some of his works.

COMMUNITY SUPPORT AND LEGAL CONTRIBUTORS

Law might not be considered a creative area by everyone, but given the long relationship that Muslims have had with sharia, and the importance of moral rectitude in Muslim life, it is worth pointing out that more than forty people associated with Al Rashid have practiced or practice law in Alberta.

Judge Ed Saddy, for example, is mentioned a number of times in this book. The Honourable Judge Edward Hyder Saddy was born in Wardlow, Alberta, on January 18, 1931. He is one of eight children born to Rikia Mary and Mahmoud Said Saddy Hage Ahmad of Jib Jinine, Lebanon. He obtained his degrees in economics and law from the University of Alberta, where he was president of the Law Club and the Western Canadian Law Students' Association. He was class valedictorian in 1959. After graduation, he spent a year travelling around the world, visiting thirty-one countries on four continents,

Judge Edward Saddy, president of
Al Rashid Mosque in the 1970s and
the first Muslim judge in Canada.

including Lebanon, Syria, Jordan, Egypt, Turkey, Iran, and Iraq.
Upon returning, he practiced law in Edmonton and was appointed
to the Queen's Council in 1975.

After successfully practicing law for twenty-seven years, he
was appointed as a judge in the Alberta Provincial Court in 1990,
the first Muslim to be appointed a judge in Canada. Judge Saddy
remained active in the Arabian Muslim Association throughout his
life, serving as president of the association for twelve years and as a
member of the board of the association for more than twenty-five
years, during which the community experienced rapid growth and
development. He was involved in the planning and negotiating the
contract for the new Al Rashid Mosque and travelled with Mahmoud
Tarrabain to Libya to finalize the granting of the generous gift
from that country that permitted the association to complete the
new mosque debt-free. After his retirement from the court in 2001,
Judge Saddy and his wife, Marcy, moved to Vancouver to be near his
daughter Rikia and his grandsons Rohan and Malcolm Naif.

I have elected to profile one currently active lawyer,
Nooreddin (Norm) Assiff. Nooreddin's roots stretch back to Lala,
Lebanon, home of his father and mother, Kamal and Fatima. It
is important to see the family connection in this story because

the success of the whole family was a concern for everyone in the community. It is also interesting to see the linkages between Lac La Biche and Edmonton.

His father's brother was Mohammed. Mohammad Ahmed Assiff, whose name appears as Mohammed Ahmed Assaff in the Arabian Muslim Association's charter, was born in the village of Lala, Lebanon, in 1904. He was one of the founders who paved the way for Kamal to come to Canada. Mohammad embarked for Canada in 1922, but was forced to stop over in Marseille, France, for a much longer period than anticipated, due to shortage of funds. He worked in France for approximately six months, which made it possible for him to raise enough money for the remainder of his journey to Canada.

When he arrived in Canada in 1923, he made his way to Frog Lake, Alberta. Five years later, he moved to Edmonton working as a travelling peddler. These were humble beginnings, travelling by foot with a suitcase strapped to his back. As finances improved, he purchased a horse-drawn buggy as his mobile store. After a few years Mohammad was able to purchase his own store as well as a rooming house, and the government contracted him to board many of the local homeless and disadvantaged people. Nooreddin witnessed Mohammad's willingness to help people in need, and it inspired him.

Mohammad quickly became involved in the Edmonton Muslim community by helping to raise funds for a new mosque. He spent many hours and days writing letters to politicians, business people, and even to churches to solicit funds for the new mosque. At times, he travelled to eastern Canada, at his own expense, hoping to raise funds for the new mosque.

In 1946, Mohammad changed his name to Sam. That year, he sold all his assets in Edmonton and moved to Lac La Biche where he started his own mink ranching operation. He met and married Malaki Abougoush in January 1949. They raised seven children: Ozzie, Fisal, Jamel, Naief, Noor, Nowf, and Gamela, all born in Lac La Biche. After his ranch was started, Mohammad (Sam) became president of the Lac La Biche Muslim Association and applied his previous experience in fundraising for a new mosque in Lac La Biche. In 1958, the Lac La Biche Mosque was completed—only the second mosque to be built in Alberta. It was there that they welcomed his brother Kamal (father of Nooreddin) and his family. Kamal worked in the asbestos mines when he first arrived, but seven years later, he owned his own store. He also drove a taxi for a number of years.

Nooreddin was the youngest of seven, and his father told him to study hard to be a doctor—"Do something important and make a difference in the community." As Nooreddin tells it, being a physician didn't quite suit him, and one of his professors, Dr. Cheung, told him he just didn't quite have it in him. Besides, he talked a lot, too much for a doctor. So he decided to try law. He pursued injury law even though he was aware of the American image of injury lawyers as "ambulance chasers" because, as he says, Canada had a cap of $4,000 on injuries, and workers, patients, children often suffered extraordinary injury without adequate assistance. He thus began working on victims' rights. He finally joined a group called the Alberta Civil Trial Lawyers Association and took Alberta's famous case of *Sparrowhawk v. Zapoltinsky*. With that case, he was able to overturn the cap and open up victim's rights law in Alberta. Now, he is president of the Alberta Civil Trial Lawyers Association, an organization of over 630 members.

He reflects, "I am most happy with my law firm—Assiff Law Office—because we deal with some of the poorest people who have no hope of getting redress, and we are only small, but we believe in supporting things like the Food Bank, because the Prophet said, 'Don't go to sleep if your nephew is not fed.' So we make sure we work hard for that community support." Yet Nooreddin admits that being a Muslim lawyer is not all rosy: "Any good Muslim lawyer will have dilemmas...Should we use the law to protect someone's dirty money, for example...But the Prophet has told us that it is a Muslim's responsibility to obey the law of the land, and that's what we must uphold" (2015). Nooreddin sees conflicts at several levels in the legal profession, but he believes the law protects and assists everyone, and lawyers must maintain that tradition.

AL RASHID-RELATED ORGANIZATIONS

Arabian Muslim Association
Al Rashid Mosque
Canadian Islamic Centre
Islamic Investment Corporation
Al Rashid Cultural Society
Helping Hands Society
Al Rashid Investments Corporation
Al Rashid Youth and Sport Club of Edmonton
National Awqaf Foundation of Canada (Awqaf Canada)
Islamic Funeral Society
Al Rashid Education Foundation
Edmonton Islamic School Society

ARABIAN MUSLIM ASSOCIATION

Board Members

Dates represent known information, made available by Al Rashid Mosque.

Imams

James Ailley (Najib Ali Al-Hadjar)	1938–1959
Hammudah Abdul-Ati	1950
Abdul M. Khattab	1964–1967
Soteia Al Jumaili	1967–1970
Ahmad Cherkawi	1970
Yousef Chebli	1982–1992
Mohsen Elbiltagy	1990
Ibrahim Alkurdy	1996
Jamal Taleb	1996–1999
Ali Jomha	1999
Mohamed Shaeesha	2001
Shaaban Sharrif	2002–2004
Maher Abbas	2004–2010

Mustafa Khattab	2010–2012
Sherif Ayoup	2012–2015
Nasser Ibrahim	2015–2018

Presidents

Darwish Teha	1938–1949
Sam Hassan	1950
Ali Kazel	1952
Mohammed Shaben	1955
Ali Tarrabain	1968
Edward Saddy	1972
Monier Hamdon	1975
Abdullah (Ed) Shaben	1979
Saleem Ganam	1982–1985
Mahmoud Ali Tarrabain	1985–1986
Ahmad Assaf	1987–1988
Khalil Rahime	1988–1989
Mohammed (Mickey) Jomha	1988–1992
Hamdan Hamdan	1992–1993
Khalid Tarabain	1993–2018

Ladies Association Members, Past and Present

We apologize if anyone was unintentionally overlooked.

Fadia Abdo

Sana Abdall

Nabiha Aboilwani

Eve Aboughoche

Fatima Aboughoche

Kadrya Aboughoche

Najla Aboughoche

Zareefi Aboughoche

Rawdah Aboughoche

Naeema Aden

Nasreen Ahmed

Naeema Ahmed

Saniya Ahmed

Naila Al Omari

Suhad Al Omari

Yasmeen Alhussien

Mana Ali

Fatin Almaouie

Raya Amiri

Amal Arabi

Fatima Hussein Assaf

Ghada Assaf

Khazma Assaf

Lamia Assaf

Wafa Assaf

Samya Awad

Sanura Awaad

Lila Awid

Khadija Azaz

Joanne Bendera

Kathleen Burtnick

Salma Chebli

Mahasin Chehadi

Ibtisam Darwish

Lila Darwish

Sahar Deeb

Amal Elbenhawy

Soad Elbenhawy

Dalal Eljaji

Kathy Elkadry

Salma Elkadri

Rehab Elmoustafa

Omaya Elmoustafa

Souhad Elomari

Gamileh Elzein

Khadija Elsafadi

Turkiee Elsafadi

Ragheeda Essawi

Naimon Farhat

Halime Faris

Sanna Fayad

Rushdia Fyith

Mary Ganam

Lila Gebara

Nada Gebara

Nora Gebara

Khadija Ghotmi

Soraya Ghotmi

Fadila Grine

Mariam Hajar

Nabiha Hajar

Nasrine Hajar

Samira Hajar

Sana Hajar

Faye Hamdon

Helwie Hamdon

Joanne Hamdon

Josephine Hamdon

Lamia Hamdan

Mariam Hamdon

Nadera Hamdan

Patricia Hamdon

Rakia Hamdon

Wafaa Hawa

Fatima Haymour

Fatin Haymour

Lila Haymour

Mariam Haymour

Nora Haymour

Reema Haymour

Anjeenah Henawi

Jana Hocheimi

Tonia Hucaluk

Hala Huoseh-Cheikh

Fatima Hussein

Waffa Hussein

Ragheda Issawi

Alice Jomha

Gorda Jomha

Jawdah Jorf

Susan Kaddah

Eman Kadri

Fatin Kadri

Nasra Kadri

Salwa Kadri

Amina Kadry

Asmaa Kadry

Naheda Kadry

Samira Kadry

Alma Kanbour

Selma Karout

Kefah Keshta

Sabah Keshta

Fatima Kassab

Anisa Khatib

Lobna Khan

Shameeza Khan

Rukia Zaman Khurshed

Remzija Lagarija

Wafaa Mahfoud

Roa Mahfouz

Bahja Mahmoud

Sumaya Mohamed

Aishi Mouallem

Gail Mouallem

Huda Mouallem

Mona Mouallem

Raefi Mouallem

Intisar Mourad

Maryam Mustafa

Samira Mustafa

Shafika Mustafa

Arabia Najmeddine

Hawaa Najmeddine

Mariam Najmeddine

Amni Nashman

Fatima Nashman

Rayya Qureshi

Shireen Qureshi

Fatima Rahall

Hala Rahall

Ihsan Rahall

Fatima Rahime

Naoel Rahime

Michele Ramisch

Rageena (Ruby) Saif

Najlaa Saleh

Rola Saleh

Naziha Sandouga

Alma Shaben

Harriet Shaben

Mona Taktak

Bahija Tarrabain

Fadwa Tarrabain

Fatima Tarrabain

Hana Tarrabain

Kathy Tarabain

Mariam Tarrabain

Ramzie Tarrabain

Eva Teha

Hayat Torbeih

Khoulood Yousef

Rawda Younes

Noha Yousif

Mona Zahra

BIBLIOGRAPHY

Abu-Laban, Baha. 1983. "The Canadian Muslim Community: The Need for a New Survival Strategy." In *The Muslim Community in North America*, edited by Earle H. Waugh, Baha Abu-Laban, and Regula Qureshi, 75–92. Edmonton: University of Alberta Press, 1983.

Abu-Laban, Baha, and Sharon McIrvin Abu-Laban. 1999. "Arab-Canadian Youth in Immigrant Family Life." *In Arabs in America: Building a New Future*, edited by Michael Suleiman, 113–28. Philadelphia, PA: Temple University Press.

Ahmed, Leila. 1982. "Western Ethnocentrism and Perceptions of the Harem." *Feminist Studies* 8 (3): 521–34.

Ahmad, Nadia B. 2014. "The Islamic Influence in (Pre-) Colonial and Early America: A Historico-Legal Snapshot." *Seattle Journal for Social Justice* 12 (3): 913–47. http://digitalcommons.law.seattleu.edu/sjsj/vol12/iss3/7.

Alberta Caregivers Association. 2008. "KWIKAIDS Information Package." Created by E. Waugh. Edmonton: Alberta Caregivers Association.

Al-Guindi, Fedwa. 1981. "Veiling Infitah with Muslim Ethnic: Egypt's Contemporary Islamic Movement." *Social Problems* 28 (4): 465–85.

Allan, Iris. 1966. *Wop May, Bush Pilot*. Toronto: Clarke, Irwin.

"Al-Rashid Mosque." 2012. *Fort Edmonton Park Blog*, July 17.
    http://www.fortedmontonpark.ca/1920-street/al-rashid-mosque/.

Amery, Zainab. 2013. "The Securitization and Racialization of Arabs
    in Canada's Immigration and Citizenship Policies." In *Targeted
    Transnationals: The State, the Media, and Arab Canadians*, edited by
    Jenna Hennebry and Bessma Momani, 32–53. Vancouver:
    University of British Columbia Press.

Arabic Canadian Community. 2015. "History of Recent Arab Immigration to
    Canada." Accessed August 3. http://www.canadianarabcommunity.com/
    historyofrecentarabimmigrationtocanada.php.

Assaf, Dany. 2013. "I'm Albertan and a Muslim, Not an 'Other' Canadian."
    Globe and Mail, September 12. http://www.theglobeandmail.com/
    commentary/im-albertan-and-a-muslim-not-an-other-canadian/
    article14279326/.

Awid, Richard. 2010. *Through the Eyes of the Son: A Factual History about
    Canadian Arabs*. Edmonton: Accent Printing.

Baker, Peter. 1976. *Memoirs of an Arctic Arab: A Free Trader in the Canadian North:
    The Years 1907–1927*. Yellowknife, NT: Yellowknife Publishing Co.

Barnett, Laura. 2011. "Freedom of Religion and Religious Symbols in
    the Public Sphere." Background paper, publication no. 2011-60E.
    Library of Parliament, Parliament of Canada. http://www.lop.parl.
    gc.ca/Content/LOP/ResearchPublications/2011-60-e.pdf.

Beinin, Joel, and Lisa Hajjar. 2014. "Palestine, Israel and the
    Arab-Israeli Conflict: A Primer." Middle East Research
    and Information Project, February. http://www.merip.org/
    primer-palestine-israel-arab-israeli-conflict-new.

Bélanger, A., and É. Caron Malenfant. 2005. "Population Projections of
    Visible Minority Groups, Canada, Provinces, and Regions 2001–2017."
    Statistics Canada, Demographic Division, catalogue no. 91-541-XIE.
    http://publications.gc.ca/collections/Collection/Statcan/91-541-X/
    91-541-XIE2005001.pdf.

Bonnell, Keith. 2008. "Defiant Levant Republishes Cartoons." *National Post*,
    January 12.

Boyd, Marion. 2004. *Dispute Resolution in Family Law: Protecting Choice, Promoting
    Inclusion*. Toronto: Ontario Ministry of the Attorney General.

Brean, Joseph. 2013. "Edmonton Police Set to Unveil Official Hijab That
    Muslim Officers Can Wear." *National Post*, November 24. http://news.
    nationalpost.com/news/canada/edmonton-police-set-to-unveil-
    official-hijab-that-muslim-officers-can-wear-on-duty.

Broadhurst, Roland J.C., trans. and ed. 1952. *The Travels of Ibn Jubayr: Being the Chronicle of a Mediaeval Spanish Moor Concerning His Journey to the Egypt of Saladin, the Holy Cities of Arabia, Baghdad the City of the Caliphs, the Latin Kingdom of Jerusalem, and the Norman Kingdom of Sicily*. London: Cape.

Cairney, Richard. 2006. "Arts Establishes Canada's First Chair in Islamic Studies." Edmonton Council of Muslim Communities. January 18. http://www.theecmc.com/media/articles/06/0118_chair.html.

Canadian Heritage. 2017. "Statement by Minister Joly on Imamat Day/ Khushali." Government of Canada Statements, July 11. https://www.canada.ca/en/canadian-heritage/news/2017/07/ statement_by_ministerjolyonimamatdaykhushiali.html.

Carney, Maria. 2015. "Are Seniors without Children the Future's Elder Orphans?" *Aeon*, August 13. https://ideas.aeon.co/viewpoints/ maria-carney-on-are-seniors-without-children-the-future-s-elder-orphans?

City of Edmonton. 2010a. "Cultural and Demographic Change." Paper 4, Focus Edmonton, City Plan. http://www.focusedmonton.ca/media/ dp_cultural%20_and_demographic_change.pdf.

———. 2010b. "Edmonton City Trends, Third Quarter 2010." Available from the City of Edmonton, Department of Community Services.

Commission of Inquiry into the Actions of Canadian Officials in Relation to Maher Arar. 2006. *Report of the Events Relating to Maher Arar: Analysis and Recommendations*. Ottawa: Public Works and Government Services Canada. http://www.sirc-csars.gc.ca/pdfs/cm_arar_rec-eng.pdf.

Corbett, E.A. 1992. *Henry Marshall Tory: A Biography*. Edmonton: University of Alberta Press.

Doucette, Chris. 2012. "Expand Burka Ban, Says Muslim Group." *Toronto Sun*, January 22. http://www.torontosun.com/2012/01/22/ expand-burka-ban-muslim-canadian-congress.

Dunn, Ross E. 1986. *The Adventures of Ibn Battuta: A Muslim Traveler of the Fourth Century*. Berkeley: University of California Press.

Edmonton Public Schools. 2017. "Dr. Lila Fahlman." Accessed November 14. http://lilafahlman.epsb.ca/aboutourschool/schoolprofile/.

Edmonton Council of Muslim Communities. 2005. *Towards Understanding of Muslims in Canada*. 2nd ed. Edmonton: ECMC. http://www.theecmc.com/ docs/ECMC%20Towards%20Understanding.pdf.

Edmonton Federation of Community Leagues. 2017. "Going back Almost 100 Years: EFCL Was Born out of the Need for a Unified Voice." Accessed April 7. http://efcl.org/about-us/history/.

Edmonton Public School Board. 2017. "Arabic Bilingual: Program Description."
     Accessed April 5. https://www.epsb.ca/programs/language/
     arabicbilingual/.

Eickelman, Dale F., and James P. Piscatori, eds. 1990. *Muslim Travellers:*
     Pilgrimage, Migration, and the Religious Imagination. Berkeley: University
     of California Press.

Emon, Anver. 2005. "A Mistake to Ban Sharia." *Globe and Mail*, September 13.

Fife, Robert. 2017. "Ottawa Pays Out $10.5-million to Khadr amid Potential Legal
     Battle." *Globe and Mail*, July 6. https://www.theglobeandmail.com/news/
     politics/omar-khadr-settlement-federal-government-guantanamo-bay/
     article35581403/.

Freeze, Colin, and Karen Howlett. 2005. "McGuinty Government Rules
     Out Use of Sharia Law." *Globe and Mail*, September 15.
     https://www.theglobeandmail.com/news/national/
     mcguinty-government-rules-out-use-of-sharia-law/article18247682/.

Gibb, Camilla, and Celia Rothenberg. 2000. "Believing Women: Harari and
     Palestinian Women at Home and in the Canadian Diaspora." *Journal*
     of Muslim Minority Affairs 20 (2): 243–59. doi: 10.1080/713680360.

Gorham, Beth. 2008. "Khadr Was a Child Soldier, His Lawyers Say."
     Toronto Star, January 18.

Government of Alberta. 2007. "Detailed Population Projections December
     2007." http://www.alberta.ca/home/CapRegionFiles/FINAL_REPORT_
     Appendix_B.pdf.

———. 2010. *Aging Population Policy Framework*. http://www.seniors-housing.
     alberta.ca/documents/Aging-Population-Framework-2010.pdf.

Government of Canada. 2017. "Government of Canada Eliminates Conditional
     Permanent Residence." Notice, April 28. http://www.cic.gc.ca/english/
     department/media/notices/2017-04-28.asp.

Hamdani, Daood. 1997. "Canada's Muslims: An Unnoticed Part of Our
     History." *Hamdard Islamicus* 20 (3). Reprinted at http://muslimcanada.
     org/cdnmuslm.htm.

———. 2013. "Canadian Mosque and Pakistani Church Share More than
     the 2013 Anniversary." *Common Ground News Service*, March 26.
     http://www.commongroundnews.org/article.php?id=32797&lan=en.

———. 2015. "Canadian Muslims: A Statistical Review." *Islamic Horizons*
     44 (6): 24–27.

Hamdon, Evelyn Leslie. 2010. *Islamophobia and the Question of Muslim*
     Identity: The Politics of Difference and Solidarity. Winnipeg, MB:
     Fernwood Publishing.

Hodgson, Marshall G.S. 1974. *The Venture of Islam*. Volume 1, *The Classical Age of Islam*. Chicago: University of Chicago Press.

Human Rights Watch. 2007. "The Omar Khadr Case: A Teenager Imprisoned at Guantanamo." Background briefing. http://www.hrw.org/legacy/backgrounder/usa/uso607/.

Hume, Jessica. 2011. "Cancelled Debate Highlights Tension among Canadian Muslims." *National Post*, February 7. http://news.nationalpost.com/holy-post/cancelled-debate-highlights-tension-among-canadian-muslims.

Husaini, Zohra. 1999. "Muslims in North America." In *Muslims in Canada: A Century of Achievement*, 10–20. The Canadian Islamic Centre (In-house mosque publication).

———. 2011. *A Quest for Justice: Universal Human Rights and Canadian Muslim Women*. Edmonton: Canadian Council of Muslim Women.

Itkowitz, Colby. 2016. "From Tortured Terrorist Suspect to Entrepreneur: How This Canadian Father Got His Life Back." *Washington Post*, April 26. https://www.washingtonpost.com/news/inspired-life/wp/2016/04/27/from-accused-terrorist-to-canadian-entrepreneur-maher-arar-is-finally-getting-his-life-back/?utm_term=.e0a376c4cadc.

Jarrah, Carmen Taha. 2015. *Smuggled Stories from the Holy Land*. Dearborn, MI: Mosaic Design Book Publishers.

Kernaghan, Jennifer. 1993. "Lord Cromer as Orientalist and Social Engineer in Egypt, 1882–1907." MA thesis, University of British Columbia.

Khan, Adnan R. 2014. "Muslim Brotherhood: The New Islamist Bogeyman in Canada." *Maclean's*, June 2. http://www.macleans.ca/news/world/the-muslim-brotherhood-the-new-islamist-bogeyman-in-canada/.

Ladha, Mansoor. 2008. *A Portrait in Pluralism: Aga Khan's Shia Ismaili Muslims*. Calgary, AB: Detselig Enterprises.

Lawyers' Rights Watch Canada and the International Civil Liberties Monitoring Group. 2012. "Briefing to the Committee against Torture, 48th Session, May 2012, on the Omar Khadr Case." http://www.lrwc.org/ws/wp-content/uploads/2012/04/LRWCCLMG.CAT_.on_.Canada.re_.Khadr_.18.04.pdf.

Levett, Andrea, Jane Badets, and Jennifer Chard. 2003. "Ethnic Diversity Survey: Portrait of a Multicultural Society." Statistics Canada, catalogue no. 89-593-XIE. http://www.statcan.gc.ca/pub/89-593-x/89-593-x2003001-eng.pdf.

Lewis, Bernard. 2010. *Faith and Power: Religion and Politics in the Middle East*. New York: Oxford University Press.

Lorenz, Andrea. 1998. "Canada's Pioneer Mosque." *AramcoWorld* 49 (4): 28–31. http://archive.aramcoworld.com/issue/199804/canada.s.pioneer. mosque.htm.

Malak, Amin. 1993. "The Shahrazadic Tradition: Rohinton Mistry's Such a Long Journey and the Art of Storytelling." *Journal of Commonwealth Literature* 29 (2): 108–18.

——. 2008. "Toward a Dialogical Discourse for Canadian Muslims." In *Belonging and Banishment: Being Muslim in Canada*, edited by Natasha Bakht, 74–84. Toronto: TSAR Publications.

Maloof, Patricia S., and Fariyal Ross-Sherif. 2003. *Muslim Refugees in the United States: A Guide for Service Providers*. Washington, DC: Center for Applied Linguistics.

Manji, Irshad. 2004. *The Trouble with Islam: A Wake-Up Call for Honesty and Change*. Toronto: Random House Canada.

——. 2007. *Faith without Fear*. PBS documentary.

Marshall Cavendish Corporation. 2010. *Islamic Beliefs, Practices, and Cultures*. Tarrytown, NY: Cavendish Square Publishing.

McDonough, Sheila, and Sajida Alvi. 2002. "The Canadian Council of Muslim Women: A Chapter in the History of Muslim Women in Canada." *Muslim World* 92 (1/2): 79–97. doi: 10.1111/j.1478-1913.2002.tb03733.x.

Mernissi, Fatema. 1991. *The Veil and the Male Elite: A Feminist Interpretation of Islam*. Translated from French by Mary Jo Lakeland. London: Perseus Books.

Metcalf, Barbara D. 1996. "Introduction: Sacred Words, Sanctioned Practice, New Communities." In *Making Muslim Space in North America and Europe*, edited by Barbara D. Metcalf. Berkeley: University of California Press. UC Press E-Books Collection, 1982–2004.

Meurrens, Steven. 2011. "Sponsorship Bars and Conditional Permanent Residency: Coming Soon to the Spousal Sponsorship Program?" *UNB Law Journal*, 62.

Mohanty, Chandra. 1984. "Under Western Eyes: Feminist Scholarship and Colonial Discourses." *boundary 2* 12 (3): 333–58.

Mustapha, W. 1989. "The Islamic Cultural Paradigm." In *Multicultural and Intercultural Education: Building Canada*, edited by Sonia V. Morris, 207–13. Calgary, AB: Detselig Enterprises.

Nesbitt-Larking, Paul. 2007. "Canadian Muslims: Political Discourses in Tension." *British Journal of Canadian Studies* 20 (1): 1–24.

Norman, Bob. 2002. "The Tale of Two Mosques." *Miami New Times*, August 8. http://www.miaminewtimes.com/2002-08-08/ news/a-tale-of-two-mosques/full/.

Pimenti-Bey, Jose V. 2002. *Othello's Children in the "New World": Moorish History and Identity in the African American Experience*. Portland, OR: First Books.

Quig, Paula. 2004. "Testing the Waters: Aboriginal Title Claims to Water Spaces and Submerged Lands—An Overview." *Les Cahiers de droit* 454:659–92. http://www.erudit.org/revue/cd/2004/v45/n4/043812ar.pdf.

Quiggin, Tom. 2014. *The Muslim Brotherhood in North America (Canada/USA): Sabotaging the Miserable House through the Process of Settlement and Civilization Jihad*. Terrorism and Security Experts of Canada Network. https://counterjihadreport.com/tag/terrorism-and-security-experts-of-canada-network-tsec/.

Rangaviz, David. 2011. "Dangerous Deference: The Supreme Court of Canada in *Canada v. Khadr*." *Harvard Civil Liberties Law Review* 46:253–69.

Razavy, Maryam. 2010. "Faith-Based Arbitration in Canada: The Ontario Sharia Debates." PhD diss., University of Alberta.

Reel Girls Media. 2010. *Al Rashid: The Story of Canada's First Mosque*. Video featuring Karen Hamdon, Mounee Hamdon, and Baha Abu-Laban, etc. Edmonton, AB.

Renard, John. 2015. *The Handy Islam Answer Book*. Detroit, MI: Visible Ink Press.

Saddy, Guy. 2008. "The First Little Mosque on the Prairie." *The Walrus*, October 12. https://thewalrus.ca/the-first-little-mosque-on-the-prairie/.

Schuessler, Ryan. 2014. "In Iowa, a Lasting Symbol of American Islam." *Al Jazeera America*, February 13. http://america.aljazeera.com/features/2014/2/in-iowa-a-lastingsymbolofamericanislam.html.

Soharwardy, Syed. 2002. "Muslim Migrants in Canada: Victims of Undeclared Racism and Discrimination." Reproduced on Yahoo public group, Islamic News Updates and Informative Articles from around the Word for Muslims and Non-Muslims, December 29. https://groups.yahoo.com/neo/groups/IslamicNewsUpdates/conversations/topics/2556.

Spence, Donald, dir. 2007. *Giving Up and Holding On*. Film written by Earle Waugh. Alberta Religious Diversity Series.

Statistics Canada. 1991. 1991 *Census*. Census Data Sets. Accessed October 31, 2017. http://www12.statcan.gc.ca/datasets/Index-eng.cfm.

———. 2003. "Religions in Canada, 2001 Census." http://www5.statcan.gc.ca/olc-cel/olc.action?objId=96F0030X2001015&objType=46&lang=en&limit=0.

———. 2009. "Region of Birth of Recent Immigrants to Canada, 1971–2006." Last modified November 20. http://www12.statcan.ca/census-recensement/2006/as-sa/97-557/figures/c2-eng.cfm.

———. 2015. Table 427-0003. "Number of Non-Resident Travellers Entering Canada by Country of Residence (Excluding the United States), Monthly (Persons)." CANSIM. Accessed July 16. http://www5.statcan.gc.ca/cansim/a26?lang=eng&id=4270003.

———. 2016a. *Educational Indicators in Canada: An Introductory Perspective.* www.statcan.gc.ca/pub/81-604-x/2016001/ch/cha-eng.htm.

———. 2016b. "Education, Training and Learning." Last modified October 7. https://www.statcan.gc.ca/pub/11-402-x/2010000/chap/edu/edu-eng.htm.

———. 2017. "2011 National Household Survey: Data Tables: Religion." Last modified February 14. http://www12.statcan.gc.ca/.

Statistics Canada, Census Operations Division. 2003. "Census 2001: Analysis Series: Religions in Canada." Statistics Canada, catalogue no. 96F0030XIE2001015. http://publications.gc.ca/Collection/Statcan/96F0030X/96F0030XIE2001015.pdf.

Strategic Research and Statistics. 2005. *Recent Immigrants in Metropolitan Areas: Edmonton: A Comparative Profile Based on the 2001 Census.* Ottawa: Citizenship and Immigration Canada. http://publications.gc.ca/collections/Collection/MP22-20-6-2005E.pdf.

Sturcke, James. 2008. "Sharia Law in Canada, Almost." *The Guardian* (News blog), February 8. https://www.theguardian.com/news/blog/2008/feb/08/sharialawincanadaalmost.

Suleiman, Michael. 1999. "Islam, Muslims, and Arabs in America: The Other of the Other of the Other." *Journal of Muslim Minority Affairs* 19 (1): 33–48.

Tamari, Salim. 2000. "The Dubious Lure of Binationalism." *Journal of Palestine Studies* 30 (1): 83–87. doi: 10.2307/2676483.

United Nations High Commissioner of Refugees (UNHCR). 2015. *Global Trends: Forced Displacement in 2015.* http://www.unhcr.org/576408cd7.

United Nations Relief and Works Agency (UNRWA). 2017. "Palestine Refugees." Accessed November 14. https://www.unrwa.org/palestine-refugees.

Vassanji, M.G., ed. 1985. *A Meeting of Streams: South Asian Canadian Literature.* Toronto: TSAR Publications.

Waugh, Earle H. 2002. "Social Policy and Islam in Canada." Unpublished paper produced for Mill Woods Senior Society, November.

———. 2010. "Canada: Pluralism." Rev ed. In *Encyclopedia of Religion in America*, edited by C.H. Lippy and P.W. Williams, 385–95. Washington, DC: CQ Press.

Waugh, E.H., and D. Goa, eds. 2013. "Commemorative Volume in Honor of I. Abu-Rabi." Special issue, *Religious Studies and Theology: An Interdisciplinary Journal* 32 (2).

Waugh, Earle, and Jenny Wannas. 2003. "The Rise of a Womanist Movement among Muslim Women in Alberta." *Studies in Contemporary Islam* 1:1–15.

Waugh, Earle H., Baha Abu-Laban, and Regula B. Qureshi, eds. 1983. *The Muslim Community in North America.* Edmonton: University of Alberta Press.

Waugh, Earle, Maryam Razavy, and Rabia Sheikh. 2011. *Embracing 2030: The Edmonton Muslim Community.* Unpublished report (available from the authors).

Wikipedia. 2015. S.v. "Fry, John Wesley." Accessed August 3. http://en.wikipedia.org/wiki/John_Wesley_Fry.

Wikipedia. 2017. S.v. "John Wesley Fry." Last modified September 4, 9:32. https://en.wikipedia.org/wiki/John_Wesley_Fry.

Zogby, John, Regina Bonacci, John Bruce, Rebecca Wittman, and Patricia Malin. 2001. "A Poll of Arab-Americans since the Terrorist Attacks on the United States." Zogby International. Accessed October 31, 2017. https://d3n8a8pro7vhmx.cloudfront.net/aai/pages/9711/attachments/original/1431962418/ArabAmericansAttitudes_September11Attacks_2001.pdf?1431962418.

Personal Communications with the Author

Abu-Laban, Baha. 2002. Personal communication.

Arid, Summayah. 2015, July 10. Interview.

Assiff, Nooreddin (Norm). 2015, July 3. Interview.

Awid, Richard. 2014, October 10. Interview.

Chadi, Sine. 2015, January 5. Interview.

Chebli, Yousef. 2015, February 3. Interview.

Deeb, Muhammad. 1994. Personal communication.

Elsafadi, Waleed, and Anwar Elsafadi. 2015, June 22. Interview.

Emami, Muhammad. 2012. Personal communication.

Hafez, Soraya Zaki. 2013, September 17. Opening remarks on occasion of Al Rashid's seventy-fifth anniversary.

———. 2014, September 16. Interview.

Hamdon, Sydney. 2015, May 5. Interview.

Jarrah, Carmen Taha. 2014, December 27. Interview.

Jomha, Mickey. 1977. Personal communication.

———. 1981. Personal communication.

Jorf, Jawdah. 2015, March 16. Interview.

Kadri, Salwa. 2015, February 5 and June 11. Personal communication.

Mansour, Moe. 2015, June 19. Interview.

Mouallem, Omar. 2015, July 6. Interview with the author.

Nelson, Peggy. 2015, January 12. Personal communication (phone).

Perry, Buff. 2015, May 12. Personal communication.

Saddy, Edward. 2015, May–June. Personal communication.

Salama, Sameeh. 2015, June 10. Interview.

Saleh, Issam. 2008. Interview.

Tarrabain, Khalid. 2006, November 8. Interview.

———. 2014, June 24. Interview.

Tarrabain, Mahmoud (Bill). 1977, September 20. Interview.

———. 1981, October 23. Interview.

INDEX

Names prefixed by *Al* are alphabetized under the element
following the article.
Bold page numbers indicate photographs.

feminism, 121–27

Ferran, Bedouin, 11, 26

Fort Chipewyan, 30, 31

Fry, John Wesley
    approached about land for
        mosque, 31, 37, 38, 39
    and building of mosque, 52, 53
    as mayor, 32
    on opening of mosque, 57

fur trade, 26

Fyith, Majeda, 187

Ganam, Ameen, 67

Ganam, Saleem
    activism of, 80, 81
    and M. Ali, **110**
    and building of new Al Rashid
        mosque, 95
    and Edmonton Islamic
        Academy, 173
    and fight for control of Al
        Rashid, 111, 112, 113, 114, 115
    as fundraiser for new Al Rashid,
        100–01, 102, 103
    and Iran, 85
    outreach by, 83–85
    protests Iraq War, 156
    and school, 129
    work for Al Rashid, 109–10

Generation of Change, 116

Gibbons, Ed, 198

Giving Up and Holding On (film), 86

Great Britain, 62

Hafez, Soraya Zaki, 129–30, 131, 154,
    167, 190, 197–98

Haider, Gulzhar, 173, 174

halal, 46, 137–38

Hamas, 194

Hamdan, Hamdan, **38**

Hamdan, Maryam, **119**

Hamdon, Ali, 30, 37–38, 52

Hamdon, Hilwie Teha Jomha, **31**–32,
    33, 52, 53, 219

Hassann, E.M.M., 38

Hawrelak, William, 93, 104

Haydar, Ranya, 219

Hehr, Kent, 193

Heritage Festival, 147–48

hijab controversy, 168–70, 181

homosexuality, 193

honour killings, 191–92

Husaini, Zohra, 190, 198

Hussain, King, 101

Indigenous peoples, 12, 83, 135–36

Interfaith Council, 84

interfaith dialogue, 143, 152, 188, 200

Iranian Muslims, 149

Iranian Revolution, 79–80, 82–83, 85

Iraq War, 156

Islam
    blending of identity with Arab,
        5, 17
    as civic religion, 77
    conservative movement within,
        140–41
    and conversion of Canadians to,
        19
    cultural cohesion of Sham
        village life, 9–11
    current view of in the West,
        74–77
    and education, 128–32
    feminist movement, 8–9
    fragmentation into separate
        groups, 7, 69–70
    and hybrid identities, 200

AL RASHID

Building and Supporting Community

THE AL RASHID COMMUNITY IS A LEADER in North America with a proven track record of success—from founding the first mosque in Canada and building a state-of-the-art school to offering hundreds of programs and services, including the brand-new ARCA banquet facility. Today, Al Rashid continues to meet and satisfy the evolving needs of its community.

Al Rashid supports the Edmonton Muslim community through innovative programs in five primary areas: Religion, Education, Health and Wellness, Culture, and Endowment (Awqaf).

Al Rashid Education Foundation (AREF)

The Al Rashid Education Foundation (AREF) is the cornerstone of Al Rashid's education program. This not-for-profit organization was founded in 2013 to make a positive contribution to the lives of Canadian students who are either from racialized communities or recent

immigrants to Canada. AREF endeavours to produce a lasting legacy of world-leading intellectuals and researchers in all academic disciplines, thus empowering a dynamic community of high achievers and nation builders.

AREF fulfills this mandate by offering scholarships to students pursuing post-secondary education. AREF scholarships are awarded to applicants who demonstrate a high level of academic, community, and leadership achievement. AREF is funded through the generous contributions of community leaders who place a high value on education and on developing successful and motivated student leaders who contribute to the advancement of their communities within Canadian society and around the world.

Awqaf Canada

The National Awqaf Foundation of Canada (Awqaf Canada) was incorporated in January 2014 as a not-for-profit organization. Awqaf Canada envisions a society where immigrants and minorities in Canada are valued, respected, and have the opportunity to live and work to their full potential. Through its efforts, Awqaf catalyzes the growth and development of communities of immigrants and minorities in Canada through the development of social enterprises and endowment projects, which empower them to become effective contributors, builders, and leaders.

OTHER TITLES FROM THE UNIVERSITY OF ALBERTA PRESS

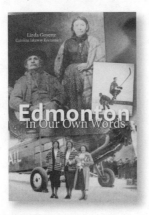

Edmonton In Our Own Words

**LINDA GOYETTE &
CAROLINA JAKEWAY ROEMMICH**

Linda Goyette and Carolina Roemmich have
tapped Edmonton's collective memoir through
written records and spoken stories. Citizens
with diverse viewpoints speak for themselves,
describing important events in Edmonton's
social, political, and economic development.

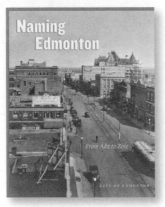

Naming Edmonton

From Ada to Zoie

CITY OF EDMONTON

With over 1,300 sites, 300 photographs, and
detailed maps, *Naming Edmonton* gives life to the
personal stories and the significant events that
mark this city. Use this comprehensive local
history as a guide to revisit Edmonton's streets,
parks, neighbourhoods, and bridges in an
exploration of the signs of our origins and
our times.

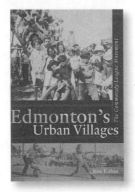

Edmonton's Urban Villages

The Community League Movement

RON KUBAN

No other major city in North America owes as
much to its community league movement as
Edmonton, Alberta. The Edmonton Federation
of Community Leagues (EFCL) has left a living
legacy of sports, cultural, and civic initiatives
for the improvement of Edmonton, and has also
provided an important lesson on how to create
vibrant communities.

More information at www.uap.ualberta.ca